International Education

INTERNATIONAL EDUCATION

EDUCATION

Its History and Promise for Today

THEODORE M. VESTAL

Foreword by Robert Leestma

PRAEGER

Westport, Connecticut
London

Library of Congress Cataloging-in-Publication Data

Vestal, Theodore M.
    International education : its history and promise for today /
Theodore M. Vestal ; foreword by Robert Leestma.
      p.   c m.
    Includes bibliographical references and index.
    ISBN 0–275–94759–9 (alk. paper)
    1. International education—United States—History. I. Title.
LC1099.V38 1994
370.19'6—dc20   93–23478

British Library Cataloguing in Publication Data is available.

Library of Congress Catalog Card Number: 93–23478
ISBN: 0–275–94759–9

First published in 1994

Praeger Publishers, 88 Post Road West, Westport, CT 06881
An imprint of Greenwood Publishing Group, Inc.

Printed in the United States of America

The paper used in this book complies with the
Permanent Paper Standard issued by the National
Information Standards Organization (Z39.48–1984).

10   9   8   7   6   5   4   3   2   1

To the many heroes of international education,
sung and unsung

Contents

Part III: International Education in the Post–Cold War Era

Foreword

This book is important from beginning to end: from the opening chapters on the meaning and significance of international education through the closing chapters on recent progress at the federal level and the author's considered judgment on the need for a national strategy and how coordination of effort might be achieved. In between lies the heart of the work: the first scholarly account of the frustrating saga of the International Education Act of 1966 (IEA), its birth and brief life, but longer legacy. The IEA was the legislative centerpiece of President Lyndon Johnson's grand vision and proposed program for international education.

Although never funded directly, the IEA remains an important landmark of federal intention. Evidence is in the widespread awareness of need it helped generate, the momentum that developed around it despite the gathering political and budgetary storms of the early Vietnam era, and the program activity it stimulated even in the absence of appropriations.

The book is timely because the unfulfilled aspects of the Johnson vision and the rationale and purpose of the IEA — that the national interest in education requires strong international dimensions — are even more important today, more than a quarter century later, due to the growing international complexities and challenges that face us in the post–Cold War world. The book clearly contributes to the cause of helping international education receive the attention it deserves within the domestic milieu.

Now little known and generally underappreciated, President Johnson's vision and proposed program have long deserved to be accounted for in the history of major federal efforts on behalf of international understanding through education in the half century since the end of World War II. Thanks to Professor Vestal's dedicated effort much of this crucial gap is now largely filled, particularly with regard to the IEA. One of the insights in his account is the crucial role played by Rhodes scholars in various federal undertakings, including some of the most recent.

The story begins almost 30 years ago when President Lyndon Johnson, aided by a number of distinguished associates in and out of government, endeavored to take some giant steps toward bringing the world into U.S. education and U.S. education into the world through a combination of vision, task force, proposed program, administrative action, Executive Order, and legislation. He first sketched his vision in an address on the Mall in front of the Smithsonian Institution in September 1965. The occasion celebrated the bicentennial anniversary of the birth of James Smithson and the knowledge production and diffusion heritage of the institution that bears his name. The president's remarks were based on some basic propositions of continuing relevance, including:

The growth and the spread of learning must be the first work of a nation that seeks to be free. . . . We know today that certain truths are self-evident in every nation . . . that ideas, not armaments, will shape our lasting prospects for peace; that the conduct of our foreign policy will advance no faster than the curriculum of our classrooms; that the knowledge of our citizens is the one treasure that grows only when it is shared.

The president followed with a special message to Congress in February 1966 that proposed a sweeping program of international education and health, including what became the IEA. He called upon Congress to add a world dimension to improving the education and health of the people of the United States. He requested Congress to declare that: "Programs to advance education and health are basic building blocks to lasting peace. . . . Education lies at the heart of every nation's hopes and purposes. It must be at the heart of our international relations." He emphasized the reciprocal nature of international understanding: "International education cannot be the work of one country. It is the responsibility and promise of all nations. It calls for free exchange and full collaboration. We expect to receive as much as we give, to learn as well as to teach. Let this Nation play its part." He then proposed a broad, four-part program involving several federal agencies, private sector participation, and cooperation with international organizations, including UNESCO: "to strengthen our capacity for international educational cooperation. — to stimulate exchange with the students and teachers of other lands. — to assist the progress of education in developing nations. — to build new bridges of international understanding."

The temptation is strong to detail here the many desirable activities proposed along with the often ringing rhetoric of rationale. A sampling is

irresistible: the president called for creation of a corps of educators to
serve in our embassies abroad as representatives of U.S. education. He
sought to strengthen international studies in U.S. elementary and
secondary schools. ("No child should grow to [adulthood] in America
without realizing the promise and the peril of the world beyond our
borders. Progress in teaching about world affairs must not lag behind
progress made in other areas of American education.") He made
provision for assisting international studies in smaller and developing
colleges. He proposed establishment of an Exchange Peace Corps,
expansion of opportunities for U.S. educators to assist in summer
workshops in developing countries, growth of school-to-school
partnerships, and a range of efforts to encourage exchange programs
for students and teachers. ("Only when people know about — and
care about — each other will nations learn to live together in harmony.") The list goes on, but space here is limited and the book lies
before you.

   As it turned out, most of the two dozen specific actions called for were
to languish on the launching pad. Yet to judge progress as a whole since
then — to revisit that part of the 1960s chronicled in this book and the
subsequent accomplishments stimulated by the vision and efforts of that
period; to take stock of the cumulative and continuing contributions of
such long-standing government programs as Fulbright, NDEA and HEA
Title VI, Peace Corps, and USAID's university linkages along with those
of the many programs in the private sector and the growth of global
perspectives in education; and then to add the important new steps
forward of 1991–92 in the enactment and funding of the Boren bill, the
Bradley-Leach exchange program for citizens of the former Soviet
Union, and related progress in Title VI and Fulbright programs — is to
realize again the power of ideas, sustained effort, and how far
international education has come.

   But despite the progress since that 1966 message to Congress, such a
current and retrospective review serves also to dramatize anew the utility
of a vision and how much further education has to go in dealing with the
whole round world that increasingly presses in on our daily lives and
national destiny. U.S. education and our body politic remain
insufficiently prepared to deal with the diverse and changing international
realities that face us. The context of our existence and various dynamics
affecting our country's future have become international and multicultural
more rapidly and more pervasively than have our educational programs
for coping with them. We haven't caught up with the international past
yet, let alone the present state of world affairs and prospects for the

foreseeable future. That other nations haven't either provides neither consolation nor relief.

President Johnson would have applauded several recent developments at home and abroad, including the genuine peace dividend represented by the National Security Education Act of 1991 with its trust fund, grant provisions for higher education comparable to those in the IEA, and available budget. He certainly would have welcomed the recent global manifestation of some of the ideas he held so dear — the World Conference on Education for All held in Jomtien, Thailand, in March 1990 and the resulting Declaration and Framework for Action to Meet Basic Learning Needs developed by the participating 155 countries, 20 intergovernmental organizations, and 150 nongovernmental groups. He would have been pleased by the U.S. involvement, especially the subsequent follow-up response: establishment of an increasingly dynamic private/public U.S. Coalition for Education for All with a multichannel mission of building bridges for mutual understanding through international cooperation in education.

The address on the Mall and the special message to Congress provide compelling context for what this book is about. They convey a feeling for the heady days of a few years in the 1960s when it seemed that a golden age might be dawning for international education. Most of the ideas remain fresh, good for the soul generally, and resonate no less today.

Thus I believe the reading of this book is best begun at the back rather than at the front — "back to the future." Start in the Appendix with President Johnson's address on the Mall in September 1965, and follow with the succeeding item, his message to Congress in February 1966. His closing points in the latter echo his remarks on the Mall and provide a running start for Chapter 1:

We can generate growing light in our universe — or we can allow the darkness to gather. . . . The choice between light and darkness . . . between knowledge and ignorance, is not one that we can ignore. . . . The International Education and Health Acts of 1966 present an opportunity to begin a great shared adventure with other nations. I urge the Congress to act swiftly for passage of both measures. Our national interest warrants it. The work of peace demands it.

The twenty-eighth anniversary of that message is marked by at least five promising developments. This book is going to press. The National Security Education Act is becoming operational. More U.S. citizens than ever are realizing the need to know more about the rest of the world, to become internationally competitive through systematic reform of education, and to cooperate internationally on education matters of common concern. If enough policymakers, educators, and parents, along with the mass media, work together to foster international understanding through education, it would augur well for the republic.

Some concluding thoughts in this rumination on the past, present, and future of international education: when one considers what is today, what might have been, and what needs to be, one wonders how the present situation (status, crosscurrents, needs, opportunities) may change during the next decade or two or by that symbolic moment less than half a dozen years away when the twenty-first century arrives. How, then, will education at home and abroad be attending to such realities as international trade and interwoven economies, global financial markets, and the worldwide telecommunications revolution; the increasing interdependence of nations and peoples; ethnic, religious, and cultural diversity and sometimes strife; emerging democracies and market economies; population growth and ecological consequences; poverty, illiteracy, malnutrition, disease, and underdevelopment; nation building and disintegration; human rights; arms control and nuclear waste disposal; intergenerational responsibility for the global environment; peacemaking in national and regional conflicts; and international cooperation in coming to terms with these and other facts of life on planet Earth?

In short, how adequately will education be dealing with international realities, perspectives, issues, problems, and prospects in appropriate context: how the world, including systems aspects, is and came to be, works or does not work, yet might or could — along with the implications for citizenship in the twenty-first century? And of particular significance for the United States with its special leadership role in the world: how will all of this be reflected in the results of our nation's recent, historic commitment to national education goals, coherent curriculum frameworks, and voluntary world class standards?

Acknowledgments

I am indebted to the Lyndon Baines Johnson Foundation for a grant-in-aid of research for this book. The staff of the Lyndon Baines Johnson Library was most helpful, and I am especially appreciative of the assistance of archivists Linda Hanson, Shellynne Eickhoff, and Nancy Keegan Smith. Invaluable typing and word processing aid was provided by Marilyn Steel and Jim Hellwege of the Department of Philosophy of Oklahoma State University and Leann Anderson of the University of Tulsa. Robert England and William Parle, consecutive heads of the Political Science Department of Oklahoma State University, have provided consistent support for my efforts.

Several major actors in the story of the International Education Act (IEA) of 1966 and champions of international education ever since — Paul A. Miller, Douglass Cater, John Brademas, Robert Leestma, and Glen Taggart — read my manuscript, suggested additional lines of inquiry, and offered constructive criticism that helped strengthen the work. Martin Hurwitz and Charlene King of the National Security Education Program Office, Jynks Burton of the Alliance for International Education and Cultural Exchange, and Rebecca Cooper of Senator David L. Boren's staff provided helpful information about the National Security Education Act (NSEA). I also thank Charles M. Vestal, of the Department of English, University of Illinois, for his careful editorial critique of the entire manuscript.

International Education

1

The Challenge of International Education

In the post–Cold War world, the United States most immediately faces challenges of global revolutions in technology, weapons proliferation, population growth and migration, economic and political aspiration, national disintegration, resource scarcity, and environmental decay. These simultaneous upheavals are all of immediate consequence to Americans attempting to deal effectively with the complicated agenda of international affairs. Indeed, the American people in general are now more concerned about a broader range of international problems than ever before in their peacetime history.[1]

Yet, as Richard Lyman, president emeritus of Stanford University, points out, "We are as a people astonishingly ill-prepared for this situation, ill-equipped to understand it and too ill-informed to provide the context for intelligent policy-making regarding international matters."[2]

Lyman's assertions are backed up by numerous reports and polls that document U.S. citizens' and students' lack of knowledge about other societies and cultures, foreign language skills, and geographic literacy.[3] While international education and the study of foreign languages have received less emphasis in the United States during the past 25 years, our economic competitors have been following the opposite path. For example, every student graduating from high school in Japan is required to have studied English for at least two years, and the European Community (EC) has announced that by the end of the decade, all high school students will have to demonstrate fluency in two foreign languages in order to graduate. The EC also plans to send 10 percent of its students to study abroad.

By contrast, a very small percentage of U.S. students study abroad for credit each year — less than 1 percent of the more than 12 million undergraduates in the United States. Few Americans study foreign languages and cultures, and schools have difficulty finding foreign language teachers. In 77 percent of U.S. colleges and universities, students can earn a bachelor's degree without taking any foreign language courses.[4]

Senator David Boren (D-OK) notes that

To compete economically and to protect our diplomatic and national security interests, we need to think internationally. This means improving our skills in the areas of international and regional studies and developing more foreign language fluency. If we fail to do so, we will be ignoring a critical threat to our national security and to our ability to remain a world leader.[5]

While policy makers, responding to the current global transformation, ponder anew the national psyche and the collective consciousness, the need for improved international education in the United States and the dangers of neo-isolationism also need to be reexamined. As Norm Peterson counsels, there is a need to impress on policy makers the idea that "domestic problems are no longer purely amendable to domestic solutions."[6]

Americans, now more than ever, need to understand both Western values that historically have shaped their society and the values of other cultures that are transforming that society. A comprehension of foreign languages and cultures and, even more importantly, an understanding of the social, political, and economic factors affecting international relations would appear critical to a modern education.

U.S. education generally and higher education specifically have a responsibility to develop the level of perception needed to make intelligent policy choices in the international arena. A lack of understanding of other peoples and cultures distorts citizens' interpretation of world events. Walter Lippman pointed out the dangers to humankind if the pictures that people have in their heads do not sufficiently correspond to the reality of the world outside: people make mistakes because an important part of human behavior is reaction to inaccurate pictures.[7]

The U.S. business community especially suffers from deficiencies in international education. Such developments as the creation of new European markets, foreign ownership of a large portion of the U.S. federal debt, and giant increases in foreign trade have diminished the economic sovereignty once enjoyed by Americans. To compete in a world of complex interdependence, U.S. business people must know more about their economic partners and foes. Consider these facts:

1. One-fourth of everything grown or made on earth is exported.
2. Imports make up 31 percent of U.S. consumption.[8]
3. The United States sells two of five acres of its farm produce abroad.
4. The U.S. share of world trade was 15.4 percent in 1970; 13.6 percent in 1975; and 12.3 percent in 1988.[9]
5. One of every six U.S. manufacturing jobs produces for export.
6. One of every seven dollars of U.S. sales is to someone abroad.
7. One of every three cars, nine of every ten television sets, two of every three suits, and every video recorder sold in the United States is imported.
8. One of every four dollars of U.S. bonds and notes is issued to foreigners.[10]

It is obvious from these statistics that the nation must have people better trained to work effectively in the global marketplace. As former Governor of Virginia Gerald L. Baliles observed:

How are we to sell our products in a global economy when we neglect to learn the languages of the customer? How are we to open overseas markets when other cultures are only dimly understood? How are our firms to provide international leadership when our schools are producing insular students?[11]

A series of studies in recent years by government bodies, higher education associations, and foundations have underscored these and other educational concerns and advocated improved international education as a remedy.[12] Reports of the Association of American Colleges, the National Endowment for the Humanities, the National Institute of Education, the American Association of State Colleges and Universities, and the Carnegie Foundation for the Advancement of Teaching have focused on questions about the quality and relevance of undergraduate international education.

President Carter's National Commission on Foreign Language and International Studies reviewed the state of international education in the United States and was "profoundly alarmed" by what it found. The commission noted the "scandalous incompetence" of the United States in foreign languages and unanimously recommended increased federal support for research, instruction, and graduate study in foreign languages and cultures.[13] Politicians, corporate leaders, and educators agreed that the situation was bad and that something should be done to correct it. Rhetoric surpassed deed, however, and federal government initiatives in international studies were underfunded or not funded at all.

In 1987 the Coalition to Advance Foreign Languages and International Studies (CAFLIS), composed of some 165 organizations, was created to serve as a forum for diverse groups that shared a common interest in making the country "more internationally competent and globally competitive by increasing and improving international education and expanding international exchanges."[14] The organization, funded for a period of two years by foundations, published an impressive plan of action to enhance international competence in the United States. The coalition's recommendations, like those of several predecessor organizations during the past quarter century, were duly noted by federal officials, and no meaningful action was taken. The CAFLIS program failed to generate a sense of urgency to compel thoroughgoing, widespread change by the federal government.

Richard D. Lambert notes that repeated efforts to address the challenge of international education "have been of limited effectiveness because of the enormity of the problem, the immense dispersion of the education system, and the lack of agreement on just what the content of that knowledge and understanding should be and to whom it should be given, when, where, and how."[15]

Within institutions of higher education, international education, in competition with more entrenched programs for scarce financial resources, usually received low priority. The common attitude toward international programs by university administrations was "We love them but we don't fund them."[16] A few less-than-adequately coordinated efforts by universities and businesses addressing their specific needs or playing to their particular strengths were the only counters to the ongoing problem. Although some individual programs produced excellent results, most were isolated pockets of progress in an otherwise indifferent nation.

Even so, international education survived and sometimes prospered, supported by local resources on certain campuses. Some international programs supported completely or in part by the federal government have encouraged university, private, and foundation financial support through gifts and grants that, in some cases, exceed the government grants. Nationwide, this development has been uneven in terms of courses and fields covered, but there has been growth, albeit at a glacial pace that is almost imperceptible in the general campus milieu. Collectively, the international education activities of all U.S. colleges and universities represent a substantial investment and a sizeable resource. Their impact is diminished both at the campus level and nationally, however, by their scattered, uncoordinated nature.

The most important federal initiative in international studies came during the Eisenhower administration in 1958 with the passage of the National Defense Education Act (NDEA). The NDEA was a response to the technological threats posed by the space program of the Union of Soviet Socialist Republics (USSR). The act forged a partnership between the government and higher education inducing colleges and universities to develop high-quality graduate programs in science, math, foreign languages, and area studies. Federal support (in constant dollars) for international studies reached a high point in the late 1960s, when funding of the NDEA was at its apex. From there, international education went into two decades of decline, with neither Congress nor the presidency giving the field high priority.

The only proposed full-scale, long-term effort to strengthen the international dimensions of colleges and universities throughout the nation was made in 1966, when the IEA was passed.[17] The act authorized grants for international studies and research at both the undergraduate and graduate levels to improve the overall capability and versatility in global affairs of the country as a whole. At the time of its passage, a number of observers thought the impact of the IEA within 10 or 15 years would be comparable to "some of the great changes wrought by federal support for the sciences."[18]

Unfortunately, the IEA never received an appropriation — a victim of the Vietnam War. Perhaps the best straightforward explanation of what happened to the IEA was provided by Douglass Cater some 20 years after the demise of the act:

In the age of Pax Americana, we devote scant resources to developing the generations of future leaders who will be sophisticated about what can and cannot be done in building international comity. . . . But we are not very good, despite our outlay of dollars, in winning friends or educating ourselves in the world's ways. This at least, is the motive behind LBJ's [Lyndon Baines Johnson's] sponsorship of the International Education Act of 1966 which seeks to enhance the learning component of all our foreign assistance programs and to build centers of international studies in American universities. The act is hailed as a logical extension of Johnson's domestic education programs, and it sweeps through Congress with hardly a dissenting vote. It emerges just when LBJ, having delayed overlong in facing the combined cost of guns and butter and costly social programs, is obliged to ask Congress for additional taxes. He knows all too well that at last angry money men in Congress have him where they want him. Not one dollar is appropriated for the International Education Act.[19]

Despite that defeat, the seeds of an expansive federal program in international education had been sown. Some of the ideas of the IEA were kept alive in programs in the Department of Health, Education, and Welfare (HEW), and later, in the Department of Education (ED). The NDEA also survived, as Title VI of the Higher Education Act, but two decades of inflation, reductions in purchasing power of the dollar, and benign neglect sorely cut into annual appropriations. By 1991, such support as there was for international education came principally from the financially strapped budget of the ED. Federal programs in international education amounted to a woeful 0.13 percent of total U.S. education funding. Federal funds represented 6 percent of the amount spent by universities and private sources in international programs.[20]

Although the IEA lay dormant, a relatively small but persistent group inside and outside higher education continued to champion its cause and to awaken the academic community and its patrons to the need to improve Americans' competence in international studies. Those familiar with the IEA's content recognized the act as a model of a well-planned federal strategy whose design remained salient.[21] They sought means to resurrect the IEA, but federal government financial assistance for international programs was never adequate to implement a sustained national effort.

By mid-1991, the higher education community, operating in this frustrating milieu, was resigned to passing the reauthorization of the Higher Education Act, Title VI — the successor legislation of the NDEA — "within modest authorization levels."[22] Although rumors of a "peace dividend" were bruited about, prospects for new or more generous funding were not rosy.

Therefore, there was joyful surprise when the seeds of the IEA germinated in an unexpected garden. In July 1991, Senator Boren, chairman of the Senate Intelligence Committee, proposed the NSEA, a major international education initiative, to increase opportunities for undergraduates to study abroad and to support the training of more specialists in languages and area studies. The act was put together by cutting classified segments of the multibillion-dollar intelligence budget and was developed in part (and probably of necessity to get it through the intelligence committees of both houses) to provide the federal government's national security departments and agencies with a larger and better-trained pool of experts on critical regions and languages around the world.

The NSEA, which eventually was enacted by Congress and signed into law on 6 December 1991 by President Bush, provides for the establishment of a $150 million trust fund, the income from which will be used to finance continuing scholarship, fellowship, and grants programs.[23] Of the $150 million appropriated for this purpose, up to $35 million may be spent on programs in the initial year. The remainder will go into the trust fund. The interest from a trust fund of $115 million will generate limited revenue, an annual appropriation of only about $12 million for the programs in subsequent years. Still, the Boren program represents a 41 percent increase in federal funding of international studies in the first year and a 14 percent increase thereafter.[24] And there is the possibility that Congress will add to the trust fund in the future. In addition, funding increases were approved for the ED's international education programs in 1991, and major revisions were made in the authorization of the programs in the Higher Education Act in 1992.

The NSEA signaled that the federal government was again committed to major financing of international fields critical to the nation's interest. Higher education now might be enabled to provide more organized knowledge and highly trained personnel essential to safeguard the welfare and interests of the nation and to continue the search to determine conditions, policies, and actions to create a more stable and peaceful world.

Buoyed by Boren's success, other senators, in 1992, championed bold measures to increase educational and cultural exchange programs. Senator Ernest Hollings (D-SC), chairman of the Senate appropriations subcommittee that funds the United States Information Agency (USIA), led a successful effort to increase total appropriation for fiscal year 1993 for exchange programs to more than $223 million — an increase of more than $29 million or 15 percent over the previous year's funding. Congress also passed an aid program originally proposed by Senator Bill Bradley (D-NJ) — the Freedom Exchange Act, a $50 million exchange program with the former republics of the Soviet Union.[25]

Guardians of the international education enterprise in Congress are led by former Rhodes scholars Senators Boren and Bradley, and, at an earlier time, as we shall see, they were guided by Congressman John Brademas. It remains to be seen whether another Rhodes scholarship alumnus, President Bill Clinton, will endorse long-term federal support of international education with the same vigor.

The enactment of the NSEA and the new or expanded exchange and international education initiatives herald an opportune time for the federal government and the higher education community to clarify their goals and to strengthen their commitments to enhance U.S. competence in world affairs. The times demand bold measures to consolidate existing programs, replace outdated provisions with activities focusing on today's challenges, and provide better linkages between the various components of international education.

Lessons from the past may be helpful to those attempting to do this. A comprehensive model for a nationwide international education program was developed by the IEA in 1966, and its design is just as salient now as it was 25 years ago. This model needs only a fine tuning in light of the post–Cold War international education initiatives to make it applicable to current conditions.

A history of the IEA and an analysis of its legacy incorporated in the initiatives of the 1990s may enlighten the work of those who are attempting once again to bring the national government more vigorously into the support of international education. All involved in the effort might well ponder the inscription above an entrance to the University of Michigan's William L. Clements Library: "In darkness dwells the people which knows its annals not."

The chapters that follow attempt to shed some light on the annals of international education during the past three decades. Part I explores what international education is and reviews federal activities in this field. Part II traces the history of the IEA and conjectures upon what its impact on the country would have been had the act been funded during the Johnson administration. To keep the events surrounding the passage of the IEA in a broader perspective, occasional reference is made to historical milestones that occurred in the United States and abroad during 1965–67. Part III analyzes the post–Cold War initiatives and their place in the mosaic of international education and speculates on the needs of the nation in the future.

NOTES

1. Robert E. Ward, *Report of the Committee on International Studies at Stanford*, Stanford University, 25 February 1985, p. 12.

2. "World Class Institute," *Stanford Observer*, February 1989, p. 1. For an illustration of the ill-preparedness of the United States to deal with rapidly changing global events, see Allen H. Kassof, "Meager Resources Could Stymie Our Ability to Study the Changes in Eastern Europe," *Chronicle of Higher Education*, 31 January 1990, p. A48.

3. See, for example, Philip Shenon, "Governors Warning of an Ignorant U.S.," *New York Times*, 26 February 1989, p. 14; *The Gallup Survey*, 27 July 1988; Stephen S. Birdsall, "America's Geographic Illiteracy," *Focus* 36 (Summer 1986): 1; Arthur Levine, "And the Capital of Kankakee Is . . . ," *Phi Delta Kappa* 67 (March 1986): 535; Wayne C. McWilliams, "What University Students Know about Foreign Affairs: A Six Nation Study," unpublished paper presented at International Studies Association Conference, Anaheim, Calif., March 1986; "*Deja Vu*," *Change* 18 (January/February 1986): 50.

4. George Lardner, Jr., "Language Education for National Security," *Washington Post*, 19 July 1991.

5. "Boren's International Education Bill Becomes Law," Press Release, U.S. Senator David Boren, 6 December 1991, p. 1.

6. Paul Desruisseaux, "Education Leaders Urge U.S. Strategy for Coordinating International Exchanges," *Chronicle of Higher Education*, 25 November 1992, pp. A27–28.

7. Walter Lippman, *Public Opinion* (New York: Macmillan, 1965), pp. 18–19.

8. Donald A. Ball and Wendell H. McCulloh, Jr., *International Business: Introduction and Essentials* (Homewood, Ill.: Irvin, 1990), p. 28.

9. Subhash C. Jain, *International Marketing Management* (Boston, Mass.: PWS-Kent, 1990), pp. 3, 11.

10. Michael R. Czinkota and Ilbba A. Ronbainen, *International Marketing* (Chicago, Ill.: Dryden Press, 1990), p. 7.

11. Gerald L. Baliles, "Chairman's Overview," *America in Transition: The International Frontier*, Report of the Task Force on International Education (Washington, D.C.: National Governors' Association, 1989), p. v. See also, for example, Business-Higher Education Forum, Northeast-Midwest Congressional Coalition, and Congressional Clearinghouse on the Future, *An Action Agenda for American Competitiveness* (Washington, D.C.: Business-Higher Education Forum, 1986); Sven Groennings, "The Global Economy and Higher Education," *The Atlantic Commuity Quarterly* 25 (Winter 1987–88): 470–78.

12. James B. Holderman, *Critical Needs in International Education: Recommendations for Action*, Report to the Secretary of Education by the National Advisory Board on International Education Programs (Washington, D.C.: Government Printing Office, December 1983); Michael I. Sovern, *Annual Report 1982–83 Academic Year* (New York: Columbia University, 1983); Edwin A. Deagle, Jr., *A Survey of United States Institutions Engaged in International Relations Research and Related Activities* (New York: Rockefeller Foundation, 1981); Elinor G. Barber and Warren Ilchman, *International Studies Review* (New York: Ford Foundation, 1979).

13. James A. Perkins, *Strength Through Wisdom: A Critique of U.S. Capability*, Report to the President from the President's Commission on Foreign Languages and International Studies (Washington, D.C.: Government Printing Office, 1979).

14. CAFLIS, "International Competence: A Key to America's Future," Executive Summary of the Plan of Action, December 1989; see also, "CAFLIS Update: The Final Stretch," 7 April 1989; "CAFLIS Update: Consensus Reached," 14 July 1989. Other recent studies of note include Liaison Group for International Educational Exchange, *Exchange 2000: International Leadership for the Next Century* (Washington, D.C.: National Governors' Association, 1990); *America in Transition: The International Frontier* (Washington, D.C.: National Governors' Association, 1989).

15. Richard D. Lambert, *Points of Leverage: An Agenda for a National Foundation for International Studies* (New York: Social Sciences Research Council, 1986), p. 131.

16. C. Peter Magrath, quoted in Barbara B. Burn, *Expanding the International Dimension* (San Francisco, Calif.: Jossey-Bass, 1980), p. 106.

17. 20 U.S.C. sec. 1171 *et seq.*; 80 Stat. 1066–1073 (1966).

18. 14 February 1967, Supplemental Budget Request, Ex Ed Box 3, LBJ Library.

19.   Douglass Cater, "What Did LBJ Know and When Did He Know It?" *Washington Post*, 19 July 1987, p. C7.

20.   "Boren's International Education Bill Becomes Law," Press Release, U.S. Senator David Boren, 6 December 1991, p. 2; Wayne Clifton Riddle, "Foreign Language and International Education: The Federal Role," CRS Report for Congress, Congressional Research Service, The Library of Congress, 20 November 1989, Technical Revision, 7 February 1990.

21.   Telephone interview with Glen Taggart, 8 May 1989.

22.   Memo, Miriam A. Kazanjian, NASULGC, to Persons Interested in the Reauthorization of the Higher Education Act, Title VI, International Education Programs, July 1991. See also Report of the Interassociation Task Force on HEA–Title VI/Fulbright-Hays (102(b)(6)), *Recommendations on the Reauthorization of the Higher Education Act of 1965, as Amended for Title VI, International Education Programs and Fulbright-Hays (102(b)(6))*, Washington, D.C., May 1991.

23.   Title VIII of H.R. 2038, the Intelligence Authorization Act for Fiscal Year 1992.

24.   "Boren's International Education Bill Becomes Law," Press Release, U.S. Senator David Boren, 6 December 1991, p. 3.

25.   Scott Jaschik, "Congress Votes to Expand Exchanges with Former USSR," *Chronicle of Higher Education*, 14 October 1992, p. A35.

I

PROTEAN INTERNATIONAL EDUCATION AND ITS CONNECTIONS WITH THE FEDERAL GOVERNMENT

2

What Is
International Education?

"International education" has different meanings for different people. As an academic subject, the field has been plagued by the use of a multiplicity of definitions. Such terms as "international studies," "international programs," "intercultural programs," "transnational programs," "foreign area studies," "non-Western studies," and "international relations" are used widely and interchangeably.[1] One of the most succinct definitions is that of Harvard historian John K. Fairbank, who defined the subject matter of international studies as "the non-us" of humankind.[2] A vagueness of meaning, leaving room for different interpretations of "international education," has haunted federal initiatives in the field, and the IEA was attacked for a lack of specificity in its passage through the legislative process.

During congressional hearings on the IEA, there was a consensus that international education has at least three major strands: content of curricula, movement of scholars and students concerned with training and research, and arrangements that engage a system of education in technical assistance and educational cooperation programs beyond its national boundaries.[3]

In preparing answers to congressional questions regarding the IEA, representatives of HEW further defined international studies as

Education in foreign institutions or studying abroad — or studying subjects or disciplines from a world-wide approach, such as world population developments, economics of development, or international banking. The broadest meaning encompasses all subjects and specialties which have international implications.[4]

In 1969, Robert Leestma, then associate commissioner for International Education and director of the Office of Education's Institute of International Studies, divided the concerns and activities of international education into seven general categories:

1. The traditional study of other lands and other peoples in elementary, secondary, and higher education.
2. Interdisciplinary approaches to the specialized study of world affairs, international relations, and foreign policy, particularly in colleges and universities.
3. Comparative and cross-cultural studies in a variety of subjects and disciplines.
4. Educational exchange and study abroad — the movement of persons for firsthand immersion in other cultures.
5. Technical assistance to educational development in other countries through various foreign aid programs.
6. International cooperation in intellectual exchange and educational development through international organizations and multilateral arrangements (for example, United Nations Educational, Scientific, and Cultural Organization [UNESCO] and the Southeast Asian Ministers of Education Organization).
7. Intercultural education — the study of various subcultures that make up a nation. The ethnic diversity of America makes this category as valid at home as it is abroad.[5]

A decade later, Leestma described the elements of "global education," the label increasingly applied to international studies by the field in 1979:

1. Unity and diversity of humankind: a concern with the commonalities of people, with the fact that certain basic human concerns and needs are shared by all men and women; at the same time, there is a concern with the differences within the family of man.
2. International human rights: basics to human dignity and the achievement of the individual's potential.
3. Global interdependence: perception of the world as a planetary ecosystem — an interconnected web of interacting physical, biological, and social subsystems.
4. Intergenerational responsibility: human use of the earth viewed as a special kind of living trust, each person having obligations for the maintenance of the health of the planet during his or her lifetime.
5. International cooperation: recognition that many of the planet's major problems can be solved or alleviated only through transnational cooperation of some sort — bilateral, regional, or worldwide.[6]

Sven Groennings contends that international education encompasses two domains different in tradition, substance, constituencies, finance, and policy development. One domain is the education component of cultural diplomacy and nation-building. This focus is related to foreign policy, diplomatic history, technical assistance under contracts with the government and foundations, and related issues involving the university in world affairs. Much of the field of exchange of persons, including the Fulbright program and International Visitors, is conducted within this framework of foreign policy.

The other domain is campus-based and focuses on curricular developments and strategies that promote the learning of international substance within the disciplines, on interdisciplinary bases, and within broad fields ranging from the liberal arts to professional schools; foreign language study and English as a second language (ESL); study abroad; foreign students; and institutional planning of internationally focused studies and programs. In this domain the federal government's policy is significant, defining the legal parameters for foreign students' stay and providing limited financial support for area studies, undergraduate program development, international business education programs, and institutional linkages abroad.

Groennings believes that because of the split traditions, international education is broadly regarded not as a distinctive field but rather as a collection of topics or problems having international aspects, an approach applicable to a great number of fields, or even a movement:

Yet there are growing professional organizations and networks; central administration of disparate international programs and activities is increasingly common on campuses; integrated planning of all such activities is becoming more widespread; and an emerging literature suggests that international education is becoming a field of study.[7]

International studies, whether a field of study or a number of fields, are thus conducted in a variety of ways at the undergraduate, graduate, and professional school levels at home and abroad. These programs are commonly based on the conviction that quality education must reflect and encompass knowledge of diverse societies and cultures as well as the realities of global interdependence.

Graduate programs in universities usually focus on a significant area of the world (such as Latin America) or a civilization (such as Islam) or comparative studies of more than one area or civilization (for example, international relations, comparative politics). These programs concentrate on the development of curriculum offerings and research pertaining to the areas of study. Such programs are normally in the humanities and social sciences and may include a field experience ranging from one summer to a full year.

Professional school programs prepare students to work in transnational, intercultural settings. Because technical competence alone may be insufficient preparation for successful work in a different culture, students are   sensitized to the diversities of societies and institutions that are encountered in a global economy.

International programs at the undergraduate level are significant in three ways: as part of a twentieth century liberal education; as preparation of students who will terminate their formal education after college but who need strong international competence for their careers; and as preparation for students who will continue international studies at the graduate level. In his 1989 study *International Studies and the Undergraduate*, Richard D. Lambert analyzed international studies under four rubrics: study abroad, foreign language instruction, internationally focused concentrations and courses, and the internationalization of the campus as a whole.[8]

At the undergraduate level, some colleges and universities offer courses with an international focus in the belief that sensitization to at least one other major culture is essential to understanding one's own culture and to appreciating the phenomenon of cultural similarity and diversity. Programs of this type may provide opportunities for the immersion of students in a foreign culture through study or work experience abroad. Another approach is through interdisciplinary studies (on a topic such as peace) or comparative studies (such as politics of South Asia). Less frequently, an attempt is made at "infusion" of disciplines through the introduction of international content throughout the undergraduate curricula.

These disparate efforts are admirable, but the existence of some international programs on campus reaching a limited segment of the student body is not seen as sufficient by those who are committed to the diffusion and integration of the international dimension. Changing undergraduate curricula to reflect a more global perspective will not be a simple task. Indeed, an old academic saw states that changing a curriculum is as easy as moving a graveyard. Only a visible and sustained commitment to institutionalizing the international dimension, preferably financed from off-campus sources, seems to generate the interest and support of the faculty and administration as a whole.

U.S. higher education has also been an important source of contractual help to U.S. government assistance programs abroad. The land-grant universities with strengths in science and agricultural technology have played an especially significant role in U.S. Agency for International

Development (USAID) programs that place hundreds of faculty abroad annually. Faculty returning from such foreign experience have brought new perspectives to their classes and have stimulated student and faculty awareness of world conditions.[9] During the past 35 years, most major U.S. universities have participated in some form of technical assistance under contracts with the government.

Since the mid-1960s, however, development assistance involving U.S. higher education, measured in constant dollars, has declined. Part of the decline is attributable to the increased use of consultants from the private sector, sometimes called "beltway bandits," who have been awarded contracts that previously were held by universities.

In 1975, Congress enacted Title XII of the Foreign Assistance Act of 1961 (FAA) to strengthen foreign program capabilities in universities and colleges and to enlist more effective use of their faculty. Programs under the FAA assist in upgrading the educational and human resources of those less-developed countries that are aided by USAID programs to further their national development efforts by reducing illiteracy, extending basic education, and increasing manpower training skills related to development. Much of the training is performed under contracts generally related to specific development projects agreed upon by the host government and the USAID mission in that country. Presently, about 50 universities participate in this program.[10] U.S. universities also assist in development work abroad financed by international organizations such as the World Bank.

The most successful aspect of international education in the early 1990s is seen in the number of foreign students studying in the United States. Indeed, one-third of all students worldwide who study abroad enroll in higher education in the United States. Their impact on the economy of the United States is substantial: they spend about $5 billion annually. In the past five years, more than 50 percent of the students have been Asian, with the largest numbers coming from China, India, Japan, and South Korea.[11]

In 1991–92, there were 419,585 foreign students (58.7 percent Asians) from 186 countries and territories attending more than 2,000 colleges and universities throughout the nation — a 3 percent increase over the previous year.[12] The top fields of study for the international students were business (20 percent), engineering (18 percent), mathematics and computer sciences (9 percent), and physical and life sciences (9 percent).[13] Slightly less than half of the students (46 percent) were enrolled in graduate programs. About 75 percent of international students use funds from family or other non-U.S. resources as primary sources of financial support. In contrast, there were only 21,579 foreign students in the United States in 1966–67.[14]

The number of U.S. students studying abroad has also increased dramatically since 1965–66, when there were 18,000. In 1989–90, there were more than 70,727 students (less than 3 percent of the total U.S. student population) who received credit from U.S. institutions in study-abroad programs. More than 77 percent of them studied in Western Europe, mainly in the United Kingdom (U.K.), Germany, and France. Only about 1,200 Americans study in Japan, in contrast to the more than 36,000 university students from Japan currently in the United States.

The field of study choices of U.S. students abroad are significantly different from those of foreign students in the United States. Most U.S. students study liberal arts, foreign languages, and social science, and only 6.7 percent choose engineering, physical and life sciences, and mathematics and computer sciences combined.[15]

Students from the United States primarily engage in three kinds of study abroad programs: those for exposure to other cultures and languages; those for training in disciplines and languages; and those for advanced studies (with research and the study of languages being dominant).

The barriers to more students from the United States studying abroad are not necessarily financial. According to a study by the State University of New York, impediments to study abroad are more likely to arise from advising, curriculum requirements, and related degree requirements than from lack of finances.[16] These encumbrances may be eased in colleges and universities as new educational exchange programs funded by the federal government make overseas study more attainable for U.S. students. In the 1990s, major changes are due for the numbers, destinations, and fields of study of U.S. students abroad.

The flow of foreign scholars coming to work in the United States is also significant. In 1991–92, there were 62,148 foreign academics, 47 percent Asian and one-third from Europe, teaching and doing research in U.S. universities. This contrasts to the 10,084 foreign scholars, 43 percent from Europe, who were in the United States in 1973–74.[17]

International education, then, regardless of how one slices it, exists in various guises in U.S. colleges and universities. The pluralism and diversity of higher education in the United States has made possible a variety of initiatives, a situation that offers many advantages, but the uncoordinated, ad hoc approach to international education within the academy leaves the challenge of infusing U.S. education with global perspectives far from fulfilled. The federal government may be the only entity with the magnitude and wherewithal to braid the strands of international education into a meaningful pattern to better serve the national interest. The government is not a newcomer in the field.

NOTES

1. Maurice Harari, "Internationalization of Higher Education," in *The International Encyclopedia of Higher Education*, Vol. 5, ed. Asa S. Knowles (San Francisco, Calif.: Jossey-Bass, 1977), pp. 2293–301; Robert A. McCaughey, *International Studies and Academic Enterprise: A Chapter in the Enclosure of American Learning* (New York: Columbia University Press, 1984), pp. XI–XVI.

2. John K. Fairbank, "Assignment for the '70s," *The American Historical Review* 74 (1969): 868.

3. Eighty-ninth Congress, Second Session, House of Representatives, Report No. 1539, "International Education Act of 1966," 17 May 1966, Report from Committee on Education and Labor.

4. "Notebook Concerning International Education and Health, 1966," Questions and Answers, What Are International Studies? p. 2, Box 44, Office Files of Cater, LBJ Library.

5. Robert Leestma, "OE's Institute of International Studies," *American Education*, May 1969, p. 6.

6. Robert Leestma, "Education for a Global Age: What is Involved?" *Vital Issues* 28 (March 1979): 1–6.

7. Sven Groennings, "Syllabus, Spring Quarter 1989, EHI 993: Critique of Educational Literature in International Higher Education," Institute of Higher Education, University of Georgia, Photocopy, pp. 1–2.

8. Richard D. Lambert, *International Studies and the Undergraduate* (Washington, D.C.: ACE, 1989), p. 1.

9. E. Boyd Wennergren, Donald L. Plucknett, Nigel J. H. Smith, William L. Furlong, and Joan H. Joshi, *Solving World Hunger: The U.S. Stake* (Washington, D.C.: Consortium for International Cooperation in Higher Education, 1986) pp. 31–33; AID-University Cooperation in Technical Assistance, *Building Institutions to Serve Agriculture* (LaFayette, Ind.: Purdue University, 1968) pp. 3–27; Sidney C. Sufrin, *Technical Assistance — Theory and Guidelines* (Syracuse, N.Y.: Syracuse University Press, 1966) pp. 44–45, 88–89; Richard A. Humphrey, ed., *Universities and Development Assistance Abroad* (Washington, D.C.: ACE, 1967).

10. Wennergren, *Solving World Hunger*, p. 31.

11. Paul Desruisseaux, "Education Leaders Urge U.S. Strategy for Coordinating International Exchanges," *Chronicle of Higher Education*, 25 November 1992, pp. A27–28.

12. *Open Doors 1991/92* (New York: Institute of International Education, 1989), p. 11.

13. Desruisseaux, "Education Leaders," pp. A27–28.

14. Digest of Education Statistics, 1966, National Center for Education Statistics, U.S. Department of HEW, OE (Washington, D.C.: Government Printing

Office, 1967), p. 120. Statistics for the 1966–67 academic year are from *CQ Almanac*, Eighty-ninth Congress, Second Session, 1966, p. 307.

15.   *Open Doors 1991/92*, p. 85.

16.   National Association of State Universities and Land Grant Colleges, Division of International Affairs, "Workshop on the Reauthorization of Title VI of the Higher Education Act," University of Pittsburgh, 2–3 March 1990, p. 19.

17.   Desruisseaux, "Education Leaders," pp. A27–28.

3

Federal Government Involvement in International Education

Historically, public concern for international affairs has never been widespread in the United States. Americans considered themselves geographically isolated, and domestic affairs dominated the nation's agenda until well into the twentieth century.

There was one notable exception, in the field of education, to the generally isolationist national attitude. In 1862, Senator Justin Morrill, author of the Morrill Act, which led to the establishment of the U.S. system of land-grant colleges and universities, recognized the challenges to the United States posed by international competition:

Our artisans are to contend with the skill and wealth of many nations, and our farmers are sorely pressed by the competition of agricultural products which change and rapid communication pushes to the front in all markets both at home and abroad. To successfully withstand this formidable rivalry, our countrymen need ... that fundamental instruction which is founded on the widest and best experiences of mankind.[1]

Morrill's views were ahead of their times, however, and the more usual world view of Americans was limited.

These attitudes changed during World War II, when an understanding of other nations became essential to our defense. The ensuing post-war rebuilding of war-damaged countries, the Cold War, the end of the colonial era, and creation of newly independent states throughout Asia and Africa all had significant effects on the United States. It was obvious that the United States could no longer remain isolationist, and the Marshall Plan and the system of economic and military alliances entered into by the United States and its allies gave evidence of the need for

Americans to know more about the international dimensions of their lives.

The federal government began to play a more important role in post–World War II higher education with the passage of the G.I. Bill that brought veterans, many of whom had returned from military service overseas, to campuses in the United States. The Fulbright Act of 1946, created with funds made available through the renegotiation of outstanding European debts to the United States, provided for the exchange of scholars and students between the United States and foreign countries.

"It was my thought then, and it is now," wrote Senator J. W. Fulbright, "that if large numbers of people know and understand the people from nations other than their own, they may develop a capacity for empathy, a distaste for killing other men, and an inclination to peace."[2]

Under the Fulbright program, the State Department Bureau of Educational and Cultural Affairs (CU) was, by 1966, sending 2,500 Americans abroad to study and bringing 6,000 foreign scholars and teachers to the United States. Beginning in 1961, the Fulbright educational exchanges were supported (and still are) through congressional appropriations in the Mutual Educational and Cultural Exchange Act of 1961.

The U.S. Advisory Commission on Public Diplomacy (ACPD) was created by Congress in 1948 to provide broad, bipartisan oversight of the international broadcasting, public affairs, and educational exchanges activities of the nation. Under supervision of ACPD, USIA conducted extensive education programs at U.S. missions abroad. USIA was to become the major government agency involved in educational and cultural exchanges, although many other federal government agencies and private foundations are also involved in international exchange and training programs.

Beginning in the 1950s, Point Four programs (under the auspices of the Foreign Operations Administration and, later, the International Cooperation Administration) sent U.S. advisors, frequently recruited by universities, to Third World nations to assist in their development programs. In 1961, the USAID was created to administer such overseas technical-assistance programs, usually through contracts with U.S. land-grant and other universities.[3] In 1966, USAID had contracts with 72 universities to train technical personnel for programs in 39 nations. USAID gave high priority to educational activities, including training of teachers and local agricultural extension agents, establishing agricultural universities, and assisting in the construction of new schools.

The National Science Foundation (NSF) Act of 1950 rejuvenated research in higher education by creating and sustaining a first-class science establishment based primarily in universities in the United States. The NSF supported the exchange of U.S. and foreign scientific personnel as well as the development of international science education programs. The NSF fostered the interchange of information among scientists from the United States and abroad and provided support for the translation of foreign scientific information.

The NDEA passed through the leadership of Senator Carl Elliott (D-AL) in 1958, the year after the Soviets' launch of Sputnik I shocked Americans into a reevaluation of the state of education in the United States. The NDEA represented an effort by the United States to regain international leadership not only in science and math but also, through Title VI of the act, in foreign languages and area studies. In addition, Title VI and its subsequent amendments supported fellowships in international fields.[4] Administered by HEW, the NDEA provided the most direct assistance to universities for continuing work in international studies.

The NDEA, passed by a Democratic Congress during Eisenhower's Republican administration (the act being shepherded through the legislature by Lyndon Johnson as majority leader of the Senate), was a landmark in federal higher education policy. Although it was conceived as a temporary, emergency program aimed at producing scientific manpower, it became a permanent and broader program well before its initial four-year authorization expired. The NDEA represented a great leap forward in the size and scope of federal activity in higher education. It was also the first omnibus education bill, combining a variety of loosely related titles that could have been separate bills.[5]

A few state governments also built up international studies competence in their public universities during the 1950s and 1960s. The state legislatures of California and Michigan were among the more generous in their appropriations to assist their universities develop programs in international education.

Starting in the 1960s, significant numbers of Americans went overseas in the Peace Corps with two missions: to learn about their host countries and to teach their hosts about the United States. In assisting in Peace Corps training programs, more than 100 U.S. universities learned some practical lessons about preparing Americans to work in developing nations.

The Fulbright-Hays Act (the Mutual Educational and Cultural Exchange Act), passed in 1961, authorized grants to teachers and prospective teachers of foreign languages for study in the United States and abroad. In addition, Special Foreign Currency Funds (so-called PL-480 funds) authorized pursuant to the Agricultural Trade Development and Assistance Act of 1954 as amended were made available for educational purposes in nations where the sale of grains and other commodities under the Food for Peace program had left the United States with surplus funds in the currencies of recipient countries. One of the most successful programs financed under this act was the University of the State of New York's Educational Resources Center in New Delhi, which developed educational materials about India for use in U.S. schools and colleges.[6]

By the mid-1960s, the varied involvement of the federal government in international education was criticized for its reliance on the academy for performance of a precise task, often by a specific scholar or a single department of a college or university, and frequently on a one-time basis. "The government regards intellectuals as astrologers to be summoned in for instant answers," wrote Herman Wells, Chancellor of Indiana University, "or as servile plumbers to be called on to patch up bits and pieces of a machine which they had no real hand in designing."[7] Such a situation was conducive to uneven development of international expertise throughout the nation and did not stimulate total university commitment to global education.

Outside the government, in the decade before the IEA, a few large foundations provided support to international activities, primarily in leading private universities. The Ford Foundation was a major pioneer and supporter of international education until 1970, when it turned to other priorities. The Ford Foundation also took a major interest in solving the educational needs of the growing nations of the world.[8]

The Carnegie Corporation supported programs utilizing U.S. academicians in teacher training, curriculum reform, and educational research at universities in Africa, the Caribbean, and the South Pacific. The Rockefeller Foundation, likewise, was interested in the development of higher education in Asia, Africa, and South America and also made large commitments to international agricultural research. In 1962, the Ford Foundation and the Carnegie Corporation helped finance the formation of a new private, nonprofit educational foundation, Education and World Affairs (EWA), to strengthen the international teaching, research, and service dimensions of U.S. colleges and universities. William W. Marvel, EWA's president, explained the foundation's creation as stemming "from the belief in university and foundation circles that, given the new scale of international effort by American higher education, there should be at least one organization devoting itself full time to the review, analysis and assessment of the directions in which we are moving."[9] EWA, joined by the associations representing higher education in Washington, was to play a significant role in formulating the IEA.

In 1966, the federal government and private foundations were at the zenith of support for international education. After the passage of the IEA and the subsequent decision by Congress not to appropriate funds for the act, interest in and financial support for international education from both sources declined. As a result, growth in the number of international programs and specialists depended more heavily upon local resources in the 1970s and 1980s.

NOTES

1. Quoted in Sven Groennings, "American Higher Education's Comparative Advantage in our Global Economy," Keynote Address, Fourteenth Annual Meeting, Association for the Study of Higher Education, Atlanta, Ga., 4 November 1989, p. 10.

2. J. William Fulbright, "The Creative Power of Exchange," *Exchange* 11 (Summer 1975): 4. On the Fulbright-Hays Act, see *A Quarter Century: The American Adventure in Academic Exchange* (Washington, D.C.: Board of Foreign Scholarships, 1971) and Walter Johnson and Francis J. Colligan, *The Fulbright Program: A History* (Chicago, Ill.: University of Chicago Press, 1965).

3. See, generally, Edward W. Weidner, *The World Role of Universities* (New York: McGraw-Hill, 1962), Chapter 9.

4. Clarence B. Lindquist, *NDEA Fellowships for College Teaching, 1958–68; Title IV, NDEA of 1958*, U.S. Department of HEW, OE, 1971; Barbara B. Clowse, *Brainpower for the Cold War: The Sputnik Crisis and National Defense Education Act of 1958* (Westport, Conn.: Greenwood Press, 1981).

5. Lawrence E. Gladieux and Thomas R. Wolanin, *Congress and the Colleges* (Lexington, Mass.: Lexington Books, 1976), p. 9.

6. Ward Morehouse, "Importing India's Educational Riches," *American Education*, May 1969, USOE, Washington, D.C., pp. 14–19.

7. Letter, Herman Wells and Bill Marvel to LBJ, 24 January 1967, Ex Ed Box 3, LBJ Library.

8. Robert E. Ward, *National Needs for International Education*, CSIS Monograph (Washington, D.C.: Center for Strategic and International Studies, Georgetown University, 1977), p. 12. For a more detailed analysis of support of international education by private foundations in the 1960s, see Department of Labor and Health, Education, and Welfare Appropriations for 1970, Hearings Before a Subcommittee of the Committee on Appropriations, House of Representatives, Ninety-first Congress, First Session, pp. 982–84.

9.   William W. Marvel, "The University in World Affairs: An Introduction," in Allan A. Michie, *The University Looks Abroad: Approaches to World Affairs at Six American Universities* (New York: Walker, 1965), p. xviii.

4

The Mosaic of
International Education

To better understand the complexity of international education in its many forms and varieties in the United States, it may be helpful to view it as a work of art — a giant mosaic composed of small tiles representing all of the institutions and individuals who contribute to the total picture.[1] The present-day mosaic looks like a Jackson Pollock design. The pieces appear to have been set in the wall at random. There is little or no relationship between the tiles. Many stand in isolation — sometimes splendid, but often just lonely. Huge gaps appear on the mosaic where pieces should have been placed. Some tesserae (the major foundations) have fallen out and have never been restored.

At the heart of the mosaic, central to the design, are the tiles of higher education. Close inspection of the tiles of any institutional pattern, the college or university configuration, reveals a complex collage of different-sized tesserae. Some are pure gold and give a sparkling effect, while others are only fragments or shards that lack luster. The tile arrangements of the university centers of excellence have survived in a better condition than others, perhaps not only because of the durability of the materials but also because the artists in charge have had the capability of replacing tesserae, should any fall out. However, only a few of the institutional arrangements enjoy such largesse. Few show much planning; they are not well-thought-out works. Without a coherent pattern in the center, the nationwide mosaic fails as a work of art.

What is needed is a national cartoon of the mosaic to indicate how the tiles should be arranged to follow contours of design rather than being set in a haphazard way. Leaving the arrangement to the whims of an uncoordinated committee of artists has not worked. A quarter of a century ago, a masterpiece of a cartoon of the national mosaic (the IEA) was designed by master painters, well-known figures in their day. Today's master painters, whose works are well-known, need to be commissioned to refine the cartoon, which could then be executed by expert mosaicists, who may vie with each other in the subtlety of their work and their ability to transpose the original designs of the masters into mosaic.

The center of the design is vital. Experience indicates that the center, the higher-education mosaics, will be properly planned and crafted only if commissions make it worthwhile for the mosaicists to organize their studios and craftsmen to effectively carry out the work. Financial support of the arts may also encourage new craftsmen and artist guilds to join the labors.

Once that is done, there are several techniques or ways of handling the setting of the tiles into the cement and numerous kinds of cements, plasters, and waterproof mastics from which to choose, according to circumstances. The operations are simple in principle, but instruction and practical guidance from an experienced mosaicist are recommended before one attempts any important work.

Durable materials are necessary, because a work of this magnitude will require several years to plan and execute. Recent trends in artistic circles have brought about a favorable situation for a national mosaic; a genuine revival of interest in its creation seems to be forming, in which case, procedures, supplies, and facilities for artists to execute the mosaic will become more widespread and standardized.

The United States badly needs an artistically designed monumental mosaic of international education — a state-of-the-art composition with the tesserae arranged to show a brilliant effect. New commissions (the NSEA, the Freedom Exchange Act, increased USIA educational exchanges, and revisions in the Higher Education Act) have been granted by the only financial angel (the U.S. government) with enough resources to sustain the effort to create such an important work of art. Is the nation on the verge of a renaissance of the art of the mosaic?

NOTE

1. Robert Leestma wrote of "The Mosaic of International Education" in "OE's Institute of International Studies," *American Education*, May 1969, USOE, Washington, D.C., p. 8. Techniques of mosaic work are described in Ralph Mayer, *The Artist's Handbook of Materials and Techniques* (New York: Viking, 1971), pp. 375–77.

LBJ on his way to deliver remarks at the Bicentennial celebration of the Smithsonian Institution, 16 September 1965. (Photograph by Yoichi R. Okamoto)

Wilbur Cohen, LBJ, and John Gardner. (Photograph by Yoichi R. Okamoto)

Congressman John Brademas and Senator Howard Cannon with LBJ. (Photograph by Frank Wolfe)

Douglass Cater, Assistant to LBJ, with Senator Wayne Morse. (Photograph by Yoichi R. Okamoto)

II

A NATIONAL MODEL:
THE IEA OF 1966

5

The History of the IEA and
Its Major Actors

The history of the IEA is a mixed story of brilliant initial success followed by disheartening failure as political events altered the public policy agenda of the nation. A description of the defeat of the IEA is an important story, if only because of the issue's contemporary significance. It is a story that provides insights into the realities of politics in Washington and highlights some of the factors that hinder the federal government's support for international education today.

The IEA was introduced in Congress in 1966 at a time when an extraordinary transformation of federal education policy was taking place during the administration of President Lyndon B. Johnson. Major new federal commitments were already in place, including the landmark Elementary and Secondary Education Act and the Higher Education Act of 1965. Other federal initiatives would follow, including the National Endowments for the Arts and the Humanities; Teacher Corps; Project Head Start; Follow Through; guaranteed student loans; college work-study; scholarships for the needy; school breakfasts; public television; and aid for school construction, developing institutions, the handicapped, community colleges, and bilingual education. A total of 47 educational laws were enacted during the Johnson administration, and federal education programs increased from approximately 20 to 130. During the 1960s, federal aid to schools and colleges surged from $1.8 billion to more than $12 billion annually.[1]

The IEA was passed in the midst of this euphoric success in the fields of education, and its passage was illustrative of the legislative process during the Johnson administration. The president publicly outlined the main points of the act in a major policy address and subsequently proposed specific actions in an educational message to Congress. The general content of the act was planned by a powerful presidentially

appointed task force of distinguished government officials and academicians. Congressional leaders of both House and Senate introduced the
bill and provided initial enthusiastic support for its passage, aided by
members of the White House staff who were energetically involved in
seeing the act through the legislative process. Strong endorsement of the
act came from representatives of higher education and in newspaper
editorials in the national press. A leading intellectual journal of the time,
The Saturday Review, ran a laudatory cover story on the IEA.[2]

Yet, with all of this support, the timing of the act's passage in the final
days of the Eighty-ninth Congress precluded its receiving an appropriation before adjournment. Only three months later, a new Congress
convened with a different attitude toward international education and
the president's programs, and the IEA was never funded. Rapidly
changing priorities of government in the 1960s, the vagaries of the
legislative process, and the ambivalence of academicians toward
international education contributed to the stillborn funding of the act,
which brought an end to that serious effort to strengthen international
education nationwide. It was a great cause laid upon a soul unfit because
of concerns about the war in Southeast Asia and urban rioting in the
United States.

A caveat about the failure of the IEA to gain an appropriation should be
noted. Most of the principal actors in the IEA story ascribe the disappointing outcome to the times and, especially, to that powerful variable,
the Vietnam War. Still, the question can be raised about whether the act
would have been funded in any case. There were other opportunities to
fund the law after 1967, the annus horribilis for the international education enterprise. An old axiom of Congress holds that acts get passed and
laws get funds when the national interest is clearly at stake. Some of the
nation's best and brightest leaders in government and academe could not
convince the hard-nosed legislators that the IEA met that test. In many
other instances, Congress found means to fund education at all levels,
directly and indirectly. Why not the IEA?

Federal funding for international education has been passed most
successfully when brigaded with practical and strategic concerns: national
defense (the NDEA); public diplomacy (without a clear differentiation
between educational exchanges on the one hand and the overt effort to
control public opinion in other nations on the other in educational and
cultural exchanges of USIA); and intelligence (the NSEA). Congress in
the post–Cold War era will probably stand by its old axiom. Funding for
IEA-like programs then will depend upon the recognition of policy
makers of the importance and relevance of international education to the

national interest of the United States. The major actors in the IEA saga endeavored to make such a compelling case in 1966–67.

Each actor in the decision-making process in national legislation tries to leave his/her own personal thumbprint on the final document.[3] This was certainly the case with the IEA, in which a number of major and minor actors contributed to the policy-making and policy-defeating process. Some of these players appeared to have greater personal impact, and some, less than their positions and their degree of involvement would lead one to suspect.

In addition to President Johnson, the most significant participants in the development and passage of the IEA were Douglass Cater in the White House, Representative John Brademas in Congress, Charles Frankel and William Marvel with the Presidential Task Force, and John Gardner and Paul A. Miller in HEW. The backgrounds of these men may provide clues about their interest in international education and their motivation in seeing the act implemented.

Lesser actors will be dealt with as they appear in the IEA drama. It should be noted that although opponents of the act used all means at their disposal to defeat the IEA, some friends, by their serendipitous actions, may have contributed to the ultimate failure of the act.

President Johnson gave the IEA its impetus and then, strangely, let it wither at the end. One of the hallmarks of the Johnson administration's Great Society was a strong commitment to innovation, especially in education. The president wanted the federal role in education to produce qualitative improvements. Because Johnson's only occupation other than public service had been as a public school teacher, he took a special interest in that field. As a consequence, the presidency was centrally involved in the education policy process throughout the Johnson administration.[4]

As Frankel noted, "The President's eyes lit up when education was discussed."[5] Gardner thought it natural that this "education president" should emphasize international education, because a president tends to give his own distinctive imprint to foreign policy.[6] Unfortunately, Johnson's foreign policy will be remembered more for its Southeast Asian imprint.

The president was not inexperienced in international matters. For six of eight Eisenhower years, Johnson, as majority leader, had steered foreign policy bills through the Senate, a task that required him to "know everything that could be known about the pending legislation."[7] While vice president, he sat in on National Security Council and cabinet meetings and insisted on a full reading of State Department cable traffic every day.

Johnson also visited some 25 foreign countries while vice president. Before each such visit, he received a complete briefing on U.S. relations with the country involved. Tom Wicker, a critic of Johnson's lack of experience in foreign affairs, felt that the trips abroad were largely ceremonial and "due to his informal and extroverted manner, not entirely successful."[8] Nevertheless, Johnson was well-traveled and had been exposed to cross-cultural contacts when he succeeded to the presidency.

The president also admired intelligence. According to Jack Valenti, "To have a Phi Beta Kappa key, to be a Rhodes scholar, to have graduated from a university in the higher reaches of your class was to the President an unerasable mark of achievement . . . the President gloried in brains."[9] It was ironic that those academicians that Johnson admired the most were to be among his severest critics during his administration.

On the White House staff, the key participant in the fields of education and health was Douglass Cater, special assistant to the president. Cater, who held two degrees from Harvard, had been the Washington editor and national affairs editor of *Reporter* magazine from 1950 to 1964 before joining Johnson's staff. During his time as a journalist, he had been an Eisenhower Exchange Fellow and a visiting professor at Princeton and Wesleyan.

Wilbur Cohen (secretary of HEW in 1968 after Gardner's retirement), in describing Cater's unique role as a presidential assistant solely concerned with education and health, praised "his relationship with the Budget Bureau, the Congress, the Commissioners of Education, the Secretaries, and the Washington educational lobby."[10] Many educators admired Cater as "someone they could talk to" who, in turn, had the ear of the chief executive.[11]

Valenti described Cater's role in getting education bills passed by Congress: "It was Doug Cater who rode point, clearing the way with stubborn congressmen and sometimes paranoid academicians and school professionals who saw darkly what the rest of us saw clearly."[12] Cater was closely involved with the IEA from its inception until its death, and it was he who made the last appeal for help to the physician who might have saved the act.

Charles Frankel was professor of philosophy at Columbia University when the president appointed him assistant secretary of state for education and cultural affairs in August 1965. Frankel had spent virtually his entire career at Columbia, where he received his B.A. (Phi Beta Kappa) and Ph.D. before joining the faculty in 1939. He was a Fulbright professor at the University of Paris in 1953–54. His liberal political credentials were attested to by his membership on the board of directors of the New York State Civil Liberties Union from 1959 to 1964.

In the spring of 1965, Frankel wrote *The Neglected Aspect*, a study of U.S. educational and cultural policy abroad, in which he noted that "the relations between societies and the prospects of any major government's foreign policies, depend on the activities and attitudes of the intellectual community." *The Neglected Aspect* suggested programs that the government might develop to give intellectual workers a more active and useful part to play in international affairs.[13]

The success of this work was a factor in Frankel's presidential appointment. In Washington, he exercised considerable influence on the Task Force on International Education and the drafting of the IEA. Frankel came to Washington at the urging of John Kenneth Galbraith, who told him, "You ought to get into the State Department. It will broaden your horizons. You'll find that it's the kind of organization which, though it does big things badly, does small things badly too."[14]

Another New Yorker, William W. Marvel, president of Education and World Affairs, contributed ideas that helped shape the IEA and rallied support for the act from foundations and universities. A Princeton graduate (Phi Beta Kappa) and Ph.D., he had taught international relations at his alma mater, Yale, and West Point. Marvel had served as a State Department cultural relations officer in Nicaragua and as a program officer for the director of mutual security in the executive office of the president. He was an officer of the Carnegie Corporation in New York for ten years (where he was a colleague of John Gardner) before becoming president of EWA in 1962. During the time of the Kennedy and Johnson administrations, EWA was a dynamic center for research and publication about international aspects of higher education.

Under Marvel's direction, EWA fostered communication and cooperation between the academic and governmental communities, both in the United States and abroad. Marvel believed that "scholars and research people have much to say and much to contribute to policy makers, and that a constructive dialogue will produce a significant flow of benefits in the other direction as well." He maintained that effective interchange was not only desirable but also absolutely vital to the role that the United States was playing in world affairs.[15]

Marvel was a protege of Herman B. Wells, chancellor of Indiana University and a member of the EWA board. Wells also was to play an important role in the IEA story as consultant to the Brademas Task Force on International Education. At the time of the passage of the IEA, Marvel, along with Brademas, wrote cover story articles for the *Saturday Review* that gave the act wide national exposure.

The driving force for the IEA in Congress was John Brademas (D-IN), a Phi Beta Kappa and magna cum laude graduate of Harvard and a Rhodes scholar (he earned a doctorate in social studies from Oxford). He had worked as a congressional assistant, served on Adlai Stevenson's staff during the 1956 presidential campaign, and taught political science at St. Mary's College (Notre Dame) before his election to the House in 1958. Brademas, described as an intellectual in politics, admired new ideas and fresh approaches to problems.[16]

In 1961, Adam Clayton Powell, Jr., chairman of the House Education and Labor Committee, appointed a Special Subcommittee on Education that included Brademas among its members. The subcommittee launched the first systematic survey of federal activities related to higher education, and its recommendations led to the passage of the Higher Education Facilities Act of 1963.[17]

Also in 1961, Powell created an Advisory Group on Higher Education and named Brademas as chairman. This five-member bipartisan study group investigated unmet needs of higher education in fields that contributed most directly to national security and economic growth. The advisory group produced a set of unanimous recommendations that included giving "special attention to ways of fostering high-quality basic research on the learning process with a view to improving the effectiveness of teaching and learning at all levels" and extending NDEA programs "to increase the effectiveness of college teachers in all fields."[18]

The work of the advisory group and the special subcommittee signaled the emergence of a higher education interest in the House that was distinct from elementary and secondary education.[19] In addition, the appointment of the Advisory Group on Higher Education, chaired by Brademas, established a precedent within the House Committee on Education and Labor that bore directly on Chairman Powell's creating a Task Force on International Education shortly after the IEA was introduced.

By 1966, Brademas had already played a significant role in shaping Project Head Start, the Elementary and Secondary Education Act of 1965, and the Higher Education Act of 1965 and was well on his way to earning the sobriquet "Mr. Education" in the House. Brademas was sponsor and floor manager of the IEA in the House and chaired a bipartisan Congressional Task Force on International Education that held extensive hearings on the act. The bill reported by the task force and the House Committee on Education and Labor contained the major provisions of the IEA that were eventually passed by Congress. The work of

Brademas, more than that of any other member of Congress, refined, shaped, and molded the international education ideas of the president into law.[20]

John W. Gardner, as secretary of HEW, was the most eloquent spokesman for the IEA during congressional hearings on the act. He had been president of the Carnegie Corporation before joining the Johnson administration in 1965. With credentials as an intellectual, he brought a level of establishment prestige unprecedented for his department. Gardner attracted bright and talented assistants to HEW and "provided the Department with leadership and an ambiance that made it the kind of place where bright young lawyers, analysts, educators, scientists, doctors, and social workers wanted to be."[21]

Gardner was educated at Stanford and the University of California, where he received his Ph.D., and he had taught psychology at the University of California, Connecticut College, and Mt. Holyoke. During World War II, he served as an officer in the U.S. Marine Corps and head of the Latin American section of the Federal Communications Commission. As early as 1948, when he was vice president of the Carnegie Corporation, Gardner questioned whether Americans were doing their "homework in foreign affairs." In an article in the *Yale Review*, he identified at least three audiences that would benefit from improved international education: adult citizens, college-age students, and "experts highly trained with respect to the various areas of the world." The latter group Gardner characterized as "that pitifully small corps of experts on each of the various areas of the world."[22] In 1964 he had chaired President Johnson's Task Force on Education that provided many of the ideas for the administration's education program, including several in the field of international education.

Gardner's assistant secretary for education was Paul A. Miller, who had been selected by President Johnson to direct the implementation of the IEA. The president of West Virginia University at the time of his appointment, Miller began work in Washington in July 1966 and made preparations to implement the IEA as soon as it was passed. Subsequently, he led the administration's efforts to get an appropriation for the act. Miller had a strong background in international activities of land grant universities, having worked at Michigan State University (MSU) (where he had received his Ph.D.) from 1947 to 1961, serving as a professor and provost. His mentor had been MSU President John A. Hannah, who had developed one of the best programs of international education at a major land grant institution (and who, like Miller, had been an agricultural extension specialist).

All of these major actors in the passage of the IEA were activists who had been university instructors and veterans of the military. They all had experience abroad, either in government service or in academic exchange programs, and were articulate spokesmen for public policy issues. Most were honor graduates of prestigious private universities, and all held advanced degrees. Gardner, Cater, and Frankel were nationally known authors, and Marvel, Frankel, and Gardner were friends who had worked together for a number of years in New York. All knew the benefits accruing from international education, and they were painfully aware of higher education's shortcomings in that field. Their heroic efforts almost brought about a revolutionary change in internationalizing U.S. education, but ultimately, the political realities of 1967 foreclosed the promise of their undertaking.

NOTES

1. Hugh Davis Graham, *The Uncertain Triumph: Federal Education Policy in the Kennedy and Johnson Years* (Chapel Hill: University of North Carolina Press, 1984), p. xix; see also Hugh Davis Graham, "The Transformation of Federal Education Policy," in *The Johnson Years, Volume One, Foreign Policy, the Great Society, and the White House*, ed. Robert A. Divine (Lawrence: University Press of Kansas, 1987).

2. *Saturday Review* 49 (20 August 1966): 47–48, 50–61, 67–71.

3. Wilbur J. Cohen, "Education Legislation, 1963–68, From Various Vantage Points," in *Educating a Nation: The Changing American Commitment*, A Symposium on Education, ed. Kenneth W. Tolo (Austin, Tex.: LBJ School of Public Affairs and University of Texas at Austin, 1973), p. 34.

4. Norman C. Thomas, *Education in National Politics* (New York: David McKay, 1975), p. 228.

5. Charles Frankel, *High on Foggy Bottom* (New York: Harper & Row, 1968), p. 10.

6. Ibid.

7. Glen T. Seaborg, *Stemming the Tide* (Lexington, Mass.: Lexington Books, 1987), p. 14.

8. Tom Wicker, *JFK and LBJ: The Influence of Personality Upon Politics* (New York: William Morrow, 1968), p. 153.

9. Jack Valenti, *A Very Human President* (New York: W. W. Norton, 1975), p. 156.

10. Cohen, "Education Legislation," p. 37.

11. Chester E. Finn, *Scholars, Dollars, and Bureaucrats* (Washington, D.C.: Brookings Institution, 1978), p. 196.

12. Valenti, *A Very Human President*, p. 84.

13. Charles Frankel, *The Neglected Aspect of Foreign Affairs: American Educational and Cultural Policy Abroad* (Washington, D.C.: Brookings Institution, 1966); Frankel commented on his "Spring '65 thesis" in *High on Foggy Bottom*, p. 17.

14.   Frankel's *High on Foggy Bottom* is a diary of his experiences in the Department of State.

15.   William W. Marvel, "Preface," in Richard H. Wood, *U.S. Universities: Their Role in AID-Financed Technical Assistance Overseas* (New York: EWA, 1968), p. 8.

16.   Lawrence E. Gladieux and Thomas R. Wolanin, *Congress and the Colleges* (Lexington, Mass.: Lexington Books, 1976), pp. 137–38.

17.   Ibid., p. 253.

18.   "Congressional Action for Higher Education," House of Representatives, Report of the Advisory Group on Higher Education, Committee on Education and Labor, Eighty-first Congress, Second Session, January 1962, pp. 9, 5.

19.   Gladieux and Wolanin, *Congress and the Colleges*, p. 253.

20.   John Brademas with Lynne P. Brown, *The Politics of Education: Conflict and Consensus on Capitol Hill* (Norman: University of Oklahoma Press, 1987), p. 20.

21.   Joseph A. Califano, Jr., *A Presidential Nation* (New York: Norton, 1975), p. 196.

22.   John W. Gardner, "Are We Doing Our Homework in Foreign Affairs?" *Yale Review* 37 (March 1948): 400–408.

6

The IEA as Part of Johnson's Legislative Program

In the summer of 1965, the Johnson administration was a Janus facing an escalating war in Southeast Asia and a War on Poverty in the United States. In Vietnam, President Johnson authorized General William C. Westmoreland, commander of U.S. Forces, to commit ground troops to direct combat against the Vietcong. U.S. B-52 heavy bombers carried out their first World War II–style mass bombing of Vietcong targets. Secretary of Defense Robert S. McNamara announced that an additional 21,000 U.S. soldiers had been deployed in South Vietnam, bringing the total number of U.S. troops to more than 70,000.

In the United States, Sargent Shriver was in the forefront of Johnson's war on poverty, directing the Office of Economic Opportunity. The Civil Rights movement continued its drive for equality for all Americans, and its efforts contributed to the enactment of the Voting Rights Act of 1965.

At the same time, the White House staff began work on its legislative program for 1966 under the direction of Joseph Califano, special assistant to the president. Califano coordinated the work of the "sub-presidency," all those who serve the president on a continuing or ad hoc basis, in an institutional capacity or otherwise, in the exercise of his responsibilities.[1] As Wilbur Cohen observed, much governmental decision making is made "by the relevant people meeting together *ad hoc*, and that's done largely by the President's main assistants like . . . Califano, or the Budget Bureau in the field of budget."[2]

A foreign observer noted at the time:

The search is on for useful things for the Johnson Administration to do next. . . . For all its Great Society label, the greater part of the legislation that has been passed represents the fulfillment of hopes deferred from previous Administrations. Mr.

Johnson wants to do something new of his own and the nooks and crannies of the executive departments are once more being combed for ideas.[3]

International education was one of the ideas that was combed out of the White House to be a part of a new legislative package in education. In May 1965, Ervin Duggan, an assistant to Cater, prepared a memo outlining an international education program (at his boss's request and with his review and approval) and suggested that "if a major program in this area is worked out (the Johnson Plan?), we might think of a major address by the President announcing his initiatives." Duggan thought such a speech might be delivered at the opening of an important international conference at a major university or at the UN General Assembly. He envisioned the address having "the sort of impact" that President Kennedy's "Strategy of Peace" speech had in 1963.[4]

Duggan's memo also contained a digest of suggestions for a program from Sam Smith; Harry McPherson, assistant to the president; Gardner; Kenneth Holland, president of the Institute for International Education; Senator William Fulbright (D-AR); Roger Fisher, professor of law at Harvard University; and S. Dillon Ripley, secretary of the Smithsonian Institution.

Commissioner of Education Francis Keppel was assigned the development of the program. Keppel, in turn, asked Frankel, who had been appointed but not confirmed as assistant secretary of state, to draft the international education section. This Frankel did in the offices of EWA in New York City, where he established a temporary headquarters until he was confirmed by the Senate on 11 September 1965.[5] On that very day, the number of U.S. forces in Vietnam surpassed 125,000.

Frankel's most important recommendation was for legislation to provide long-term grants to colleges and universities to help them develop new programs in international education. Such grants would assist the renovation of curricula and strengthening of faculties in the interest of the institutions' basic education programs. To Frankel, international education meant "an enlarged international perspective in education generally." Under the programs he advocated, the federal government would have done more than simply give financial support to higher education. It would have put its moral authority behind efforts to reduce the parochialism of U.S. schools and would have created a firmer foundation on which to base giving of long-term assistance to higher education — assistance that would "be given not to meet an emergency, or to buy specific services, but for the straightforward reason that the country has a permanent education interest in understanding and cooperating with other countries."[6]

Frankel's draft went to Keppel as an undated memorandum entitled "A Program in International Education," in which he advocated a "Johnson Doctrine" for international affairs. Central to this doctrine would be "a domestic program in international education" in which educational resources would be marshalled to promote U.S. understanding of other countries. Using rhetoric that would appear later in a presidential address, Frankel proclaimed that "the Great Society does not stop at the water's edge."[7]

The Bureau of the Budget's (BOB) International Division, which was to consistently serve as a less-than-enthusiastic supporter of international education, described Frankel's program design as "quasi-heroic" in "packaging" a grand "Johnson Doctrine" to take the Great Society abroad but as essentially barren of new ideas. The BOB was critical of the program's being anchored in education and excluding "health, personal security, social justice: all the other instruments for the international war on poverty, disease, ignorance, prejudice." The program was seen as establishing "OE [U.S. Office of Education] beachheads abroad" through a network of educational attachés to help Frankel's cultural affairs officers run "the local U.S. alumni office." Worst of all, from the BOB point of view, it ignored the problems of turf battles within the federal bureaucracy by asserting that "if the basic premises and purposes of such a program can be clearly defined, the problem of parceling out operational responsibility for it to various agencies *should settle itself.*"[8]

Also in the late summer, Marvel sent a memo to Cater, Keppel, and Frankel, spelling out his ideas on "The New Peace Offensive: A Johnson Program in International Education." Marvel stressed the need for bringing together the many separate aspects of international education — "a wide variety of programs launched individually over the last twenty years to meet different needs and opportunities" — and to combine them "with certain new elements, producing a unified program based on a restated, systematic philosophy." He suggested a restructuring of the governmental machinery by establishing "a semi-autonomous, founda-tion-like agency, similar to the National Institute for Educational and Technological Cooperation suggested by John Gardner in *AID and the Universities.*" Such an agency would have "close linkage" with the OE and would have the assistant secretary (CU) as its "policy chief."[9]

During Frankel's first day at the Department of State, Cater requested him to write a draft of a speech for LBJ to deliver at the centennial celebration of the founding of the Smithsonian Institute. Frankel wrote a first draft that provided an outline for Johnson's plan for international education that would be as imaginative and enterprising as the ones in domestic affairs. Cater put it into "Johnsonian prose," and after Califano had reviewed the draft, the speech was presented to the president on 14 September 1965.[10]

In the Smithsonian address, delivered two days later on the south side of the Mall to an audience of 500 scholars and scientists from 90 nations, the president announced "a new and a noble adventure" in international education. He invited all nations to share in and contribute to a five part program:

First, to assist the education efforts of the developing nations and the developing regions.

Second, to help our schools and universities increase their knowledge of the world and the people who inhabit it.

Third, to advance the exchange of students and teachers who travel and work outside their native lands.

Fourth, to increase the free flow of books and ideas and art, of works of science and imagination.

And fifth, to assemble meetings of men and women from every discipline and every culture to ponder the common problems of mankind.[11]

The president promised to present such a program to Congress in the following year. To carry out his proposals, Johnson stated that he had directed a special task force chaired by Secretary of State Dean Rusk and including Gardner among its members "to recommend a broad and long range plan of educational endeavor."[12]

In the lofty rhetoric typical of Johnson's speeches, the president declared that "the growth and the spread of learning must be the first work of a nation that seeks to be free. . . . We mean to show that this Nation's dream of a Great Society does not stop at the water's edge: and that it is not just an American dream." The president quoted De Toqueville: "Men cannot remain strangers to each other or be ignorant of what is taking place in any corner of the globe." He concluded, "We must banish that strangeness and the ignorance."[13]

Johnson's oratory did not match the noble sentiments of the occasion. According to Frankel, "his tone was flat, and people around me, representing more than eighty countries, seemed not to be listening."[14] The *New York Times* was on strike at the time, limiting press coverage in the United States. One U.S. college president, however, wrote Johnson that the Smithsonian address was "the most important speech" of his career.[15]

The address was widely reported by the foreign media. President Bourguiba of Tunisia had been impressed by the Smithsonian speech and indicated that he was interested in setting up a Tunisian-U.S. education foundation using excess foreign currencies.[16]

Ten days after the Smithsonian celebration, Rusk, Gardner, Cater, McPherson, Keppel, and Frankel met to discuss priorities among the five basic objectives of the Smithsonian speech. The group talked about the formation of a semiautonomous agency to manage international education programs, composed of a board of directors representing the major agencies concerned and chaired by the assistant secretary of state for educational and cultural affairs.[17]

At this point, the international education initiative merged with the study and staff review of other components of the administration's legislative program that had begun in August. Many of the ideas for legislation came from secret, presidentially appointed, outside task forces. Proposals from task forces were further refined by White House staff into a presentation for the president. The president then approved or added some other ideas. Following the president's final decision, the subpresidency prepared the legislative program for presentation to Congress: first, the preparation of the state of the union message and the budget message for presentation to Congress, followed by preparation of bills and messages on the particular parts of the legislative program.[18]

The use of outside task forces as a supplementary source of ideas for a president's legislative program had been initiated by President Kennedy. President Johnson, in planning his activist program of public policy initiatives in 1964, made the task force a central feature in the development of his legislative agenda. The task force process suited Johnson's style of management, with its reliance on ad hoc, informal bodies, the maintenance of personal control of process by the White House, and the retention of flexibility by means of confidentiality.[19]

The president wanted "to get the advice of the best brains in the country on the problems and challenges confronting America," and he wanted "their help in devising the best approach to meeting them." Johnson instructed the task forces to develop "*practical* program ideas," but he reserved for the government the right "to exercise judgments later about what was feasible." The president also demanded that the task forces "operate without publicity."[20]

The strict requirement for staff secrecy fostered complete candor, even boldness, in task force recommendations while maintaining the president's mastery of the process. Public discussion and development of adverse reactions were avoided while the president considered his policy options and their political feasibilities and consequences. Thus, the outside task forces were free to be bold and innovative; they were not to be concerned with political or budgetary considerations; and they were to give confidential, off-the-record recommendations.[21] Cater found that the task forces produced "a remarkable number of good ideas . . . at the appropriate stage in the legislative planning process."[22]

The objectives of the Smithsonian address became the focus of the work of such a task force on international education appointed by the president on 1 October and chaired by Secretary Rusk. The Rusk Task Force enjoyed a large and powerful membership and strong presidential backing. Its membership included five university and college presidents — Harvie Branscomb of Vanderbilt University, Margaret Clapp of Wellesley College, John Fischer of Columbia University Teachers College, Charles Odegaard of the University of Washington, and Harry Ransom of the University of Texas — and high-ranking federal officials — Secretary Gardner of HEW, Commissioner Keppel, Peace Corps Director Sargent Shriver, USAID Director David Bell, USIA Director Leonard Marks, and Director of the National Science Foundation Leland Haworth — Cater and McPherson from the White House, and Frankel as de facto chair. The other members were Herman Wells of the Indiana Foundation; Professor John Hope Franklin of the University of Chicago; Harold Howe II, executive director of the University of North Carolina's Learning Institute; Pauline Tompkins, general director of the American Association of University Women; James Linen III of *Time*; Mrs. Arthur Goldberg; and Marvel.[23]

Cater reported to the president that the international education task force had a "broad regional mix with three Negroes, three women, and the number kept to fourteen to maintain an effective working group."[24] The membership of the Rusk group was typical of the Johnson task force representing the world of the bureaucracy, which would be finally responsible for implementing the ideas; the world of expertise outside of government; and a White House special assistant. Such representation made it possible for the administration to anticipate the reactions of different constituencies that would be served or alienated by the recommendations of that task force and make them a part of the process in developing the programs.[25]

The Rusk Task Force published its first-round summary of ideas and proposals suggested to implement Johnson's five objectives on 12 October 1965. Most of the initiatives and suggestions made to the president were from the late summer memos of Frankel and Marvel. Arthur Goldberg, U.S. ambassador to the UN, also made suggestions that Frankel considered particularly well thought out.[26] To supplement this first report, specific papers were requested from selected governmental agencies, private individuals, and private organizations.[27] During the time the Rusk Task Force was gathering its information, the number of U.S. troops in Vietnam had reached 148,300.

On 1 December, Frankel sent task force members a summary of Department of State Field Posts' proposals to implement the president's five points that he found "fascinating."[28] The next day, Marvel offered to work full time for the following two months on Rusk Task Force matters and to use the offices of EWA as a "nerve center for continuity" for the next six to eight months until the IEA was in place.[29] Marvel's offer was accepted, and he and the staff of EWA carried on valuable work on behalf of international education during the next several months.

On 3 December, Secretary Rusk submitted the "Report of Task Force on International Education" to President Johnson. In his transmittal letter, Rusk gave "special thanks . . . to William Marvel . . . who has served as special adviser to the chairman of the Task Force." The report was a forcefully written document that addressed the problem of Americans' need to know more about the rest of the world and suggested ways to meet that requirement.

The report began by stating the necessity for a long-term view of improving the international dimension of U.S. education:

Over the long run, the U.S. education system has as much power as any other agency to promote understanding and sympathy with other nations or to stifle such understanding and sympathy at their roots. . . . We are charting only the first steps on a long road. Where education is concerned, time is necessary. . . . The national interest requires that college graduates be informed about the world beyond America's borders and the changes taking place in it.

The program promulgated by the task force was "based on a different and new premise — that educational relations with other nations merit being treated as a permanent and important aspect of foreign affairs on the same level with other enduring aspects of foreign policy like commercial relations."[30]

The task force recommended "that a new dimension be added to the Federal Government's interest in education" through a program that would "dramatically lift educational levels at home and abroad."[31] The program was described in detail in materials collected by the task force from 31 organizations and individuals involved in international education. Several of the proposals followed up some general recommendations that had been made by the Gardner Task Force on Education dealing with support for foreign universities, exchange programs, and training in international affairs in U.S. universities.[32] This confirmed Wilbur J. Cohen's observation that "the task force may have served its paramount significance in serving as a legitimating agent for ideas already in existence."[33]

Cater recalls that there were few initiatives in the task force recommendations that needed authorizing legislation: "What was needed was galvanizing institutional arrangements within the federal government as well as new funds and higher priorities for funding that could be used under the broad umbrella of International Education."[34]

On 15 December, Cater presented the president with staff recommendations based on the report of the task force. Cater thought the recommendations constituted "a dynamic first year program which will capture the imagination of people at home and abroad." He told the president that the 1966 Legislative Program for International Education would reflect Johnson's concern that "throughout the world, as in our own nation, *education* must be the first work of these times."[35] Under the proposed program, leadership "for the entire governmental effort in this field" was to be provided by a new Center for Educational Cooperation (CEC) in the OE.[36]

Cater, as the White House specialist in education, dealt both with the congressional liaisons in departments and the strategic committee members that handled related legislation in Congress. He arranged for authorship of bills in the two Houses, checked on the positions of strategically located members of Congress, and conducted head counts of committee members or of the members of the Houses. He also contacted outside sources knowledgeable about the effects of legislation or the attitudes of interest groups.[37] When the international education legislation was being prepared for presentation to Congress, Cater sampled the opinion of college and university presidents, who were generally enthusiastic about the idea.

Early in 1966, Cater reported to the president that "I think we were successful in selling [Senator William] Fulbright on your international education program." The senator had noted, however, "that this educational initiative would be much better if we could get that damn Vietnam war off our back," but then he added that the new program would serve as a useful antidote to the war in Vietnam.[38]

Fulbright declined to sponsor the IEA reasoning that it would be better to treat it as domestic legislation because it provided only for grants to U.S. colleges and universities and would be mainly administered by

HEW. The administration then turned to Congressmen John Brademas and Adam Clayton Powell (D-NY), chairman of the House Committee on Education and Labor, to sponsor the IEA in the House of Representatives and to Senator Wayne Morse (D-OR), chairman of the Senate Labor and Public Welfare Committee, to introduce the act in the Senate.[39]

Brademas described the significance of the interaction between the executive and legislative branches in passing the IEA: "It is not enough for a president to lay his ideas before Congress and then sit in the White House awaiting results. If a president's proposals are to become law, they must strike a responsive chord in legislators willing to sponsor and guide them through the obstacle course on Capitol Hill."[40] The passage of the IEA demonstrates that, even when ideas for legislation come from elsewhere, it is often a congressman — in this case, Brademas — who transforms the ideas into law.

In his state of the union message on 12 January, the president put international education into a "foreign aid" category by declaring:

This year I propose major new directions in our program of foreign assistance to help those countries who will help themselves. We will conduct a worldwide attack on the problems of hunger and disease and ignorance. We will place the matchless skill and the resources of our own great America, in farming and in fertilizers, at the service of those countries committed to developing a modern agriculture. We will aid those who educate the young in other lands, and we will give children in other continents the same head start that we are trying to give our own children. To advance these ends I will propose the International Education Act of 1966.[41]

On 2 February 1966, President Johnson reported the findings of the Rusk Task Force and the proposed legislative program in a special message to Congress on world health and education in which he urged the passage of the IEA. The president said, "We would be shortsighted to confine our vision to this nation's shorelines. The same rewards we count at home will flow from sharing in a worldwide effort to rid mankind of the slavery of ignorance and disease."[42]

President Johnson made some two dozen proposals containing details of a program whose broad outline he had set forth in his Smithsonian address. He proposed a unified, integrated program "to strengthen our capacity in international educational cooperation, to stimulate exchange with the students and teachers of other lands, to assist the progress of education in developing nations, and to build new bridges of international understanding." The president's message indicated that the varied but interrelated aspects of international education constituted an important area of national concern and responsibility.[43]

In advocating this new approach to international education, President Johnson indicated that many agencies and departments of the federal government would be involved in its implementation through new legislation, executive orders, and departmental directives. The president specifically charged HEW with "a broad authority to help strengthen our country's capacity to carry on this noble adventure."[44]

NOTES

1.   Emmette S. Redford and Richard T. McCulley, *White House Operations, The Johnson Presidency* (Austin: University of Texas Press, 1986), p. 1.

2.   Transcript, Wilbur J. Cohen Oral History Interview, 10 May 1969, tape 4, AC 72-26, p. 10, LBJ Library.

3.   "The Great Educator?" *The Economist* 216 (25 September 1965): 1203–04.

4.   Memo, Ervin S. Duggan, assistant to Douglass Cater, to Cater, 13 May 1965, "International Education 1966 (2)," Box 44, Office Files of Cater, LBJ Library; Letter, Cater to Vestal, 16 May 1989.

5.   Transcript, Charles Frankel Oral History Interview, AC 80-51, 29 January 1969, by Paige E. Mulhollan, p. 3; Letter, Marvel to Cater, 24 August 1965, "International Education, 1965 (1)," Box 44, Office Files of Cater, LBJ Library.

6.   Charles Frankel, *High on Foggy Bottom* (New York: Harper & Row, 1968), pp. 35–37.

7.   Memo, Frankel to Keppel, undated, Subject: A Program in International Education, "International Education, 1965 (2)," Box 44, Office Files of Cater, LBJ Library.

8.   Memo, International Division to Cannon, 1 September 1965, Container 412, OMB Records Div., Nat. Archives, cited in Hugh Davis Graham, *The Uncertain Triumph: Federal Education Policy in the Kennedy and Johnson Years* (Chapel Hill: University of North Carolina Press, 1984), p. 248.

9.   Memo, Marvel to Cater, Keppel, and Frankel, 17 August 1965, Subject: The New Peace Offensive: A Johnson Program in International Education, "International Education, 1965 (2)," Box 44, Office Files of Cater, LBJ Library; see also John W. Gardner, *AID and the Universities* (New York: Education and World Affairs, 1964).

10.   Memo, Cater to LBJ, 14 September 1965, "Memos to the President, September 1965," Box 14, Office Files of Cater, LBJ Library; Frankel Oral History, p. 3; Frankel, *High on Foggy Bottom*, p. 39. Tracing the history of presidential speech writing poses a challenge for the historian. In addition to Frankel's claim to authorship of the Smithsonian address that the record would appear to verify, two others profess being involved. Cater stated, "I had been the draftsman of the President's speech at the Smithsonian" (Transcript, Douglass Cater Oral History Interview, 8 May 1969, tape 2, p. 1, LBJ Library); and Ralph Flynt said he had "a considerable part in writing the Smithsonian speech and in drafting the message of 2 February 1966, out of which the IEA came" (interview, Ralph C.M. Flynt, deputy assistant secretary for international education, office of assistant secretary for education, 23 July 1968, The History of the Office of Education, Appendices, LBJ Library).

11. *Public Papers of the Presidents of the United States, Lyndon B. Johnson, 1965*, Vol. II (Washington, D.C.: U.S. Government Printing Office, 1966), p. 1005.

12. Ibid.

13. Ibid., pp. 1005–6.

14. Frankel, *High on Foggy Bottom*, p. 41.

15. Letter, George Angell to LBJ, undated, attached to Memo, Cater to LBJ, 6 October 1965, "Memos to the President, October 1965," Box 14, Office Files of Cater, LBJ Library.

16. Memo, Cater to LBJ, 27 July 1966, Box 15, Office Files of Cater, LBJ Library.

17. Presidential Task Force on International Education, 25 September 1965, pp. 5–7, "International Education," Box 10, Office Files of McPherson, LBJ Library.

18. Redford and McCulley, *White House Operations*, p. 92.

19. Ibid., p. 78.

20. Ibid., p. 79, citing the president's remarks attached to a memorandum from Bill D. Moyers, 9 June 1964, Ex FG 600, WHCF, LBJ Library.

21. Redford and McCulley, *White House Operations*, pp. 80, 84.

22. Transcript, Douglass Cater Oral History Interview, 8 May 1969, tape 2, p. 14, LBJ Library.

23. Book Telegram, Cater to Members of Task Force on International Education, 4 October 1965, "International Education, 1965 (1)," Box 44, Office Files of Cater, LBJ Library; Graham, *Triumph*, p. 113.

24. Memo, Cater to LBJ, 1 October 1965, "Memos to the President, October, 1965," Box 14, Office Files of Cater, LBJ Library.

25. Norman C. Thomas, *Education in National Politics* (New York: David McKay, 1975), pp. 178–84; Graham, *Triumph*, p. xxi. A most helpful work on President Johnson's task forces is Nancy Keegan Smith's "Presidential Task Force Operations during the Johnson Administration," 18 pp. mimeographed, June 1978, LBJ Library.

26. Memo, Elinor P. Reams, CU/PRS, to Cater and McPherson, Ambassador Goldberg's Suggestions for the President's New Program, 1 December 1965, "International and Domestic Education," Box 44, Office Files of Cater, LBJ Library.

27. OA #1234 Work Book #1, President's Task Force on an International Program, 12 October 1965, Submissions from the Private Sector that have been Reproduced as of November 9, 1965, "Materials on the Task Force on International Education (1)" and "Materials on the Task Force on International Education (2)," Box 40, Office Files of Cater, LBJ Library.

28. Memo, Frankel to Members of the Task Force, Summary of Field Posts' Proposals to Implement the President's Five Points, 1 December 1965, "International and Domestic Education," Box 44, Office Files of Cater, LBJ Library.

29. Memo, Marvel to Cater and Frankel, Continuity in International Program Development During Next Six to Eight Months, 2 December 1965, "International Education, 1966 (2)," Box 44, Office Files of Cater, LBJ Library.

30. Letter, Rusk to LBJ, 12 March 1965, p. 2, "Report of Task Force on International Education, November 1965," Box 40, Office Files of Cater, LBJ Library.

31. Ibid., p. 5.

32. Robert Eugene Hawkinson, *Presidential Program Formulation in Education: Lyndon B. Johnson and the 89th Congress*, Department of Political Science,

University of Chicago, Ph.D. dissertation, 1977, p. 191.

33. Wilbur J. Cohen, "Education Legislation, 1963–68, From Various Vantage Points," in *Educating a Nation: The Changing American Commitment*, A Symposium on Education, ed. Kenneth W. Tolo (Austin, Tex.: LBJ School of Public Affairs and University of Texas at Austin, 1973), p. 34.

34. Letter, Cater to Vestal, 16 May 1989.

35. Memo, Cater to LBJ, 16 December 1965, Subject: 1966 Legislative Program for International Education, "International Education, 1966 (1)," Box 44, Office Files of Cater, LBJ Library.

36. Memo, Cater to LBJ, 15 December 1965, "Memos to the President, December 1965," Box 14, Office Files of Cater, LBJ Library.

37. Redford and McCulley, *White House Operations*, pp. 60, 93–94.

38. Memo, Cater to LBJ, 10 January 1966, "Memos to the President, January 1966," Box 14, Office Files of Cater, LBJ Library.

39. Frankel, *High on Foggy Bottom*, p. 74. Califano contrasts LBJ's poor relationship with Fulbright ("an example of total break") with the president's good relationship with Morse ("the 'how-to' of presidential personality politics") in Joseph A. Califano, Jr., *A Presidential Nation* (New York: Norton, 1975), p. 196.

40. John Brademas with Lynne P. Brown, *The Politics of Education: Conflict and Consensus on Capitol Hill* (Norman: University of Oklahoma Press, 1987), p. 19.

41. *Public Papers of the Presidents of the United States, Lyndon B. Johnson,1966*, Vol. I, State of the Union, 12 January 1966 (Washington, D.C.: U.S. Government Printing Office, 1967), pp. 3–12.

42. *Public Papers of the Presidents of the United States, Lyndon B. Johnson,1966*, Vol. I, Message to the Congress Proposing International Education and Health Programs, 2 February 1966 (Washington, D.C.: U.S. Government Printing Office, 1967), p. 128.

43. Ibid., pp. 128–36; Rose Hayden estimated that the price tag of LBJ's programs in international education and health was $524 million (Rose L. Hayden, *Federal Support for International Education: Assessing the Options* [Washington, D.C.: National Council on Foreign Studies, 1985], pp. 14–21).

44. *Public Papers of the Presidents of the United States, Lyndon B. Johnson, 1966*, Vol. I, Message to the Congress Proposing International Education and Health Programs, 2 February 1966 (Washington, D.C.: U.S. Government Printing Office, 1967), p. 128.

7

The IEA Before the House of Representatives

On the same day that the president delivered his message on World Health and Education, Secretary Gardner submitted a draft bill to Speaker of the House John McCormack (D-MA), and Brademas and Adam Clayton Powell (D-NY), chairman of the Education and Labor Committee, introduced identical bills in the House.[1] The bill would authorize a domestic program, administered by HEW, of grants designed to strengthen the resources and capabilities of U.S. colleges and universities in international studies and research.

In a press release, Powell called the proposed act "one of the greatest contributions to international understanding in the history of this country . . . a Magna Charta of international education." He predicted that "history will record this day as the beginning of an international renaissance in learning."[2] Grayson Kirk, president of Columbia University, was equally enthusiastic, calling the act "the best and most comprehensive program of support for international education activities that has ever been devised."[3]

Brademas took a special interest in the IEA and persuaded Chairman Powell to create a task force to handle the legislation.[4] On 24 February 1966, Powell appointed Brademas as chair of a bipartisan task force of seven House Education and Labor Committee members to conduct hearings on the proposed legislation.[5] The members of the task force were Democrats Carlton R. Sickles (MD), August F. Hawkins (CA), William D. Hathaway (ME), William D. Ford (MI), and Patsy Mink (HI) and Republicans William H. Ayres (OH), Alphonzo Bell (CA), and Albert H. Quie (MN).

Herman B. Wells, former president of Indiana University and an internationally recognized authority on the subject of the legislation, served, at Brademas' request, as an unpaid but invaluable consultant to the House task force. Earlier, Wells had been a member of the Rusk Task Force. Marvel assigned EWA staff member Peter N. Gillingham to work as counsel for the Brademas Task Force. In addition, EWA maintained a Washington office to provide a liaison with higher education associations and to assist in the lobbying effort for the IEA.

While the task force hearings were being held, Cater assembled a group of private foundation leaders at Airlie House for a weekend meeting to discuss "how the foundations could get behind" the president's international education program.[6]

Seven days of hearings, a long time for a measure of this kind, were conducted by the task force from 30 March to 7 April. The task force heard testimony from 26 witnesses in a seminar-like setting that covered virtually all significant aspects of international education. Testifying as administration witnesses were Gardner, Frankel, Bell (USAID), Marks (USIA), and Warren Wiggins, acting director of the Peace Corps.[7] Representatives Robert McClory (R-IL) and Westin E. Vivian (R-MI) also testified. The 19 nongovernmental witnesses included administrators and faculty from universities, colleges, and schools; representatives of state education departments, educational associations, and scholarly and professional societies; and spokesmen for private foundations, labor, and business.[8] All of the witnesses endorsed the proposed legislation, although they suggested changes of emphasis or coverage.

The testimony of the witnesses led to two major conclusions: first, that in the conduct of foreign policy, the federal government had drawn heavily upon the resources of colleges and universities without sufficient concern for the strengthening and replenishing of their intellectual capital, and second, that the increasing responsibilities of world leadership made it necessary for the nation to increase systematically the competence of institutions of higher education to teach students and to accelerate research on international issues and problems.[9] The task force concluded that the federal government had a clear responsibility to support and strengthen the capabilities of U.S. colleges and universities for international studies and research. The testimony before the task force established the magnitude of the need and the importance to the nation of an educational system with high competence in world affairs.

In opening the task force hearings, Brademas emphasized that the IEA dealt with domestic education programs and had nothing to do with educating people in other nations. Indeed, the authors of the act stressed the domestic nature of the bill throughout the legislative process — although some of their congressional colleagues refused to hear or feigned deafness at strategic moments.

In his testimony as the first witness, Gardner set the tone that was to be echoed by later witnesses: "I believe very deeply that we are talking here about one of the gravest challenges the American people face." In commenting on the growing need for an international dimension in education, Gardner noted: "Today international and domestic concerns are woven together inextricably in the fabric of life of people everywhere on earth. The nations of the world can ignore this only at their peril."[10]

In a masterly analysis of the IEA, Gardner stressed the president's concern for international education, the growing need for an international dimension in education, the enduring national interest in the field, and the unique global responsibilities of the United States, requiring an informed citizenry. He noted that the NDEA benefited relatively few students and argued that "it is of greatest importance to American undergraduate learning that we expand from the NDEA training of specialists concept and establish a broad base in the colleges and universities for educating our young people as generalists and citizens."[11]

Gardner emphasized that the bill did "not propose that the United States undertake to educate the world" but that it offered an "opportunity . . . for genuinely collaborative" action between universities and the federal government.[12] He believed that sustained federal support for universities and colleges should be determined by national needs and the particular strengths of individual institutions.

Gardner forcefully concluded his testimony by stating: "In a world of great peril and promise, this International Education Act of 1966 will help us to lessen the peril and to increase the promise — not only for our Nation but for people all over the world."[13]

Frankel, Bell, Marks, and Wiggins, the heads of the major governmental agencies involved in foreign affairs, appeared before the task force the following day and testified that there was no conflict between their existing responsibilities in international education and those that would be assigned to HEW under the bill. These officials believed that the IEA would strengthen the basic resources available to other federal agencies in carrying out their international responsibilities. They also agreed that the interests of their agencies in international education were not only interrelated but also mutually supportive.[14]

Testimony by representatives of the private sector pointed out that if colleges and universities were to meet the demands placed upon them in the field of international affairs, additional support from federal funds would be needed. The task force noted that "however valuable the financial support provided by state, local, and private sources for international studies and research programs in colleges and universities, such financing is no longer adequate."[15]

Federal financial support under the IEA was centered in the grant programs, and three principal themes emerged from the testimony concerning their administration: "the need for criteria and guidelines in selecting institutions for support, a long-term federal commitment, and broad-gage support of a wide diversity of programs."[16]

Both witnesses and task force members emphasized that higher education's needs for funding of international studies were so great and the funds proposed in the bill so limited that it was essential to establish clear and usable criteria for their allocation. Witnesses cited such desirable standards as faculty competence, imaginative leadership, and institutional commitment to improve the quality and broaden the scope of teaching and research capabilities in international studies.[17]

The task force found that a long-term federal commitment to the objectives of the act was essential if the programs were to become an integral part of educational institutions. In the past, the short-term and project-oriented nature of federal programs in international education had led some institutions and individuals to regard the subject as peripheral to the primary concerns of a university. The task force felt that this situation could be ameliorated by sustained financial backing, as demonstrated both by the support of international studies by major foundations and by the experience of the federal government in providing grants for scientific research.[18]

The record of past experience with governmental and private support of international studies led the task force to believe that federal grants under the IEA would not result in reliance upon federal financing. On the contrary, several witnesses had testified that the IEA would likely stimulate higher levels of support for international education from the resources of the recipient institutions, from state and local governments, and from private sources.[19]

William Dix, librarian of Princeton University, representing the Association of Research Libraries, admired the coordination of programs contained in the bill:

Teachers and scholars who have been struggling to solve the countless problems of international cultural relations through scores of uncoordinated instruments and agencies, public and private, effective and fumbling, found in his [President Johnson's] words for the first time the prospect of a serious and organized attempt at the highest governmental level to develop an effective U.S. program in international education.[20]

The task force was interested in seeing "broad support" under the act given to a diversity of high-quality programs. Broad support referred both to supporting the balanced growth of an institution as a whole and to supporting a wide diversity of programs.[21]

According to Frankel, the Brademas Task Force indicated that the administration was not asking "for anything like the amount of money that was needed."[22] Many witnesses agreed. In his testimony, Ward Morehouse, director of the Office of Foreign Studies, State Education Department, University of the State of New York, cited the findings of a conference of international studies directors that attempted to forecast what funding would be required to have any pervasive impact on college undergraduates. The amount required in a ten-year period was "something in the order of $300 million."[23]

Dean Stephen Bailey of the Maxwell School of Syracuse University testified to the importance of infusing an international dimension into all undergraduate curriculums both to provide students with a better understanding of an interdependent world and to prepare students for graduate training in international studies. "The encouragement of non-Western studies in undergraduate colleges will not only serve to sustain and enliven the liberal arts but will also furnish help where it is likely to yield the highest returns," said Bailey. "The quality of graduate education depends upon the quality of the undergraduate experience."[24]

J. George Harrar, president of the Rockefeller Foundation, testified that a broader distribution of graduate centers across that nation was needed.[25] The responsibility of the federal government to develop and maintain such centers was pointed out by Chancellor Franklin Murphy of the University of California at Los Angeles (UCLA). "At UCLA we have graduate programs in which five different African languages are taught. Quite clearly we are not teaching those languages in order to solve the problems of California; these are not really very germane to the interests of the California citizen," testified Murphy. "This is in the national interest because it is one of the few places in the world where this concentration can be found, and students come from all over the United States for this experience." Murphy added that the nation was "buying a pool of national competence," without which it could not go forward.[26]

The potential impact of the IEA on the training of teachers and the development of a more internationally informed citizenry was accentuated in the testimony of William Carr, executive secretary of the National Education Association. "We might hope in time to develop a citizenry with more profound understanding of other peoples," asserted Carr. For him, the act's "power to make a real difference in the way people behave, the way they think, and how they act on foreign policy issues," would be multiplied if it was made clear "that improved qualifications of elementary and secondary school teachers, in terms of international information and attitudes," was a very important purpose of the entire effort.[27]

Witnesses also testified that programs under the IEA would produce the knowledge and the personnel required by U.S. business to compete in global markets and to assist in the economic development of emerging nations. The task force noted the possibility and desirability of greatly increased support of international education by private business with its unique strengths in the field.[28]

The task force took 620 transcript pages of testimony and received some 25 additional official statements of opinion. To facilitate a reader's understanding of the points raised in the testimony, Brademas insisted that the printed hearings contain subheads. As a result, the wealth of testimony in the task force report is much easier to follow in a rational, sequential way.

More than 40 formal and informal suggestions for amendments were proposed by the witnesses or suggested by task force members. More than a dozen of these were incorporated in an amended version of the bill that the task force reported with unanimous approval on 26 April. The amended bill, H.R. 14643, was considered by the Committee on Edu-cation and Labor on the next day and, with the addition of a minor amendment proposed by Chairman Powell, was approved without dissent and ordered to be reported to the House.[29] The significance of Brademas' legislative leadership again was demonstrated by the unani-mous approval of the bill by the Committee on Education and Labor, a group with a tradition of sharp partisan conflict.[30]

The bill declared that strengthened U.S. capabilities in international education were in the national interest and that it was, therefore, both necessary and appropriate for the federal government to assist in the development of resources for international study and research and in the development of trained personnel to meet the requirement of world leadership. Specific sections of the bill authorized programs to develop such resources.

Section 3 of the bill would authorize grants to universities or consortia for graduate centers of research and training in international studies. These centers might focus on a geographic area or on particular fields or issues in world affairs or on both.[31]

Section 4 would authorize grants to universities and colleges or consortia to assist them in planning and carrying out comprehensive programs to strengthen and improve undergraduate instruction in international studies.[32] In awarding such grants, three factors were to be taken into consideration: geographical distribution, institutional need, and the ability to use the funds effectively.

These grants were intended to encourage programs involving not only those departments traditionally concerned with area and international studies, such as political science, international relations, history, and languages, but also other parts of the institution, such as professional schools. The goal of these programs would be to provide exposure to international affairs, particularly to at least one non-Western area, as an element in the education of every undergraduate.[33] By studying at least one particular non-Western culture thoroughly in its own terms, an undergraduate could be "lifted out of his cultural bind as an American," abandon his egocentricity, and discover the capacity "to empathize universally."[34] More students would, thus, gain a better understanding of the complexities of world politics, and some would be attracted to graduate training in international studies.

Sections 3 and 4 of the bill also provided for grants to public and private nonprofit agencies and organizations, including professional and scholarly associations, because of the important role such groups had played in the development of international education.

Section 8 provided for an annual report to Congress on the activities carried out under the act and on other activities of the federal government in international education, particularly activities and plans to improve and coordinate the efforts of all federal agencies in this field.

Section 9 would amend Title VI of the NDEA by removing the requirement that language instruction be limited to those "not readily available" in the United States; eliminating the 50 percent matching requirement for institutions; and providing grant as well as contracting authority.[35]

The bill authorized for fiscal year 1967 a total for both sections 3 and 4 of $10 million; for fiscal year 1968, $40 million; for fiscal year 1969, $90 million; and for the fourth and fifth years of this five-year program, such amounts as Congress might later authorize.

On 17 May, the House Committee on Education and Labor issued a report on the IEA of 1966, providing strong bipartisan support of the bill. In the committee's view, the urgent need for the legislation could not be stated too strongly. The committee reported that "these strengthened educational resources will contribute both to providing the organized knowledge and highly trained personnel essential to safeguard the welfare and interests" of the United States and "to the continuing search to determine the conditions, policies, and actions which will create a more stable and peaceful world."[36]

Unlike most congressional committee reports that simply describe the bill being reported and give the arguments that justify the legislation and its cost, the report on the IEA provided what it described as "Background: The United States and International Education Today," an essay on the international dimensions of universities in the United States, relevant programs of the federal government, the reliance of the federal government on university resources, and a discussion of how the legislation relates to this analysis. The committee report pointed out that the major purpose of the bill was to strengthen universities and colleges in the United States as an essential national resource. The report emphasized that the legislation was domestic in focus and was not an educational foreign aid bill.[37]

The eight Republican members of the committee found the bill "a logical extension of the NDEA centers" devised and sponsored by a Republican administration. Funds to be distributed under the act, they said, were "seed money in the true sense of that expression for which we can expect returns far exceeding in worth the amount of money invested." In additional views, Albert H. Quie (R-MN), Charles E. Goodell (R-NY), and Edward J. Gurney (R-FL) emphasized that the bill had "nothing to do with aid to other nations to improve their educational systems," as might be implied by the misleading "grandiose terms" of the president's message.[38]

In early June, the prospects for the IEA were good, but Cater and Gardner were perturbed that the bill's "comparatively small beginning" had not attracted the support abroad that the act deserved.[39] Brademas and Frankel worried about Congress understanding that the act, despite its title, was exclusively for the support of U.S. institutions. Both men were concerned about the president's commitment to the act.[40]

On 6 June, the day the IEA was to be voted on by the House, U.S. troop strength in Vietnam exceeded 285,000. That morning the *Washington Post* printed an editorial urging passage of the bill "by a vote that will show by its size that the members, by an overwhelming majority, understand the challenge of our times."

The *Post* clearly stated what that challenge was:

Given the intimacy of the world's integration in these days of interplanetary transit, people who live on one part of this planet had better know something about the people who live on other parts of it. Perhaps there was a time when Americans could afford to be ignorant of the customs, institutions, and languages of most of their fellow-Earthlings; but that time has surely passed, at least when the U.S. assumed the responsibility of a world power.[41]

On 6 June, the bill was debated under a suspension of the rules on the floor of the House. Under this procedure, any member recognized by the Speaker may make a motion to suspend the rules and pass a particular bill. A favorable vote by two-thirds of those present is required for passage. Debate is limited to 40 minutes, and no amendments from the floor are permitted. If a two-thirds favorable vote is not attained, the bill may be considered later under regular procedures.

In his opening statement, Brademas pointed out that the demands of government upon universities were steadily increasing and that rather than responding to any specific need, the act proposed to strengthen research and teaching in world affairs at both the graduate and undergraduate levels throughout the nation. Brademas reminded his House colleagues that the proposed legislation was not an educational foreign aid bill but, rather, was aimed at strengthening colleges and universities in the United States, a fact echoed in the comments of Congressmen Quie, Carlton R. Sickles (D-MD), Ogden R. Reid (R-NY), and William D. Hathaway (D-ME).[42]

Despite the disclaimer by the bill's floor manager, H. R. Gross (R-IA) opposed the measure as one that "apparently would teach some people how to write and say 'Yankee go home' better than they do now," and that would add "another layer of fat to the government's present and costly language institutes" program.[43]

McClory (R-IL), who had testified before the task force, objected to considering the bill under a suspension of the rules. He said that adequate time was needed to debate the bill, which did "nothing whatever toward reducing the number of illiterates in the world."[44] McClory maintained that the president's Smithsonian speech implied that the IEA would help eliminate illiteracy in underdeveloped nations. Brademas replied that the overseas aspects of the administration's international education program were being handled by executive actions or amendments to foreign aid legislation.[45]

In bringing debate to a close, William D. Ford (D-MI) commended "the gentleman [Brademas] who singlehandedly has spearheaded the efforts . . . and has done an outstanding job in assembling points of view from throughout our country, from private enterprise and Government and education sources."[46]

The House passed the bill by a vote of 194 ayes, 89 nays, and 148 not voting. Although the suspension procedure is generally used for noncontroversial measures, the act received only five votes more than the necessary two-thirds majority for passage. A majority of Republicans voted against the bill.[47]

A few months later, the Brademas Task Force published "International Education: Past, Present, Problems and Prospects," Selected Readings to Supplement H.R. 14643. Brademas called the volume a landmark in its field, and it was a splendid compilation of published and previously unpublished materials covering not only the programs authorized by the IEA but also the entire spectrum of issues and problems in international education. The work, which made the sum total of international education experience more readily available, was distributed widely by Brademas' office, HEW, the Government Printing Office, and EWA.

The book was assembled by Allan A. Michie of Education and World Affairs and included some 19 articles with titles such as "Higher Education and World Affairs," "Internationalizing the Curriculum," "Educational Exchanges," "Education and Development," "Organizing for International Education," and "International Education: The Prospect." In his introduction to the book, Brademas noted that although international education had different meanings for different people, all the activities bore upon international studies. Brademas urged colleges and universities, as they shaped their programs, to "plan in terms of the way each of their activities in international education interacts with and affects the others."[48]

NOTES

1. *Congressional Record*, 2 February 1966, p. 1851–52; Eighty-ninth Congress, Second Session, House of Representatives, Report No. 1539 "International Education Act of 1966," 17 May 1966, Report from Committee on Education and Labor, p. 8; HEW Subject Files, Microfilm #59, PL 89-698, LBJ Library.

2. Press Release, U.S. House of Representatives, Committee on Education and Labor, 2 February 1966, attached to Memo, Cater to LBJ, 3 February 1966, "Memos to the President, February 1966," Box 14, Office Files of Cater, LBJ Library. Powell's laudation of the IEA was one of his last hurrahs. On 23 September 1966, he was to be stripped of his powers by the House Education and Labor Committee.

3. Memo, Cater to LBJ, Report on International Health and Education Bill, 3 February 1966, "Memos to the President, February 1966," Box 14, Office Files of Cater, LBJ Library, includes solicited statements from Kirk; J. George Harrar, president, Rockefeller Foundation; Clark Kerr, president, University of California; Pendleton Herring, president, Social Science Research Council; James Perkins, president, Cornell University.

4. John Brademas with Lynne P. Brown, *The Politics of Education: Conflict and Consensus on Capitol Hill* (Norman: University of Oklahoma Press, 1987), p. 19.

5. Report 1539, p. 18.

6. Memo, Cater to LBJ, 1 April 1966, "Memos to the President, April 1966," Box 14, Office Files of Cater, LBJ Library.

7. Hearings Before the Task Force on International Education of the Committee on Education and Labor, "International Education," 30 March–7 April 1966, U.S. House of Representatives, Eighty-ninth Congress, Second Session, pp. 1–453 (hereinafter cited as Brademas Task Force).

8. Ibid.

9. Report 1539, pp. 8–9.

10. Brademas Task Force, pp. 22, 13.

11. Ibid., p. 17.

12. Ibid., pp. 13, 15.

13. Ibid., p. 19.

14. Report 1539, p. 9.

15. Ibid., pp. 9–10.

16. Ibid., p. 10.

17. Ibid., p. 10.

18. Ibid., p. 12.

19. Ibid., p. 10.

20. Brademas Task Force, p.387.

21. Report 1539, p. 13.

22. Charles Frankel, *High on Foggy Bottom* (New York: Harper & Row, 1968), p. 123.

23. Brademas Task Force, p. 330.

24. Ibid., p. 156.

25. Ibid., p. 277.

26. Ibid., p. 381.

27. Ibid., p. 397.

28. Report 1539, p. 10.

29. Ibid., p. 18.

30. Norman C. Thomas, *Education in National Politics* (New York: David McKay, 1975), p. 129.

31. Report 1539, p. 19.

32. Ibid., pp. 19–20.

33. Ibid., p. 11.

34. Richard D. Lambert, "Comment: Comparativists and Uniquists," in *Approaches to Asian Civilization*, eds. William de Bary and Ainslee Embree (New York: Columbia University Press, 1964), pp. 240–42.

35. Report 1539, p. 21.

36. Ibid., p. 9.

37. Ibid., p. 14.

38. Ibid., pp. 23–25.

39. Memo, Cater to LBJ, 2 June 1966, "Memos to the President, June, 1966," Box 15, Office Files of Cater, LBJ Library.

40. Memo, William B. Cannon to Wilfred H. Rommel, assistant director for Legislative Reference, Bureau of the Budget, 14 March 1966, "Materials Concerning International Education, 1965–1966," Box 44, Office Files of Cater, LBJ Library.

41. Editorial, *Washington Post*, 6 June 1966, p. A16.

42. *Congressional Record*, 6 June 1966, pp. 12241–57.

43. Ibid., p. 12247; *1966 CQ Almanac* (Washington, D.C.: Congressional Quarterly, 1967), p. 308.

44. *Congressional Record*, 6 June 1966, pp. 12247–48

45. Ibid.

46. Ibid., p. 12244.

47. Ibid., pp. 12256–57; Memo, Cater to LBJ, 7 June 1966, "Memos to the President, June 1966," Box 15, Office Files of Cater, LBJ Library.

48. "International Education: Past, Present, Problems and Prospects," Selected Readings to Supplement H.R. 14643, prepared by the Task Force on International Education, John Brademas, Chairman, Committee on Education and Labor House of Representatives, October 1966.

8

The IEA Before the Senate

On the Senate side, the IEA's progress was much slower. The bill was introduced on 3 February by Morse, chairman of the Subcommittee on Education of the Committee on Labor and Public Welfare.[1] Morse's subcommittee was a fairly harmonious bipartisan group that had played a significant role in passing the Johnson administration's education bills during the Eighty-ninth Congress, and it had a long record of support for expanded federal aid to education that extended back to the passage of the NDEA in 1958.

Lister Hill (D-AL), chairman of the Labor and Public Welfare Committee, was primarily interested in health legislation and generally entrusted educational matters to Morse. Judgments made in Morse's subcommittee were usually sustained by the full committee and subsequently on the floor.[2]

The Subcommittee on Education was composed of Democrats Hill (AL), Ralph Yarborough (TX), Joseph S. Clark (PA), Randolph Jennings (WV), and Robert Kennedy (NY) and Republicans Winston L. Prouty (VT), Jacob Javits (NY), and Peter H. Dominick (CO). The dominant figure, however, was Senator Morse, who interpreted his role as providing "bipartisan educational policy leadership" to the Senate and the nation.[3] Morse was admired for his fair dealing and willingness to compromise in the subcommittee.

After the IEA was introduced, it languished in subcommittee until after the bill's passage by the House. Morse looked to the White House for priorities of the work before his subcommittee, and when they did not appear, he put the IEA near the bottom of his agenda.[4] Other measures such as the Economic Opportunity Act, the Elementary and Secondary Education Act (ESEA), and Higher Education bills garnered stronger support from advocates for the administration and received higher priority in the subcommittee.[5]

Morse was apparently frustrated by his inability to move the education legislation any faster than he had prior to the Senate's Fourth of July break. He thought July a "critical month" and instructed his staff "to get Senator [Jennings] Randolph (D-WV) to hold hearings on Higher Education and International Education directly after the recess so that these measures could be ready for markup."[6] The first hearing on the IEA was not held until mid-August, however. During that interim, racial riots broke out in Chicago, Cleveland, Brooklyn, Omaha, Baltimore, San Francisco, and Jacksonville and lead President Johnson to call for an end to urban rioting.

By mid-August, Morse was thinking of submitting his own bill in lieu of the IEA. He wanted stronger guarantees against federal penetration of educational institutions and thought that perhaps an independent body, composed of academic organizations, could be created that would directly administer funds for international education programs in place of HEW.[7] Frankel liked Morse's idea of a semiautonomous body, but in discussions within the executive branch, there was no interest in such an organization.

Testimony finally began on 17 August, when Gardner and Frankel appeared before the committee. Gardner again eloquently stated the case for the bill: "I do not think the importance of the IEA can be overemphasized. The first priority of this generation is international understanding — to learn the hazards and hopes of this world we inhabit and to learn how to cope with its problems." Gardner continued: "Our first step must be to strengthen our institutions of learning. Lacking such strength, we can neither engage intellectually in assistance to others nor can we develop the wisdom and judgment essential in fulfilling the almost terrifying responsibilities which we as a nation have acquired."[8]

In questioning Gardner, Morse expressed concern about "a dual administrative setup" between the Departments of HEW and State "that not only can prove to be wasteful of money but which also can result in the creation of operational problems."[9] Morse thought that the administration needed to provide more information about the overseas aspects of the IEA, and he submitted 50 questions to HEW and the Department of State to clarify the matter.

Frankel testified that the IEA dealt "with fundamental needs in a fundamental way" and added that the act would be of special importance to foreign affairs because "the role of educational systems in the 20th century is immense." He noted the pervasive interaction of international and domestic matters:

Today, the international environment of the U.S. does not begin at the oceans' edge, but penetrates almost every corner of our society. It is revealed on the news we hear, the coffee we drink, the movies we see, the political decisions we debate. And precisely because we hear so much from and about other countries, we need to have a background of information, a sense of history and a sense of the day-to-day context of events, if we are to interpret what we hear correctly.[10]

On 19 August the subcommittee heard testimony in support of the IEA from representatives of colleges, universities, and book publishers. The subcommittee was pressed for time, and witnesses were limited to ten minutes in summary of any written testimony.

Members of the subcommittee were annoyed at not being able to obtain a copy of the Rusk Task Force report. The Senators were critical of such secret documents, and they felt that such "policy-formulating material ought to be available" to them when they shaped "public policy decisions."[11] The White House stuck by its strict requirement of secrecy about task force reports, however.

After the second day of hearings, Morse apparently thought that the IEA "had very little chance" of getting out of his subcommittee. Ralph Huitt, Gardner's assistant secretary for legislation in HEW, reported that Morse "never liked the IEA and was reluctant to introduce it from the beginning."[12] According to Huitt, Morse objected to "the vague and loosely drafted language of the bill" and wanted to rewrite it. The senator, noted for his ability to fashion measures that could survive, wanted a bill with larger funding. He thought the IEA message "grandiose" and the bill "piddling."[13]

Two weeks later, however, Huitt found that Morse was "very much" in favor of the IEA.[14] The answers supplied by Gardner and Frankel to his 50 questions had pleased Morse, who stated that they removed "a great, great many of the chairman's doubts about the bill." He stated that the IEA had been in trouble before he received the clarifying statements from the two departments.[15]

On 19 September, the Senate Subcommittee on Education held its final hearings on the bill, with witnesses from academic and scholarly organizations and the Smithsonian Institution speaking in favor of the IEA.

Stephen K. Bailey informed the subcommittee that the academic community "heartily endorsed" the bill. The issue of academic autonomy raised by the IEA, Bailey said, did not seem to him a dangerous one.

"What this Act seems to reflect," he added, "is an unusual coincidence of government and educational interest. The chances of either partner seriously challenging the autonomy of the other appears to me minimal." Bailey also urged that funds authorized in the act for the first year be used strictly as planning funds to assure the wisest possible distribution of grants. He pointed out that because the act set forth a five-year program, sound preparation was possible and would give universities and colleges the time required to develop new programs.[16] In retrospect, this go-slow attitude of university leaders contributed to divisiveness within the ranks of educational organizations and was used effectively by opponents of the act to block its receiving an appropriation.

The testimony before the Senate committee reads well, but its presentation may have left something to be desired. Spokesmen for the academic community were characterized by a Senate staffer as "too vague, boring and non-critical of the bill."[17]

With hearings on the IEA completed, Morse hoped to get the bill to the Senate floor immediately after Labor Day. Instead, the Senate hearings were suspended while other matters, such as Senator Yarborough's management of the Minimum Wage Bill, had the Senate's attention.[18]

The mood in Washington was described as "irritable."[19] As Fulbright reported to Frankel, "the problem with the IEA was that people hesitated to give this administration any more broad powers."[20]

Gardner told Frankel that the outlook for the IEA was not good and that the "White House" had "told us that if we're going to get the Act passed, we'll have to do it on our own." The bill did not have high priority, and the president, who had "other problems on his tray," could not help.[21] President Johnson at that time was besieged with urban rioting, civil rights and Black Power demonstrations, antiwar protests, and concerns about inflation. In a press conference at the LBJ Ranch, the president had asserted that although it was impossible for the communists to win the war in Vietnam, there could be "no quick victory" for the United States and its allies.

It was not until 6 October that the Morse subcommittee voted out the IEA. Cater immediately contacted Senate Majority Leader Lister Hill (D-AL) to urge floor action on the bill during the following week so that the president could sign the IEA at the East-West Center in Hawaii, the first stop of a presidential tour of Asia.[22] U.S. troop strength in Vietnam was reported to be 331,000 on that day.

By that time, Hill's Committee on Labor and Public Welfare was in the midst of "long and difficult mark up sessions . . . on all sorts of controversial issues" from the poverty subcommittee and the education subcommittee. Thus, it was five days later that the Senate Committee on Labor and Public Welfare reported favorably on the bill.[23]

Finally, on 13 October, the Senate debated the bill on the floor and by voice vote unanimously passed an amended IEA. Included in the Senate version were amendments to the Mutual Education and Cultural Exchange Act of 1961 permitting foreign students to exchange their soft currency for U.S. dollars to finance their study in the United States and enabling U.S. students to use their higher education loans to study abroad; institutes for elementary and secondary teachers; and a study of the "brain drain," the reasons why foreign students failed to return to their homelands after periods of study in the United States.[24]

Senator Strom Thurmond (R-SC) voiced the concerns of the opposition during debate on the bill when he noted that the war in Vietnam should be the first priority of Congress and that it was "unwise to spend $130 million" on a domestic program.[25] Senator Fulbright countered this by stating: "If there is any hope at all for a peaceful world it will result from the kind of activity for which this bill provides."[26]

The tardy Senate action on the IEA meant that the bill would not be passed by Congress in time for the president to sign it at the East-West Center. The president did announce that he was directing Secretary Gardner to establish immediately a Center for Education Cooperation in HEW. The president also announced that a World Conference on Education would be held in the United States in 1967 and that Gardner and President James A. Perkins of Cornell University were to be in charge of its planning.[27]

In Conference Committee, the House members accepted the Senate's amendments, and the committee reported on the bill favorably on 20 October. The next day, the House, by voice vote, concurred in all the Senate amendments except one authorizing direct federal loans to students who were taking medical courses in foreign schools. Brademas explained that the amendment would have placed the secretary of HEW in the awkward position of approving or disapproving foreign medical schools when there was no professional body in the United States that was prepared to make such judgments.[28]

Opposing concurrence in the Senate amendments, McClory (R-IL) argued that the House had not had sufficient opportunity to study the changes. He said the bill would have "limited value" in improving understanding of other nations "and will do little or nothing insofar as aiding the people of the developing countries in their quest for learning." He said the bill should have emphasized studies abroad instead "of a purely domestic program of studies at home."[29]

Later, on 21 October, the Senate, by voice vote, accepted the House's deletion of the medical loan provision and sent the bill to the president. In the Senate, Morse said the bill carried out the "major objective" of the president, but he indicated that legislation would be introduced in the Ninetieth Congress to expand the program to attack educational problems abroad, "including the problem of illiteracy."[30]

The IEA had finally been passed only one day before the adjournment of the Eighty-ninth Congress, but there was not time to get the act before the appropriations committees. The requested appropriation of $1 million in planning funds to start the $131 million program was deferred to 1967. The failure to get the act funded did not displease the BOB, which reported to President Johnson that the delay in making grants was "consistent with the need for careful planning and preparation."[31]

NOTES

1. *Congressional Record*, 3 February 1966, p. 1985.

2. Lawrence E. Gladieux and Thomas R. Wolanin, *Congress and the Colleges* (Lexington, Mass.: Lexington Books, 1976), pp. 84–85.

3. Norman C. Thomas, *Education in National Politics* (New York: David McKay, 1975), p. 132.

4. Memo, Huitt to Cater, Wilson, and Manatos, 12 September 1966, HEW Subject File, Microfilm #59, PL 89-698, LBJ Library.

5. Memo, Huitt to Cater, Wilson, and Manatos, 30 August 1966; Memo, Alma E. Hughes, special assistant to Department Assistant Secretary for International Affairs, to Miller, Colmen, and Granger, 19 September 1966, "HEW 1966," Box 19 (1281), Office File of Manatos, LBJ Library.

6. Memo, Cater to LBJ, 2 June 1966, "Memos to the President, June 1966," Box 15, Office Files of Cater, LBJ Library.

7. Charles Frankel, *High on Foggy Bottom* (New York: Harper & Row, 1968), p. 129.

8. Statement of Gardner, Hearings Before Subcommittee on Education of Committee on Labor and Public Welfare, U.S. Senate, Eighty-ninth Congress, Second Session, 17 August 1966, p. 11 (hereafter, Hearings); "Congress Strengthens Foreign Studies at U.S. Colleges," *1966 CQ Almanac* (Washington, D.C.: Congressional Quarterly, 1967), p. 309.

9. Hearings, p. 62.

10. Hearings, p. 209–10.

11. Memo, Huitt to Cater, Wilson, and Manatos, 30 August 1966, "HEW 1966," Box 19 (1281), Office Files of Manatos, LBJ Library.

12. Memo, Huitt to Cater, Wilson, and Manatos, 30 August 1966, "HEW 1966," Box 19 (1281), Office Files of Manatos, LBJ Library. Morse's apologia for delayed hearings on the IEA is contained in Hearings, p. 63.

13. Memo, Huitt to Cater, Wilson, and Manatos, 30 August 1966; Memo, Alma E. Hughes, special assistant to Department Assistant Secretary for International

Affairs, to Miller, Colmen, and Granger, 19 September 1966, "HEW 1966," Box 19 (1281), Office File of Manatos, LBJ Library.

14. Memo, Huitt to Cater, Wilson, and Manatos, 12 September 1966, HEW Subject File, Microfilm #59, PL 89-698, LBJ Library.

15. Memo, Huitt to Cater, Wilson, and Manatos, 12 September 1966, HEW Subject File, Microfilm #59, PL 89-698; Memo, Alma E. Hughes, special assistant to Department Assistant Secretary for International Affairs, to Miller, Colmen, and Granger, 19 September 1966; Memo, Miller to Huitt and Halperin, 19 November 1966, "HEW 1966," Box 19 (1281), Office Files of Manatos, LBJ Library. The 50 questions and answers are in "Notebook Concerning International Education and Health, 1966," Question and Answer Index, Box 44, Personal Files of Cater, LBJ Library.

16. Hearings, pp. 458, 461, 460.

17. Memo, Ralph K. Huitt, assistant secretary for legislation to Cater, Wilson, and Manatos, 30 August 1966, quoting Roy Millenson, an aid to Senator Javits, "HEW 1966," Box 19 (1281), Office Files of Manatos, LBJ Library.

18. Frankel, *High on Foggy Bottom*, p. 167.

19. Ibid.

20. Ibid., p. 131.

21. Ibid., p. 130.

22. Memo, Cater to LBJ, 6 October 1966, "Memos to the President, October 1966," Box 15, Office Files of Cater, LBJ Library.

23. *Congressional Record*, Daily Digest, 12 October 1966, p. D568; Memo, Huitt to Cater, Wilson, and Manatos, 11 October 1966, "HEW 1966," Box 19 (1281), Office Files of Manatos, LBJ Library.

24. *Congressional Record*, 13 October 1966, pp. 26551–53; *1966 CQ Almanac*, p. 309.

25. *Congressional Record*, 13 October 1966, pp. 26563.

26. Ibid., p. 26562.

27. Memo, Cater to LBJ, 14 October 1966, "Memos to the President, October 1966," Box 15, Office Files of Cater, LBJ Library.

28. *Congressional Record*, 21 October 1966, pp. 28526–32; *1966 CQ Almanac*, p. 309.

29. *Congressional Record*, 21 October 1966, pp. 28528–29; *1966 CQ Almanac*, p. 309; Memo, Huitt to Cater, Wilson, and Manatos, 11 October 1966, "HEW 1966," Box 19 (1281), Office Files of Manatos, LBJ Library.

30. *Congressional Record*, 21 October 1966, pp. 28441–42; *1966 CQ Almanac*, p. 309. Unfortunately for international education, the senior senator from Oregon was not elected to the Ninetieth Congress, and his proposed legislation for a broader overseas program was not introduced.

31. Memo, Rommel to LBJ, 25 October 1966, pp. 4–5, Enrolled Legislation, "PL 89-698," Box 44; Letter, Cater to E. P. Anderson, 28 October 1966, Ex Ed Box 3, LBJ Library.

9

The President Signs the IEA into Law

On 25 October, President Johnson, on the first leg of a tour of Asia, cabled Brademas, congratulating him on his leadership in securing passage of the IEA. Johnson added: "Few efforts hold greater promise for building a world of progress and peace."[1]

The next day the president, in an unscheduled interruption of his tour, flew from Manila to a large U.S. base at Camranh Bay about 180 miles northeast of Saigon. Johnson lauded the U.S. troops he reviewed and told them that he was there "simply because I could not come to this part of the world and not come to see you." After a 2.5 hour visit, the president returned to Manila.

President Johnson signed the IEA (PL 89-698) at Chulalongkorn University in Bangkok, Thailand, which awarded him the honorary degree of Doctor of Political Science on 29 October. Photographs taken on the occasion show Johnson in full academic regalia, obviously enjoying the colorful proceedings and probably relieved to have his mind on something other than the war in Vietnam.

The president presented a copy of the enactment to the government of Thailand for its archives and noted that the IEA was a "far-reaching novel piece of legislation" that was a first step in a "concerted effort in international education" to extend the goals and achievements of "the Great Society" to the rest of the world. "Our goal," the president said, "is an elementary one. It is this: To give each man in the world a chance to seek the highest and deepest of human experience as he sees fit."[2] Once again, the president was broadening the scope of the IEA through his rhetoric and affirming Bill Moyers' observation that hyperbole was to Lyndon Johnson what oxygen is to life.

The somewhat misleadingly titled IEA was designed to broadly strengthen the resources and capabilities of U.S. colleges and universities in international studies and research. It was not designed to assist other nations in improving their educational systems, nor did it channel funds to individual scholars or small ad hoc research groups.

Frankel called the IEA "a new formula for the federal funding of higher education." It provided "general funds to encourage educational change and experimentation while leaving the freedom to make educational decisions to the universities."[3]

The strong federal interest in the global dimension of higher education was reflected in the introduction of the act:

The Congress finds and declares that a knowledge of other countries is of the utmost importance in promoting mutual understanding and cooperation between nations; that strong American educational resources are a necessary base for strengthening our relations with other countries; that this and future generations of Americans should be assured ample opportunity to develop to the fullest extent possible their intellectual capacities in all areas of knowledge pertaining to other countries, peoples, and cultures; and that it is therefore both necessary and appropriate for the Federal Government to assist in the development of resources for international studies and research, to assist in the development of resources and trained personnel in academic and professional fields, and to coordinate the existing and future programs of the Federal Government in international education, to meet the requirements of world leadership.[4]

The IEA would strengthen U.S. resources in international studies through a grants program administered by the secretary of HEW. Title I, based on sections 3 and 4 of the House bill, was the heart of the legislation, establishing the program of grants to be made to institutions of higher education or consortia for (1) the operation of graduate centers of research and training on geographical areas of the world, or on particular issues in world affairs, or both and (2) the strengthening and improving of undergraduate instruction in international studies through planning undergraduate programs, training faculty members in foreign countries, expanding foreign language courses, offering student work-study-travel programs, encouraging visiting scholar programs, and providing English training for foreign teachers and students.

Grants could also be made to public and private nonprofit agencies, including professional and scholarly associations, if such grants would make an especially significant contribution to strengthening the graduate or undergraduate programs in international studies of colleges and universities.

Title I also established a presidentially appointed National Advisory Committee on International Studies (NACIS) in the Department of HEW with the assistant secretary for education as chairman. The advisory committee was to advise the secretary on specific recommendations for carrying out the program of grants by 30 April 1967. Thereafter, the secretary was to prepare annual reports on the program for Congress, beginning 31 January 1968.

The act included an appropriation of $1 million in fiscal year 1967 to be used only in preparing the 1967 report. The grant program would commence in 1968 with an appropriation of $40 million, followed by a $90 million appropriation in 1969.

Title II of the IEA amended existing legislation to strengthen international aspects of several programs, including:

1. Title VI of the NDEA of 1958, which authorized grants to support university centers for instruction in modern foreign languages and related studies by (a) removing a requirement that limited instruction at NDEA centers to those languages "not readily available" in the United States (opening such centers to instruction of French, German, Spanish, and Italian); (b) removing a 50 percent ceiling on federal funding of NDEA centers; (c) permitting centers to be supported by grants as well as by contracts; and (d) transferring authority for administration of NDEA centers and language fellowship programs from the commissioner of education to the secretary of HEW.

2. Title XI of the NDEA, which authorized contracts with colleges and universities to provide "institutes in international affairs for teachers in secondary schools" and stipends for participants. The IEA authorized $3.5 million for fiscal year 1967 and $6 million for fiscal year 1968 for such institutes.

3. The Higher Education Act of 1965, which established a guaranteed loan program, the benefits of which could be used by U.S. students studying in educational institutions outside the United States that had been approved by the commissioner.

4. The Mutual Education and Cultural Exchange Act of 1961 (Fulbright-Hays Act), which authorized arrangements under which certain foreign students or teachers wishing to study in the United States could exchange their currencies for U.S. dollars. This provision would enable persons from countries with limited foreign exchange resources to obtain necessary U.S. funds to study, lecture, or do research in this country. Appropriations of $10 million in fiscal year 1967 and $15 million in fiscal year 1968 were requested for this purpose.

Title III of the IEA directed the secretary of HEW to study the "brain drain" from underdeveloped countries — students who remain in the United States after their studies are completed.

In his message of 2 February 1967, President Johnson announced that he would direct the secretary of HEW "to establish within his Department a Center for Educational Cooperation [CEC]" that would be a focal point for leadership in international education. The center was to have three main functions: to channel communications between missions abroad and the U.S. educational community; to direct programs assigned to HEW; and to assist public and private agencies conducting international education programs.[5] The president, by executive order on 14 October, empowered Secretary Gardner to establish the CEC, which was charged with the administration of the grant program under the IEA and was seen as playing a crucial role in the success of the act.[6]

The idea of the CEC had evolved from early discussions prior to the creation of the Rusk Task Force. Originally called the Institute for Educational Cooperation, the CEC was envisioned by the Rusk Task Force to be a semiautonomous agency composed of a board of directors representing the major governmental agencies concerned and chaired by the assistant secretary of state for educational and cultural affairs. The CEC was thought of as analogous with the National Institute of Health, whose director is appointed by the president.[7]

The idea of having the CEC chaired by an officer of the State Department was abandoned because of the problems foreseen in having international education closely associated with U.S. foreign policy. This sensitivity to such criticism was reflected in a *New York Times* editorial published the week the IEA was passed by the Senate:

The special significance of placing much of the responsibility for America's part in international education in the hands of HEW could and should be to remove the widely held suspicion abroad that American institutions and scholars on foreign soil are mere extensions, if not outright agents, of U.S. policy.[8]

Frankel thought that the Department of State and HEW had developed strong and effective measures for coordinating IEA programs and that Congress's favorable action rested in part on the reassurances of the two departments that coordinated arrangements had been worked out and codified in a harmonious way.[9] Frankel believed that the CEC could not exercise its coordinating function effectively if it were not part of "an operational base," an existing governmental office.[10]

The testimony of witnesses before the Brademas Task Force had urged that the center be located at a high level in HEW in order to aid the center in attracting outstanding personnel and in dealing effectively with other federal agencies having responsibilities in international education.

In his testimony before the Brademas Task Force, James Linen of *Time* listed three criteria for a successful CEC: it should be top level with stature enough to really make cooperation work between various governmental agencies; it did not need to be big, but it did need to have a very few big people in it; and it had to have sufficient authority to be respected by the educational world and the business world.[11]

The CEC was foreseen as having relatively frequent and systematic consultation with academic institutions and foundations to facilitate communications and to help the center staff implement the objectives of the act. A number of witnesses had urged the development of a close working relationship between the center and universities and colleges, "characterized by cooperation, communication, mutual understanding, and respect."[12]

Cater hoped the CEC would be located in a building that would be an "International Center" near the National Archives and Smithsonian museums in Washington,[13] an idea echoed by Miller, who saw the CEC as a lively office building that symbolized educational cooperation, a place where international visitors felt much at home. The CEC headquarters with a special center for international scholars was also considered as "an alternative for the Woodrow Wilson Memorial."[14]

Secretary Gardner decided that the center should be established directly in the secretary's office rather than in the OE, as originally suggested.[15] OE at that time was primarily concerned with programs for elementary and secondary education and was struggling to implement a greatly expanded number of grants programs mandated by Johnson administration legislation. Gardner decided that the office of the assistant secretary for education, an office too new to have many enemies, would be the appropriate place for the CEC.

Frankel agreed that the assistant secretary for education's office would permit "greater visibility, new people, a sense of fresh departure, and a chance to get international education programs closer to the academic-arts-science complex." Frankel recognized that locating the CEC in a staff office of HEW would create "complexities" and "fuzzy lines of responsibility," but he was less worried "about bureaucratic tidiness than about finding good people and giving them a fresh setting" so that they could "strike out vigorously on a new program in a new way."[16]

The assistant secretary for education position had been authorized in 1965 to serve as the principal advisor to the secretary of HEW on matters of education policy and on matters relating to the coordination of education activities within the department. In establishing the office, Gardner stated that the post would assist him in "constructive discourse" with other federal agencies, would permit an overview of federal efforts, and would assist in bringing greater cohesiveness to the education leadership in the country.[17] Francis Keppel had served as the first assistant secretary for education while remaining commissioner of education.

By the time of the passage of the IEA, Keppel had resigned from government service to return to the private sector. President Johnson asked John W. Macy, Jr., chairman of the Civil Service Commission, to assist Gardner in identifying possible candidates for the assistant secretary post. Macy recommended recruiting "a well known and successful educator in the higher education field from outside the Northeast and from a public institution."[18]

After a two-month search, Gardner recommended Paul A. Miller, president of West Virginia University, as "the right man ... [with] a unique reputation for both intellectual and administrative capabilities and a flair for innovation." Miller was a political liberal who was well regarded by the West Virginia delegation and noted for his ability to maintain close rapport with his board of trustees and the state legislatures.[19]

Miller accepted the president's appointment and "came to HEW largely for the purpose of administering the IEA and the new center."[20] Miller viewed the assistant secretary position as a staff office that provided support to the secretary on major long-range policy questions. The office was "a long-run task-oriented operation" that also nurtured new projects. In providing leadership for these programs, the assistant secretary became "involved with various aspects of the legislative and budgetary processes."[21]

At Miller's Senate confirmation hearing, when the clerk read the nominee's resume that began with his service as a county agricultural agent in the West Virginia hill country, Carl Perkins (D-KY) remarked good-naturedly: "Dr. Miller, you appear to have gone downhill in your career from the very beginning." Perkins was a Kentucky hill farmer who knew county agriculture agents and liked them.[22] Miller's subsequent encounters with some rural congressmen in committee meetings were not to be as cordial.

On 13 July, Johnson introduced Miller to the press at a White House ceremony and indicated that he would "serve as principal advisor on the International Education Program."[23] Miller inherited a small staff and other functions in the assistant secretary's office and began planning to employ additional assistants as soon as the IEA was approved. He appeared with Gardner on 17 August when the secretary testified on the IEA before the Senate subcommittee.

In early September, Miller was formulating plans to maximize the "multiplier effect" of the act by "bringing an imaginative international flavor" to teacher training colleges. By bringing an international focus to state colleges that enrolled about one-fifth of the students in higher education and supplied a substantial proportion of the nation's teachers, he foresaw "a rapid growth of interest in the field in all parts of the educational system."[24]

By mid-September, Miller had published *A Manual for the IEA of 1966* that had been developed by a task force of ten professors representing large universities, liberal arts colleges, junior colleges, and the staff of the OE's Division of Foreign Studies. The manual explained how grants were to be administered and how proposals for grants should be submitted, by what criteria and what procedures the proposals would be evaluated, and how the grants would be managed to accomplish the purposes of the act.[25]

With the passage of the IEA, the position of assistant to the assistant secretary (international education) was established to direct the planning activities incident to passage of the IEA. In addition, a special assistant to the assistant secretary was assigned to HEW from USIA. Glen Taggart, dean of International Programs at Michigan State University, where he earlier had been Miller's colleague, served as chief consultant on the IEA and played a major role in planning. An OE Fellow later joined this "interim secretariat."[26]

This small professional staff went about what Miller called the planning and consultation process, the day-to-day activities to make the CEC the focal point for all international education activities. They began work on guidelines for a program of grants to be administered through the center. The staff met with representatives of colleges and universities, foundations, professional associations, and others (averaging 40 visits per month). In addition, they represented the assistant secretary in formal meetings and conferences. These activities resulted in "ever increasing awareness of national needs in the field of international education, more specific definitions of how these needs might be met, and an assessment of the Federal supportive role."[27]

In December, the OE's Division of Foreign Studies, which was responsible for NDEA Title VI, foreign language and area centers and fellowships, was transferred to the assistant secretary's office. This was the first move to consolidate governmental international education programs in the CEC.[28]

NOTES

1. Cable, LBJ to Brademas, 25 October 1966, Ex Ed Box 3, LBJ Library.

2. *1966 CQ Almanac*, p. 309; Letter, Henry H. Wilson, Jr., to John L. Monahan, Office of the Speaker of the House, 31 October 1966, Ex Ed Box 3, LBJ Library.

3. Charles Frankel, *High on Foggy Bottom* (New York: Harper & Row, 1968), p. 115.

4. 20 U.S.C. sec. 1171 et seq.; 80 Stat. 1066–73 (1966).

5. Center for Educational Cooperation, Draft OMP-OS, 25 March 1966, "Notebook Concerning International Education and Health, 1966," LBJ Library.

6. Memo, Cater to LBJ, 14 October 1966, "Memos to the President, October 1966," Box 15, Office Files of Cater, LBJ Library.

7. Report of Task Force on International Education from Rusk to LBJ, 3 December 1965, p. 18, Box 40, Office Files of Cater, LBJ Library.

8. Editorial, *New York Times*, 18 October 1966, p. 44.

9. Memo, Frankel to Eugene V. Rostow, "Draft Executive Orders on International Education," 27 January 1967, Ex Ed Box 3, LBJ Library.

10. Memo, Frankel to Gardner, Lee, Howe, Corson, Marvel, and Cater, 30 June 1966, Ex FG 165-4 Box 245, LBJ Library.

11. Brademas Task Force Hearings, p. 309.

12. Report 1539, pp. 16–17.

13. Memo, Cater to Gardner, Ripley, and McPherson, 14 December 1965, "International Education," Box 10, Office Files of McPherson, LBJ Library.

14. Memo, Miller to Cater, 9 November 1966, Ex Ed Box 3, LBJ Library.

15. Interview with Harold Howe, II, Commissioner, OE, 12 July 1968, by Jack Broudy, Appendices: The History of the Office of Education, LBJ Library.

16. Memo, Frankel to Gardner, Lee, Howe, Corson, Marvel, and Cater, 30 June 1966, Ex FG 165-4 Box 245, LBJ Library.

17. Administrative History of Department of HEW, Vol. I, Part I, pp. 1–3, LBJ Library.

18. Letter, John W. Macy, Jr., to Gardner, 11 April 1966, Ex FG 165-4 Box 245, LBJ Library. College and university presidents named as possibilities were Meredith Wilson, University of Minnesota; Clifford Hardin, University of Nebraska; Thomas H. Eliot, Washington University; G. Homer Durham, Arizona State University; Charles E. Odegaard, University of Washington; William Friday, University of North Carolina; Douglas M. Knight, Duke University; Alexander Heard, Vanderbilt University; and Joseph M. Ray, Texas Western College. Friday was offered the position but declined. Johnson wanted James McCrocklin, president of Southwest Texas State College (Johnson's alma mater), for the post, but inquiries about McCrocklin's qualifications produced some reservations. Gardner concluded that he "would go for Paul Miller." Memo, Gardner to LBJ, 30 June 1966, Name File, "Miller, Paul A-E," LBJ Library. Gardner thanked the president for approving Miller's appointment. Letter, Gardner to LBJ, 7 July 1966, Name File, "Miller, Paul A-E," LBJ Library.

19. Memo, Macy to LBJ, 27 June 1966, Name File, "Miller, Paul A-E," LBJ Library. Miller's name first appears in the LBJ Library files as a candidate for the National Food and Fiber Commission. He was described as "an outstanding

administrator and scholar" and "a rural sociologist of some repute." Memo, Edward L. Sherman to Califano, 25 October 1965, Name File, "Miller, Paul A-E," LBJ Library. Prior to his appointment in HEW, Miller had invited President Johnson to visit West Virginia University during its centennial celebration in 1967-68. Letter, Miller to Valenti, 8 April 1966, Name File, "Miller, Paul A-E," LBJ Library.

20.   Interview with Howe, 12 July 1968, Appendices: The History of the Office of Education, LBJ Library.

21.   Norman C. Thomas, *Education in National Politics* (New York: David McKay, 1975), p. 125.

22.   Letter, Miller to Vestal, 6 February 1989.

23.   Memo, Cater to LBJ, 13 July 1966, "Memos to the President, July, 1966," Box 15, Office Files of Cater, LBJ Library.

24.   Memo, Miller to Cater, 8 September 1966, Ex Ed 13 July 1966–15 April 1967 Box 3, LBJ Library.

25.   Records of the Department of HEW, 15 September 1966, A Manual for the IEA of 1966: Comprehensive Programs in International Studies (sect. 102), "IIS(4) International Education Act of 1966," Box 160; see also Task Force, Report on Section 102 of the IEA, Office of the Assistant Secretary for Education, Department of HEW, August 1967; Report, Meeting of the Task Force, 18–19 April 1967; 12–13 March 1967, "IIS (5) Task Force on Section 102 of IEA of 1966," Box 160, LBJ Library.

26.   Administrative History of Department of HEW, Vol. I, Part I. Theodore M. Vestal, former associate director of Peace Corps/Ethiopia, was assistant to the assistant secretary (subsequently, the position was redesignated deputy assistant secretary [International Education]); Otto Shaler, recently back from a United States Information Service (USIS) tour of duty in Turkey, was special assistant; Taggart, who had just returned from a two-year assignment as vice chancellor, University of Nigeria, later was to be president of Utah State University; Miller had hoped that Taggart would be the director of the CEC once the IEA was passed; Robert Otte was the OE Fellow; Joseph Colmen, deputy assistant secretary for education, was one of the unsung heroes of the IEA story. Colmen, the former director of research for the Peace Corps, took care of a significant load of non-IEA matters in the office of the assistant secretary, thus freeing Miller to devote more of his time to international education. He was also an active advisor on the IEA to Miller and Cater.

27.   The IEA of 1966, Administrative History of Department of HEW, Vol. I, Part I, LBJ Library.

28.   Ibid., p. 2.

10

Administration Plans for Implementing the IEA

Shortly after the IEA became a law, Education and World Affairs published *International Education Act of 1966*, a monograph describing the main features of the legislation and explaining its significance to the nation. In writing about "The Opportunity and the Responsibility," William W. Marvel pointed out that although government can stimulate, give shape and direction, and provide large-scale financing, the ideas and activities that make up international education are mainly the province of schools, colleges, and universities. He noted that several provisions of the act provided for the academic community to participate in the planning process "as a fully equal partner with the government." The responsibility, according to Marvel, was wholly upon the private sector to make a decisive contribution to the further shaping of the new initiatives in international education. "What happens in the years ahead," Marvel wrote, "depends significantly on how the academic community now responds."[1] Starting in late 1966, Paul Miller and his interim secretariat set about eliciting that response in planning the implementation of the IEA.

On 21 December 1966, representatives of ten major academic associations were assembled in Washington, D.C., by the American Council on Education (ACE) to produce a general strategy for implementing the act. The executive officers and international committee members present were charged to "generally stimulate interest within their constituent institutions."[2]

The most important organizations, an unofficial establishment of higher education, that could claim to represent virtually every accredited, nonprofit postsecondary institution in the country and their leaders who were to take an active role in seeking funding for the act were the ACE, an institutional holding company made up of other more specialized higher education organizations (Richard A. Humphrey, director, Commission on International Education); the National Association of State Universities and Land Grant Colleges (NASULGC), which included both land-grant colleges and large complex institutions with extensive involvement in graduate and professional education (Russell Thackrey, executive director); the Association of American Universities, a "club of presidents" of 44 of the most prestigious public and private universities that at the time had not been active in efforts to influence federal policies (Charles P. McCurdy, Jr., executive secretary); the American Association of Colleges, representing the interests of undergraduate education, with 80 percent of its members being liberal arts colleges but with most of its money coming from public four-year colleges and arts and science units from major universities (F.L. Eric Wormald, executive vice president); the American Association of Colleges for Teacher Education, which had made efforts to add international dimensions to course requirements for prospective teachers (Edward C. Pomerory, executive director, and Frank H. Klassen, associate secretary); the American Association for Higher Education, whose membership was mainly individual professors (G. Kerry Smith, executive director); the American Association of Junior Colleges, which worked in collaboration with ACE in federal relations efforts (John Mallan, director of governmental relations); and the American Association of State Colleges and Universities (AASCU), in 1966 a new organization of public colleges and universities not belonging to the NASULGC (Allan Ostar, executive director). President Johnson, the first president to be a graduate of a state college, was to be given a citation "for his contributions to higher education" by the AASCU and the NASULGC.[3]

The ACE, as the umbrella group, represented the totality of interests in higher education to the federal government. Working in concert with its member organizations, the ACE attempted to develop a consensus within its membership, one which seemed strong in the passage of the IEA. The equivocal nature of this support was to be revealed later when decisions were made that affected various members' interests. Lobbying of Congress on behalf of the IEA by staff members of higher education associations was limited; the task was usually performed by presidents of member colleges and universities. More significant was the associations' work with Miller and his staff in developing guidelines and regulations for the IEA. Richard Humphrey of ACE played a dominant role and spearheaded the publicizing of planning activities for the act.[4]

In early January 1967, the Chinese Cultural Revolution, led by zealous Red Guards, was ravaging the People's Republic of China. In the United

States, President Johnson, selecting people recommended by Macy and Gardner, appointed a National Advisory Committee on International Studies (NACIS) as required by the law. The committee was composed of educators, representatives of labor and business, foundations, and the government; it was charged to prepare plans for implementing the IEA, but the advisory group could not be officially named until funds were available.[5]

Gardner wanted a seven-member ad hoc task force from the NACIS to further define the role of the CEC and to prepare program plans so that they could be swiftly implemented when funds were appropriated. The task force was composed of university presidents Jim McCrocklin (Southwest Texas State College), Frank Rose (University of Alabama), Harold Enarson (Cleveland State), and Jerome H. Holland (Hampton Institute); foundation officers Marvel and David Bell, vice president of the Ford Foundation; and Harry Goldberg, international representative of the American Federation of Labor and Congress of Industrial Organizations (AFL-CIO). The task force met in January and had a White House lunch with the president and Gardner in February.[6]

Other members of the NACIS were to be Harrison S. Brown, professor of geochemistry, the California Institute of Technology; Reverend Theodore M. Hesburgh, president of the University of Notre Dame; Richard K. C. Lee, director of public health and medical activities, Department of Public Health, University of Hawaii; James A. Linen III, president and director, Time, Inc.; George Cabot Lodge, lecturer, Harvard Business School; Tedoro Moscoso, chairman, Commonwealth Oil Refining Co., Puerto Rico; Henry Ollendorff, secretary general, Council of International Programs for Youth Leaders and Social Workers, Inc., Cleveland; and Rosemary Park, vice chancellor, UCLA.

Also in January, EWA was host to a meeting in New York of executives from foundations, scholarly associations, and other government agencies experienced in international research and education to plan a supplementary strategy. At that meeting, Miller announced his plan of action for the next six months. The major points were:

1. HEW's activities were to be widely publicized through journals of various educational associations and through presentations at their meetings to explain the planning and consultation process. The ACE's Bulletin on International Education was to serve as the most thorough chronicle of IEA activities.
2. The interim secretariat of HEW personnel and others loaned from private institutions and organizations were to coordinate

and evaluate reports and recommendations of groups submitting materials during the planning stage.

3. International education was to be divided into selected fields on the basis of their importance to scholarship and to the national educational interest. Working groups were to draft assessments of the selected fields during the next five to six months to provide working papers for the NACIS. More detailed analyses of the fields were to be made during the following year for publication by the CEC.

4. A series of regional conferences was to be conducted by HEW with participants selected by academic associations to gain reactions, review activities, and elicit criticisms and suggestions.

5. As soon as staff and resources were available, a national baseline study would be conducted to assess the status of international education in the United States at present so that over time, progress made possible by the IEA could be evaluated.

6. The report on international education to Congress called for by the IEA would be written, although the report was the responsibility of the National Advisory Committee, which could not be officially named until funds were appropriated for that purpose.[7]

Marvel and his associates at EWA stressed the need for careful planning within the government agencies concerned, within the academic community, and within individual educational institutions. Noting that not all higher educational institutions were at the same stage of development in their international programs, Marvel expressed particular concern about two groups of uncommitted and inexperienced colleges and universities: the four-year liberal arts colleges that had neither the resources nor the impetus to get involved and universities that had not yet given prominence to the international dimension either in their curricula or in their service activities. EWA targeted those institutions for extra encouragement and guidance so that they might move more effectively into the widening areas of international education. Such institutions could benefit from the lessons to be learned from the more experienced universities, and they would also profit from a continuing flow of information about the problems and prospects of their efforts to internationalize. To assist the colleges and universities that were just commencing international studies, and especially those that were "beginning their activities from a standing start," EWA published a series of books, monographs, and occasional papers in a variety of fields that combined features of a "how to" handbook with an overview of the essential literature of the subject.[8]

On 30 January, the president approved a White House ceremony marking the first anniversary of his message to Congress on international education. A short time later, on a gloomy day on the plaza in front of the OE building, he gave a noontime speech in praise of OE and the educational initiatives of the administration being carried out so well under the direction of Gardner and Howe (who had replaced Keppel as commissioner of OE). His audience was composed primarily of workers from HEW who had a rare opportunity to cheer their chief executive in person.[9]

On 6 February, an ad hoc advisory committee of national educational leaders worked out details of an international education assessment plan to determine national needs in various fields of educational and scholarly endeavors included within the act. In addition, plans were made for "a thoughtful summary of institutional resources and opportunities" in the field. International education was divided into 32 parts, each subject to a study by a leading scholar. These studies were to assist HEW in establishing priorities for investment under the IEA and to serve as a resource to the academic community in planning improvements in international study programs. In addition, the studies would provide basic materials for a report on the status of IEA from the secretary to the Congress. The papers were expected to be "milestone documents in the implementation of any Federally-supported programs of international education."[10]

The fields of study included 8 area studies reports, 13 profession and discipline-oriented studies, and 3 papers on undergraduate programs. The list of authors of the studies was a "Who's Who" of the leading scholars in the fields covered (for example, Gwendolen M. Carter [Africa], Henry Hart [South Asia], Lucian Pye [East Asia], and Clifton R. Wharton, Jr. [agricultural economics]). The reports from the scholars were submitted to HEW in May and were edited and distributed nationwide.

Later in February, Miller sent a "Status Report on IEA-CEC" to the IEA Steering Committee. The report spelled out guidelines and principles for a "strategy of investment" for the combined efforts of the federal sector and colleges and universities in significant fields of international education. Highlights of the plan included:

1. The strategy of investment was to be a national plan emphasizing overall capability and versatility in international affairs for the

country as a whole rather than institution-by-institution development.

2. Support would be given to centers of excellence, not only strong university centers but also national centers of resources for generating new faculty, conducting research, and providing the continuing source of personnel to staff private and public programs in the international community.

3. Grants were to be made to consortia wherever possible. Institutions demonstrating long-range commitments would be supported, as would those that could show future, present, or supporting resources. Grants would have to be of substantial size and, in many cases, be sustained over a period of time.

4. Centers of excellence would be strengthened and established to emphasize graduate training and research experience for the next generation of scholars. The centers would emphasize graduate student research training.

5. Support of undergraduate programs would be provided to bring a strong international flavor to the experience of all undergraduate students. Country-wide experiments in curriculum development and the groupings of institutions would be stressed.[11]

On 24 March, Miller spoke at an ACE seminar at the Department of State, where he explained his vision of the implementation of the act: "The IEA calls for reviews of current practices, sharing ideas among institutions, re-educating faculty, inspiring trustees, more extensive and casual travel abroad, generalizing such experience at home, and more adroit participation of foreign students and faculty on homebound campuses." Miller gave details of what he termed five points of procedure:

1. Centers of excellence were to include certain extramural duties: serving as centers of strength for schools and colleges in the immediate region. . . . for trainee programs, for adult education, and for public international service.

2. The national plan was to be kept an open document, for debate and further development, between the educational community and government centers. . . . Both should move to involve the private organizations, learned societies, and professional associations.

3. There was to be a five-year period of experimentation and innovation for undergraduate emphasis addressing such

questions as a curriculum core and how to weave area interests and disciplinary views together and then relate them both to problems.

4. Careful coordination of aims and relationships among the various agencies of government was to be emphasized.
5. American scholars and government officials were to join with colleagues elsewhere in order to find fresh ways of advancing a worldwide intellectual community.

Miller concluded by warning of "storm clouds" within the academic community's approach to the IEA, "small places fearful of being jostled aside by the large places, weak institutions looking for what they believe to be inequitable allocations, and strong institutions prepared to expose unwise dilution — problems that get in the way of trust and consensus."[12]

In April the assistant secretary's office hosted a meeting of representatives of 12 organizations involved in adult and continuing education in world affairs (for example, the Foreign Policy Association, Institute of International Education, the Experiment in International Living, National Council for International Visitors, Council on Student Travel, and world affairs councils) to discuss the role of voluntary associations in international education.[13]

Between April and July, one-day regional conferences co-sponsored by HEW and various universities or colleges or associations were held throughout the country to provide the broadest possible base for planning the administration of the IEA. The number of participants in each conference was limited to 150 who were to be invited by the major educational associations. Teams headed by Miller or Taggart and including members of the ad hoc steering committee, the interim secretariat, and representatives of the subject matter committees and EWA served as speakers and discussion leaders. The meetings followed the same format of a general session followed by small group discussions and a brief concluding plenary meeting. Summaries of the meetings were then circulated to all members of the participating associations.

Regional meetings were held in St. Louis at Washington University, Tucson at the University of Arizona, Atlanta at Emory University, Ithaca at Cornell University, Boulder at the University of Colorado, California at Stanford, Chicago under the auspices of the Associated Colleges of the Midwest, New England under the auspices of the New England Continuing Education Center, and East Lansing at Michigan State University.[14]

On 15 May, Miller submitted to Congress the report required by the IEA. The study, prepared by the interim secretariat, was entitled "International Education — Its Meaning and Possible Patterns of Development." Because no funds had been allocated for the National Advisory Committee that was responsible for writing the study, the report was published instead by the Office of the Assistant Secretary for Education.

Miller had completed a conscientious and methodical plan for implementing the IEA. One wag commented that the IEA was the best-planned unfunded piece of legislation in the history of the republic. Miller and his staff probably had done the best planning-for-implementation job that could have been done under the circumstances. The future of the IEA then shifted mainly to other parties.

NOTES

1. William W. Marvel, "The Opportunity and the Responsibility," in *International Education Act of 1966* (Education and World Affairs, 1966).

2. Ibid. See also ACE, 4 *Bulletin of International Education*, 30 December 1966, pp. 1–2, "International Education, 1967," Box 45, Office Files of Cater, LBJ Library.

3. Memo, Cater to LBJ, 15 November 1967, "Memos to the President, November 1967," Box 17, Office Files of Cater, LBJ Library.

4. Norman C. Thomas, *Education in National Politics* (New York: David McKay, 1975), pp. 142–43.

5. Memo, Cater to LBJ, 4 January 1967, "Memos to the President, January 1967," Box 15, Office Files of Cater; Memo, Cater to LBJ, 4 January 1967; Memo, Macy to LBJ, National Advisory Committee on International Studies, 3 January 1967, "Advisory Council on International Education, 1967," Box 45, Office Files of Cater, LBJ Library.

6. Ibid. Memo, Cater to LBJ, 20 February 1967, "Memos to the President, February 1967," Box 16, Office Files of Cater, LBJ Library.

7. Memo, Miller to participants, Conference on International Education, 23–24 January, 13 January 1967, "Memos to and from Paul A. Miller, 1967–68," Box 12, Office Files of Cater, LBJ Library.

8. Marvel, "Preface," in Richard H. Wood, *U.S. Universities: Their Role in AID-Financed Technical Assistance Overseas* (Education and World Affairs, 1968), p. 6.

9. Memo, Cater to LBJ, 30 January 1967, "Memos to the President, January 1967," Box 15, Office Files of Cater, LBJ Library. The president made "Remarks on the Occasion of the Centennial of the U.S. Office of Education" at 12:48 P.M. at the OE Plaza on 2 March 1967, *Public Papers of the Presidents of the United States, Lyndon B. Johnson, 1967*, Vol. I (Washington, D.C.: U.S. Government Printing Office, 1968), pp. 265–67.

10.   The International Education Act of 1966, Administrative History of Department of HEW, Vol. I, Part I, p. 3, LBJ Library.

11.   Memo, Miller to IEA Steering Committee, 24 February 1967, "Memos to and from Paul A. Miller, 1967–68," Box 12, Office Files of Cater, LBJ Library.

12.   Speech, Miller to ACE Seminar, Department of State, 24 March 1967, pp. 8–11, "International Education," Box 10, Office Files of McPherson, LBJ Library.

13.   The International Education Act of 1966, Administrative History of Department of HEW, Vol. I, Part I, p. 3, LBJ Library.

14.   Ibid.

11

The IEA and
Appropriations Committees

At the time of the passage of the IEA, Cater noted that last minute action by the Appropriations Conference had struck out the initial funding of the act, which meant that the administration would "have a continuing job of persuasion to do" as soon as the new Congress convened in January.[1] Miller would be the point man for the department in its efforts to gain an appropriation for the act. Concurrent with his planning activities, Miller prepared budget requests for review by the BOB, the largest staff arm of the executive office of the president. The director of the budget, Charles Schultze, was concerned with "tradeoffs" within the full budget for education.

Because the implementation of the IEA required an expenditure of money, the appropriations process was as vital to the existence and continuance of the program as the authorization phase. Although the House Committee on Education and Labor and the Committee on Labor and Public Welfare in the Senate are responsible for authorizing a program and setting an appropriation ceiling, it is the job of the House and Senate appropriations committees to reconcile such a claim with budgetary realities. The lack of funding for fiscal year 1967 meant that Miller had to make his request for a supplemental appropriation before the committees of both houses and then return to each committee again to state his case for the regular appropriations contained in the president's proposed budgets for fiscal years 1968 and 1969.

At that time, the House subcommittee was regarded as guardian of the treasury with a strong budget-cutting bias while the Senate subcommittee was considered an appeals court that generally restored part but not all of the cuts. The House subcommittee had a more direct impact on substantive education policies.[2]

The Congressional elections of 1966, held only a few weeks after the passage of the IEA, had a profound effect upon the chances of the act being funded by the Appropriations Committees with which Miller would have to work. The elections occurred against a backdrop of budding disaffection with war and inflation and urban riots. The Republicans gained 47 House seats, 3 seats in the Senate, and 8 governorships. Within the Democratic party, President Johnson's falling popularity and "credibility gap" were matters of concern. Party leaders feared that Republicans in alliance with anti-Johnson Democrats could control the House.

The Ninetieth Congress was to prove far more resistant to Johnson's submissions, partly because his "Goldwater majority" was considerably reduced but also because of fundamentally altered fiscal and budgetary circumstances. By the end of 1966 there were 389,000 U.S. troops in Vietnam, and the accompanying surge of Great Society and Vietnam War inflation was widely recognized and deplored.[3]

There was also a shift in the priorities of the administration, with defense expenditures and legislation concerned with the problems of the underprivileged and the inner city getting top billing. Other domestic programs, including many of the president's initiatives in higher education, were diminished or cut back.[4]

Another factor that was to affect the IEA was the death of Congressman John E. Fogarty (D-RI), chairman of the House Appropriations Subcommittee, on the opening day of the Ninetieth Congress. Since the establishment of HEW in 1953, the department's appropriations had been scrutinized under the leadership of Fogarty, whose friendly attitude toward HEW generally and toward the IEA specifically were well-known.[5]

On 6 December, shortly before his death, Fogarty had told Cater of his concern about the loss from his subcommittee of four Democrats who had been defeated in the election: Denton (IN), Duncan (OR), Farnum (MI), and Matthews (FL). Fogarty hoped the president would "bear this in mind during any conversations with the (Congressional) Leadership." He feared that if the chairman of the House Appropriations Committee, George H. Mahon (D-TX), one of the most senior and most powerful of the Democrats, put "a bunch of budget cutters on his Subcommittee, it could hurt the health and education programs badly."[6]

Since the death of Clarence Cannon (D-MO) in 1964, Mahon had been chair of both the House Appropriations Committee and its Defense Subcommittee. Those two posts gave Mahon "as much influence as any man in Congress over the federal budget." Liberals complained that he cut too deeply into domestic programs and not deeply enough into Pentagon requests. Mahon used his influence to keep "heavy spenders" off of the Appropriations Committee. He possessed a keen sense of what the House would and would not accept and tailored his bills so that they would win acceptance on the floor. During his chairmanship, there was seldom a serious floor fight on an appropriations bill.[7] Mahon was to play an influential role in the House subcommittee hearings on the IEA.

The new chair of the House Appropriations Subcommittee, Departments of Labor and Health, Education and Welfare and Related Agencies, Daniel Flood (D-PA), was the only returning Democratic member of the subcommittee. Mahon appointed "a very conservative committee with the possible exception of Neal Smith [D-IA]" without consulting Flood on his choices.[8] The new conservative Democrats, Robert (Bob) R. Casey (TX), W. R. Hull, Jr. (MO), and William H. Natcher (KY), along with three mid-West Republicans, Melvin Laird (WI), Robert H. Michel (IL), and Garner E. Shriver (KS), gave the subcommittee a definite fiscally stingy cast. In the House vote on the IEA, Flood, Smith, Casey, and Natcher had voted for the act; Hull had not voted; and Mahon, Laird, Michel, and Shriver had voted against. The subcommittee was to conduct exhaustive hearings that probed deeply into the federal role in education.

As soon as the Ninetieth Congress convened, Cater and Miller began an intensive lobbying effort to get funding for the IEA. Cater met with Mahon, who told him that "he had not realized that the funds under this Act go exclusively to American universities — not to schools overseas." Mahon said he would keep an open mind about providing "some initial funding for the IEA." Cater did not allude to the Fogarty subcommittee, believing it "too ticklish a subject to try to discuss on the staff level."[9]

Miller orchestrated a lobbying campaign by presidents of colleges and universities from the home states and districts of Chairman Mahon and members of the House Appropriations Subcommittee on Education. In late January, Cater reported to the president that Mahon had been visited or written by university presidents McCrocklin of Southwest Texas State, James Cornette of West Texas State, Frank Rose of the University of Alabama, and others. Mahon's response was favorable "after it was explained that these funds will strengthen domestic colleges." In addition, Rose had received what he thought were commitments of support from Congressmen George W. Andrews (D-AL) and Natcher.[10]

In late January, the BOB approved a request to Congress for a supplemental appropriation of $350,000 to initiate planning as called for by the IEA. The request included $200,000 to establish and staff the CEC; $75,000 to organize the National Advisory Committee on

International Studies; and $75,000 to conduct the baseline study of the capacity of U.S. colleges and universities in the field of international studies.[11]

In addition, the 1968 budget request of $36,525,000 was submitted to Congress. Of the total, $20.35 million was new funding and the remainder, $15.7 million, was a continuation of NDEA programs at the same level as 1966–67. Programs of grants to colleges and universities were to receive $18.95 million, of which $13 million was for graduate programs and $5.95 million for undergraduate programs ($40 million had been authorized for the grants program by the IEA); $100,000 was for the support of the National Advisory Committee and its annual report required by the IEA; and $1,775,000 for the CEC (of which $475,000 was support of programs previously funded under the OE budget). The CEC was to be staffed with 68 new positions appointed independent of civil service regulations and General Schedule salary levels.[12] The IEA appropriation request was miniscule in the president's $169.2 billion budget, which included defense spending of $73.1 billion.

Cater sent a memo to the president explaining the details of the IEA budget and making an appeal: "The IEA is on the books. Now we have to get money for it, and I hope you will join me in talking to every Congressman you know about this."[13]

On 28 February, President Johnson, in his message on education and health, called the IEA "an historic measure recognizing this Nation's enduring belief that learning must transcend geographic boundaries." He urged Congress to approve promptly his request for the supplemental appropriation of $350,000 for the IEA (to permit necessary planning for next year's program) as well as an appropriation of $20 million for fiscal 1968.[14] Unfortunately, the president's message was delivered only 15 days after a major tremor had shaken the academic world. Congressional attention was still focused on the revelation that the National Student Association had secretly and indirectly received $3 million from the CIA from 1952 to 1966 for use in its overseas programs. The public was shocked that a federal agency had infiltrated and subverted the world of U.S. student leaders. Government and higher education were not a happy couple.

In early March, Flood told Gardner that he was "quite pessimistic about Mahon's intentions toward HEW." Flood felt that Mahon would "press for budget cuts every inch of the way" and that he had the backing of the majority on both the subcommittee and the full committee. Flood predicted that the HEW budget would "end up with a considerable variety of small but irritating reductions throughout."[15]

Mahon, who was being lobbied by President Grover E. Murray and other representatives of Texas Tech University, indicated privately that he thought the IEA was a foreign aid giveaway. Publicly he told Murray that he was working to get him "on the [IEA] Commission when and if it is approved." This led Murray to tell McCrocklin that he was confident that he could "deliver" Mahon.[16]

On March 21, the day before Miller was to appear before the House Subcommittee to request the supplemental appropriation, the president of North Vietnam, Ho Chi Minh, turned down a peace bid by President Johnson for direct U.S.-North Vietnam peace talks.

In the subcommittee hearings, Miller had his first opportunity to testify in behalf of the act. The BOB had changed the name of the appropriation to "Higher Education for International Understanding" to emphasize the domestic nature of the IEA. Miller told the subcommittee members that "we think the IEA can become as significant and far reaching to American higher education as the Morrill Act of one hundred years ago," the legislation that established the nationwide system of land-grant colleges and universities — the first major program of federal aid to higher education.[17]

Flood entered into the record a letter from Brademas and Albert Quie (R-MI) to Chairman Mahon expressing strong support for the supplemental appropriation.[18] Miller called the subcommittee's attention to the book of selected readings produced by the Brademas Task Force and called it "one of the finest substantive documents in international education."[19]

Flood used the analogy of "the old moth-eaten phrase about the camel getting its nose under the tent" to warn the witnesses from HEW that members of his committee were wary of supplemental appropriations for new programs.[20] Natcher then asked Miller why initial funding was being sought for the IEA by a supplemental appropriation rather than by regular appropriation and wanted to know why the request should not be passed over until 1969. Miller's explanation of the history of the IEA and the BOB's recommended course of action did not satisfy Natcher, who expressed concern about starting a new program when the war in Vietnam was costing the taxpayers $2 billion a month in support of 427,000 U.S. ground forces. "Never in my lifetime," said Natcher, "have I seen people as mad and incensed over Federal spending as they are today." The congressman from Kentucky concluded by stating: "Quite frankly I am concerned about this program at this time."[21]

Miller expressed HEW's apprehension, explaining that without the
. supplemental appropriation "the position of the Department must be that

we cannot create the CEC or have the President appoint the National Advisory Committee, which means that without funding, we cannot get off dead center."[22] His statement did not move Michel, who thought that in the tight budget situation, the committee's only choice was to "thwart" new programs getting underway.[23] Remarks of the subcommittee members reflected their concern that the administration was talking about a tax increase in the upcoming fiscal year.[24]

The IEA was also getting negative signals from the House Subcommittee on the Departments of State, Justice, and Commerce. Frankel's testimony before the subcommittee was interrupted by Chairman John J. Rooney (D-NY), who remarked that "the program was moth-eaten and dead."[25]

The mood on Capitol Hill — "weariness and a feeling of having been overcommitted, abroad and at home by an Administration that enters ventures without looking down the road to where they may lead" — made Brademas pessimistic about the chances of getting funding for the IEA.[26] Senator John L. McClellan (D-AR) summed up the feelings of many congressmen when he asked "if the country hadn't had too much of all the 'international business.'"[27] Frankel noted a pettishness about professors and students at this time, quoting a congressman as saying "they're not good citizens; why should we be giving them grants [sic] and won't they go abroad and talk against us?"[28]

After the hostility of the House Subcommittee was made public, the leadership of the AASCU wrote letters to Mahon and all subcommittee members. Every member of the subcommittee who had a state college in his district heard from the college president in support of the full appropriation.[29] In at least one instance, this effort was less than helpful. Kelly Thompson, president of Western Kentucky University wrote Natcher stating that Cornette of West Texas State, president of the AASCU, had asked him

To solicit your help regarding the inequity which is felt to exist in the IEA budget requests. Specifically, as one of the 206 member institutions of ASCU [sic], Western Kentucky University would like for you to use your influence to see that a better distribution is made between the undergraduate and graduate programs in international studies. . . . It is our feeling the division of funds is out of line.[30]

Congressman Natcher replied to Thompson that he would "be glad to keep your views in mind."[31]

During the Easter recess, Miller continued to contact members of the House Subcommittee. To Miller, "it seemed clear that Mahon, Casey,

Shriver, and Laird were receptive to more discussion about the IEA."
University presidents continued to lobby their congressmen: Philip G.
Hoffman of the University of Houston met with Casey, W. Clarke
Wescoe of the University of Kansas with Shriver, and Hannah of
Michigan State University with Laird and Gerald Ford. McCrocklin and
others in Texas had enlisted Edward T. Marcus of Neiman-Marcus fame
to visit Mahon.[32]

Miller asked Natcher for an opportunity to discuss possible
retrenchment of the major foundations, the growing involvement and
interest of the academic community in the planning process, and other
basic reasons why it would be unwise to delay appropriations for a year
or two as Natcher proposed.[33]

Frank Rose of the University of Alabama, meanwhile, had called again
on the generally conservative Congressman George W. Andrews (D-
AL), who promised to solicit every member of the subcommittee to vote
for the IEA supplemental appropriation as a personal favor. Cater thought
that "it might not hurt to chide Mahon that even George Andrews is
willing to accept this program."[34]

Cater reported to the president that Natcher and Casey had given
tentative affirmative responses to local constituents, although they had
been very evasive in dealing with officials of the administration. Hull
seemed hopeless. There was, however, some prospect of moving at least
one Republican (from among Laird, Michel, and Shriver). Flood thought
Mahon, who had been consistently negative, was the key. Mahon was
expected to sit in the subcommittee meeting and vote.[35] Under Mahon's
leadership, the House Appropriations Subcommittee had become a tightly
integrated bipartisan operation. In choosing between alternative uses of
limited funds, its operational credo was "to make the maximum cut and
do the least damage."[36]

Cater made a last minute plea to Johnson:

I believe the only chance of saving the supplementals is for you to make a personal
plea to Mahon. Remind him of your offer to cut anywhere else an equivalent amount
of money. But point out that these are two programs (the IEA and the Teacher Corps)
which are vested with your personal concerns and that for him to ruthlessly abolish
them is to strike directly at your leadership. You can't believe that he wants to do
that.[37]

The president apparently did not call Mahon about the supplemental
appropriation, but later in the year he was to have a frustrating meeting
with the chairman about funding the IEA.

In mid-April, just before the Appropriations Subcommittee met, hundreds of thousands of demonstrators staged anti–Vietnam War peace parades in New York City, where the demonstration was led by Martin Luther King, Jr., and in San Francisco. At that time, Laird told Cater that it would be impossible to fund the act in the House Committee. Laird indicated that he would not oppose a small appropriation, however, if it were added in the Senate.[38]

On 19 April, the House Subcommittee held hearings on the IEA appropriation for 1968. Neal Smith (D-IA) favored the IEA, but he was in Iowa with Secretary of Agriculture Orville L. Freeman when the subcommittee met. He had informed Mahon and Flood several days in advance that he would have to be out of town, and the congressman from Iowa was assured that the request for "Higher Education for International Understanding" would not be taken up while he was away. Smith was suspicious that Mahon wanted him out of town when the IEA appropriation came up.[39]

In the hearings, Miller forcefully set forth the need for funding of the IEA: "For fifteen years the education community has been putting out to itself and to others over and over again that there is no field of effort . . . for which it is so ill prepared. . . . Conference after conference and report after report have requested assistance for a marked improvement of our resources in this field." Miller called the committee's attention to the "active planning to improve the international efforts of our colleges and universities . . . underway throughout the entire country." He added: "Current enthusiasm of our educational community underscores the belief that these funds can be efficiently used to begin this enormous task which confronts us. The IEA, if adequately supported . . . can strengthen our colleges and universities as great national resources for international understanding. This momentous program aims to correct one of the gravest weaknesses of American education." Miller ended his prepared statement emphatically and prophetically: "I think this effort has the genius of history about it. If we make no start at all there may be a very grave collapse of concern, interest, momentum, and imagination."[40]

Chairman Flood, probably trying to bring some levity to the solemn proceedings, questioned Miller about the centers of excellence scheduled for support under the act. "How could I get in a taxicab and get off at a center of excellence?" he asked.

In his reply, Miller cited Columbia University as a center of excellence with, among other strengths, a distinguished school of international studies, a substantial number of graduate students from the United States and abroad, a strong research program that was excellent in many fields, and a full-time faculty who devoted their time to the study of various aspects of international problems such as international law, rural development, and comparative education. Miller went on to discuss the 25 universities most active in international education, 10 centers striving to become excellent, and 15 developing centers showing promise of becoming better.[41]

Having heard Miller's response to Flood's friendly questions, the rest of the subcommittee members began nitpicking. As Frankel described it: "They were not really interested in the substance of the legislation"; they were "interested in making a record and cutting."[42] In addition to Chairman Mahon, Frank T. Bow (R-OH), the ranking minority member on the Appropriations Committee, who had voted against approval of the IEA during House floor debate in 1966, participated in the subcommittee hearing.

Laird raised two major objections to the funding request. He felt that the CEC as described by Miller would not coordinate all international programs of AID, the Department of Defense, the Central Intelligence Agency (CIA), and HEW as Laird thought it should. Laird had probably gotten that idea from conversations with James Linen III, the publisher of *Time*, who had served on the Rusk Task Force.[43]

It is possible, too, that Laird was privy to the Katzenbach Report of a presidentially appointed committee, composed of Gardner, Richard Helms, director of the CIA, and Nicholas Katzenbach of the Department of Justice, that had reviewed the relationships between the CIA and private U.S. voluntary organizations. The report had recommended the establishment of "a public-private mechanism to provide public funds openly for overseas activities of organizations which are adjudged deserving in the national interest, of public support."[44] Secretary Rusk, who chaired a committee to follow up the Katzenbach Report "thought serious consideration should be given to placing this responsibility in the new center for international education in HEW." The president rejected Rusk's idea.

Laird also wondered that if the IEA were "such an important thing, . . . why it was held in the BOB for a total of two months while Congress was in session." Laird finished by charging that "this thing has not been planned out to the point where this committee can move with any degree of certainty as to what we are funding."[45]

Miller replied that "cooperative planning with the academic community has been truly first rate. I doubt if many Federal programs have had better communications in terms of ten year goals and where we ought to be and how we might get there."[46]

The hearing concluded with Natcher moving to strike the IEA supplemental appropriation. The vote was eight to one, with Flood casting the only vote for the appropriation. Mahon, Bow, Casey, Hull, Laird, Shriver, Michel, and Natcher were opposed.[47] The coffin for the IEA was being prepared.

Upon hearing of the subcommittee action, Frankel noted: "Scores of people have been involved in planning the [IEA] program, hundreds of hours have been spent on it, and educators all over the country have been pushing for it — and it is disposed of in five minutes before a subcommittee that gave no evidence that it had studied any of the documents involved."[48]

On 28 April, the full House Appropriations Committee disallowed the $350,000 request to begin the IEA, saying it "was not prepared to recommend starting this new and controversial program at this time." The House passed the 1967 Appropriations Bill on 3 May by a 391 to 6 roll-call vote and sent it to the Senate.[49]

In debate on the House floor, Bow noted that "with respect to the 1967 Budget, Congress has certainly won, I believe, the indisputable right to be called the rubber stamp for the Administration on appropriations." He observed that of the $128.6 billion requested by the administration, Congress had cut less than 0.7 percent.[50] The IEA was one of a very few victims of the thin slicing of the budget by the House. The only other education measures requested by the administration that were cut from the Appropriations Bill were $30 million to help local governments face problems of school segregation and funding to expand the Teacher Corps to include 5,500 volunteers by September 1968.[51]

Having been defeated in the House, Miller and Cater shifted their attention to the Senate. Frankel felt that they were "still spinning bureaucratic wheels after the issue has become academic."[52] Senator Lister Hill (D-AL), chairman of the Senate Appropriations Subcommittee, told Cater that he would "endeavor to help in any way" he could "in behalf of funding for the IEA of 1966."[53] Hill and ranking minority member Senator Javits were also members of the Morse subcommittee that had voted favorably on the IEA only a few months earlier.

The Senate Subcommittee, which was polite if not enthusiastic in hearing Miller's testimony, included Democrats Richard B. Russell (GA), Warren G. Magnuson (WA), John Stennis (MS), Alan Bible (NV), Robert C. Byrd (WV), Spessard L. Holland (FL), and E. L. Bartlett (AL) and Republicans Javits, Norris Cotton (NH), and Clifford P. Case (NJ). The Senate Subcommittee in the past had exerted only modest influence on education policy, primarily by restoring some of the cuts made by the House.[54] On 17 May, the Senate Appropriations Committee recommended $150,000 for an advisory committee to study implementation of the IEA and for a "baseline study of U.S. needs and capabilities in international research and education."[55]

On 19 May, the Senate debated the Appropriations Bill. Senators Karl E. Mundt (R-SD) and Gordon Allott (R-CO) expressed misgivings about the administration's utilizing supplemental appropriations "to get a foot in the door" to start new programs for which regular appropriations had not been provided[56] — another telling argument against an appropriation for the IEA. The Senate passed its version of the Appropriations Bill by a 74 to 1 roll-call vote and sent it to conference with the House. The Senate bill was some $218 million more than the amount approved by the House.[57] The Conference Committee of the Appropriations Committees offered the last opportunity to get funding for the IEA.

Senator Hill gave Rose a firm commitment that he would "fight for funding in Conference." Javits was a staunch supporter of the act, and Holland promised to follow Hill's lead. Hill thought the president needed to indicate clearly his strong support for funding the IEA. He said he expected trouble in getting Mahon to recede. On the other hand, it was reported that Laird might be willing to get his fellow House conferees to recede.[58]

These speculations led nowhere, however. On 24 May, the Conference Committee filed its report sustaining the House in rejecting funds to begin the IEA.[59] The act was a dead letter on the books.

On the next day, the House and Senate adopted the Conference report by voice votes. The final bill was some $60 million less than the administration had requested.[60] Included in the casualties was the IEA.

NOTES

1. Memo, Cater to E. P. Anderson, 28 October 1966, Ex Ed Box 3, LBJ Library.

2. Norman C. Thomas, *Education in National Politics* (New York: David McKay, 1975), p. 134.

3. Hugh Davis Graham, *The Uncertain Triumph: Federal Education Policy in the Kennedy and Johnson Years* (Chapel Hill: University of North Carolina Press, 1984), p. 114.

4. Interview, Ralph C. M. Flynt, Deputy Assistant Secretary for International Education, Office of Assistant Secretary for Education, 23 July 1968, Appendix 2, The History of the Office of Education, LBJ Library.

5. Ibid.; Thomas, *Education in National Politics*, p. 101.

6. Memo, Cater to LBJ, 6 December 1966, "Memos to the President, December 1966," Box 15, Office Files of Cater, LBJ Library.

7. Michael Barone, Grant Ujifusa, and Douglas Matthews, *The Almanac of American Politics* (Washington, D.C.: Gambit, 1972), p. 813.

8. Thomas, *Education in National Politics*, p. 101; see also Memo, Huitt to Cater, 18 November 1967, "Memos to the President," Box 15, Office Files of Cater, LBJ Library.

9. Memo, Cater to LBJ, 16 January 1967, "Memos to the President," Box 15, Office Files of Cater, LBJ Library.

10. Memo, Cater to LBJ, 28 January 1967, Ex Ed Box 3, LBJ Library.

11. Memo, Cater to LBJ, 28 January 1967, "Memos to the President, January 1967," Box 15, Office Files of Cater, LBJ Library.

12. Memo, Cater to LBJ, 14 February 1967, Ex Ed Box 3, LBJ Library.

13. Memo, Cater to LBJ, 9 March 1967, Ex Ed Box 3, LBJ Library.

14. *Public Papers of the Presidents of the United States, Lyndon B. Johnson, 1967*, Vol. I, Special Message to the Congress: "Education and Health in America," 28 February 1967 (Washington, D.C.: U.S. Government Printing Office, 1968), pp. 244–58. For Cater's account of the National Student Association story that was reported 15 days before the president's address, see Cater, "What Did LBJ Know and When Did He Know It?" *Washington Post*, 19 July 1987, p. C7.

15. Memo, Cater to LBJ, 7 March 1967, "Memos to the President, March 1967," Box 16, Office Files of Cater, LBJ Library.

16. Ibid.; Letter, McCrocklin to Cater, 1 March 1967, "Memos to the President," Box 16, Office Files of Cater, LBJ Library.

17. Second Supplemental Appropriations Bill, 1967, Hearings Before Subcommittees of the Committee on Appropriations, House of Representatives, Ninetieth Congress, First Session, (hereafter, Subcommittee Hearings), p. 101.

18. Subcommittee Hearings, p. 102.

19. Ibid., p. 103.

20. Ibid., p. 104.

21. Ibid., pp. 106–8.

22. Ibid., p. 117.

23. Ibid., p. 109.

24. Ibid., pp. 98–123.

25. Memo, Frankel to Cater, Subject: Hearings on Education Officers before Chairman Rooney's Subcommittee, 7 April 1967, "International and Domestic Education," Box 44, Office Files of Cater, LBJ Library.

26. Charles Frankel, *High on Foggy Bottom* (New York: Harper & Row, 1968), p. 165.

27. Ibid., p. 202.

28. Transcript, Frankel Oral History Interview, AC 80-51, 29 January 1969, by Paige E. Mulhollan, p. 27, LBJ Library.

29. Letter, Ostar to Miller, 28 March 1967, "International Education, 1967," Box 45, Office Files of Cater, LBJ Library.

30. Letter, Thompson to Natcher, 3 March 1967, "International Education, 1967," Box 45, Office Files of Cater, LBJ Library.

31. Letter, Natcher to Thompson, 6 March 1967, "International Education, 1967," Box 45, Office Files of Cater, LBJ Library.

32. Memo, Miller to Huitt, 31 March 1967, "International Education," Box 14, Office Files of Wilson, LBJ Library.

33. Ibid.

34. Memo, Cater to LBJ, 20 April 1967, 12:58 P.M., "Memos to the President, April 1967," Box 16, Office Files of Cater, LBJ Library.

35. Ibid., 10:24 A.M.

36. Thomas, *Education in National Politics*, p. 135.

37. Memo, Cater to LBJ, 20 April 1967, 10:24 A.M., "Memos to the President, April 1967," Box 16, Office Files of Cater, LBJ Library.

38. Memo, Cater to LBJ, 20 April 1967, 4:55 P.M., "Memos to the President, April 1967," Box 16, Office Files of Cater, LBJ Library.

39. Ibid., 10:24 A.M. and 12:58 P.M.

40. Department of Labor and HEW Appropriations for 1968, Hearings Before a Subcommittee of the Committee on Appropriations, House of Representatives, Ninetieth Congress, First Session, pp. 1398, 1401, 1403.

41. Ibid., p. 1406.

42. Frankel, Oral History, p. 12, LBJ Library.

43. Hearings, Part 3, p. 1410.

44. Report, Committee (Gardner, Helms, Katzenbach) to LBJ, 24 March 1967; Memo, Cater to LBJ, 28 March 1967, 31 March 1967, "Memos to the President, March 1967," Box 16, Office Files of Cater, LBJ Library.

45. Hearings, Part 3, pp. 1416, 1414.

46. Ibid., pp. 1414–15; see also, Memo, Joseph Colmen to Cater, 10 July 1967, Ex Ed Box 4, LBJ Library.

47. Memo, Cater to LBJ, 20 April 1967, 4:55 P.M., "Memos to the President, April 1967," Box 16, Office Files of Cater, LBJ Library.

48. Frankel, *High on Foggy Bottom*, p. 191.

49. *1967 CQ Almanac*, pp. 199–200.

50. Ibid.

51. Ibid., pp. 164–65.

52. Frankel, *High on Foggy Bottom*, p. 206.

53. Letter, Hill to Cater, 5 May 1967, Education Box 4, LBJ Library.

54. Thomas, *Education in National Politics*, p. 135.

55. *1967 CQ Almanac*, pp. 201–2.

56. Ibid., p. 203.

57. Ibid., p. 202.

58. Memo, Cater to LBJ, 21 June 1967, "Memos to the President, June 1967," Box 16, Office Files of Cater, LBJ Library.

59. *1967 CQ Almanac*, p. 203.

60. Ibid.

12

Why the IEA Was Defeated: Congress

In the public policy arena, education must compete for scarce national resources with numerous other problem areas. The allocation for education is determined by policy priorities shaped by the crises and demands of the time.

During the period between the end of the Eighty-ninth Congress and the convening of the Ninetieth Congress, Vietnam had become the dominant factor changing policy priorities. The mounting expense of the war and fears of inflation made it increasingly difficult for President Johnson to bargain on Capitol Hill. There was a strong feeling in Congress that the administration had been less than candid in presenting the 1966 budget, causing a growing crisis in presidential credibility.[1] At the same time, the president may have lost the support of some southern congressmen whose constituents disliked Johnson's war on poverty and efforts to end segregation.[2]

Miller remembered the ill will stirred up within Congress and between the White House and the Hill generating

So much confusion ... that anything that was a new international departure just could not come into serious place on the agenda. In meeting after meeting I had in those days with representatives from both Houses, from key people like Senator Fulbright, I gained the impression in no uncertain terms that until the Administration got its act together on the Vietnam crisis, funding of other initiatives was out of the question.

Miller concluded that "the IEA was, in the 1967–68 period, a hostage of the Vietnam crisis."[3]

Taggart agreed, contending that the failure to get an appropriation for the IEA should be traced to "the conditions of government" at the time — especially the war in Vietnam — and not to the techniques and strategies of the act's proponents.[4] The rise in numbers of U.S. ground troops deployed in Vietnam during the time the IEA was under consideration was dramatic — from 70,000 to 427,000 — and no one could be sure how many more would be required.

Frankel noted a change in congressional attitudes toward the president in early 1966: "When I first came in the summer of '65, and went up to the Hill to present various bits of legislation or what have you, and I'd mention the President's name, and say he's personally interested in this and very eager, it was smooth sailing." But, wrote Frankel, "By February or March of the next year when you said the President had a special interest in something you might get a negative feeling."[5]

In 1967, the president's domestic programs gave top priority to problems of the ghetto, the underprivileged, and the handicapped. Miller recalls the urban crisis turning government officials almost overnight to new issues:

This happened to me: while my portfolio was largely international education, almost at once . . . I [was] hauled into responses on the new front. Of course, the War was still there, so that the resulting matrix of crosscutting tension at the White House and in the Congress found the IEA in rapid descent. While I was working on the [IEA] funding issue, I remember Douglass Cater asking me to go to work on ideas drawn from my agricultural extension background that could be adapted to urban development. So it went all along the front![6]

One critic of the Congress of that time alleged that the congressional coalition leadership used "the power of the national legislature to support domestic parochialism, to perpetuate cold war orthodoxy and to bestow a ludicrously uncritical acceptance on the excesses of the new militarism." The sheer inertial force of the huge military-industrial-technocratic-educational complex pushed aside other critical public priorities, including international education.[7]

There were, of course, institutional advantages for fiscal conservatives in the budgetary process. The sequential steps required to move an idea from proposal to program provide many points at which policy change can be blocked. In the educational policy process, approval by the House Appropriations Subcommittee was a strategic point. The IEA, like a steeplechase racer, had almost made its way over the course of obstacles, only to be tripped by the last hurdle posed by Mahon and associates.

Congressional opponents of funding the IEA rationalized their actions in several ways. Most, especially the fiscal conservatives of both parties, simply did not want to appropriate money for any new program. When war-inspired inflation set in, in the absence of a wartime mood of sacrifice, the centers of power in Congress responded with a conventional call to cut the budget.[8]

With the "guns and butter" issue paramount, congressmen, always mindful of constituency perceptions of their fiscal stewardship, were not eager to support funding of a new program — even the modest amount requested for the IEA.[9] Some congressmen, doubtlessly knowing better, justified their inaction by publicly condemning the act as a foreign aid measure; others declared that the act did not do enough for education programs of other nations.

By 1967, many congressmen had wearied of the "Johnson treatment" of "talking with them, and cajoling with them, and persuading with them" on legislative matters. According to Cohen, the more Johnson dealt, pushed, and compromised with the congressmen, the more "their natural animosity and antagonism grew."[10]

Republicans were mostly partisan sour grapes critics of the earlier successes of the Johnson legislative program. Congressman Michel (R-IL) had strongly objected to the use of secret education task forces to generate ideas.[11] The White House strategy of "pass the bill now, worry about its effects and implementation later" was bemoaned on both sides of the congressional aisle.[12]

Miller contends that many congressmen "believed that education had been given so much in the 1965–67 period that, with the advent of race and urban issues, education in general had to move over for other aspirants."[13] The major educational policy accomplishments of the Ninetieth Congress involved either coordination and consolidation of statutes on the books or adjustment and reaction to problems arising in the administration of existing programs. There was already an overdose of legislation that had been passed but was underfunded. The new programs that successfully made it through the Ninetieth Congress were, for the most part, administered along with existing legislation.[14]

Some congressmen, such as Natcher, publicly faulted the administration for using a supplementary allocation, "the camel's nose in the tent," to begin a new program such as the IEA for which a regular appropriation had not been provided. Many "budget-wedge" items had been passed in the domestic budgets, and a large number of fragmented and small categorical programs were being implemented by HEW. Privately, Natcher told Brooks Hays (D-AL) that he opposed an appropriation for the IEA "on the basis of Vietnam and war requirements generally."[15]

According to Laird, the IEA failed to win approval because it "did not implement the promised coordination of all international education programs. It was a bad bill. It did not do the job we had requested and the administration had promised so we said no money. If we had funded it we would have been stuck with it. Once you get a program like that under way you can never get rid of it."[16] Laird wanted the CEC to centralize *all* international educational activities of the federal government, including USAID, CU, the Department of Defense, and the CIA. Such coordination in HEW would have been a tall order — even under the leadership of John Gardner!

Another problem was the apparent lack of interest in the IEA by the voting public. To many in Congress, even among those who had voted for its passage, the IEA did not command voters' interest. As Laird told Miller: "There are simply no votes for this out in the public."[17]

In retrospect, Miller thinks he should have spent more time "working the corridors on the Hill" rather than preparing the long-term plan for the IEA, which he wanted to be "of genuine professional quality."[18] Congress might have been more open to an appropriation for the IEA had the proponents of the act shown more lobbying clout.

Frankel sensed a residue of congressional suspicion toward the entire program:

Congress grew increasingly negative towards the President — toward anything marked international. There got to be a quasi-isolationist sentiment. It was hard even to get internationalists behind the program. They came along but — for example, Wayne Morse, who sponsored it in the Senate put me — as he had every right to do and did a good job — through the ropes on whether there was a CIA tie-up. He was terribly worried about that. There was suspicion of the President as a result of Vietnam. Then, of course, there were other people who didn't like to vote that kind of money anyway. I think the Bureau of the Budget didn't help.[19]

Landrum Bolling, president of Earlham College, wrote Miller complaining that the cost of the war in Vietnam "which must in part be attributable to our lack of knowledge and skill in the handling of international affairs," had made it "necessary for Congress to resist any and all moves for additional spending" but that Congress, in its allocation of scarce national resources, was guilty of "an extraordinary kind of shortsightedness . . . to search for so relatively minor an economy as to abort the international education programs."[20]

Finally, a major problem was the lack of an enduring champion for the IEA in Congress, someone who made the funding of the act "a focused and continuing project, carrying his personal signature of open, aggressive, and continuing support." Brademas had championed the IEA, but his efforts and those of others on the Hill and in the academic community may have peaked in getting the act passed. When the funding of the IEA was addressed belatedly in the midst of the dissension over Vietnam, "the strength of the movement had been rather spent."[21]

NOTES

1. John C. Donovan, *The 1960's: Politics and Public Policy* (Lanham, Md.: University Press of America, 1980), p. 84; Harry McPherson, *A Political Education* (Boston: Little, Brown, 1972), p. 178.

2 Transcript, Wilbur J. Cohen Oral History Interview, 10 May 1969, tape 4, AC 72-26, p. 15, LBJ Library.

3. Letter, Miller to Vestal, 6 February 1989.

4. Telephone interview with Glen Taggart, 8 May 1989.

5. Transcript, Charles Frankel Oral History Interview, AC 80-51, 29 January 1969, by Paige E. Mulhollan, p. 9, LBJ Library.

6. Letter, Miller to Vestal, 6 February 1989; see also Memo, Miller to Cater, 16 July 1967, "Memos to and from Paul A. Miller, 1967-68," Box 12, Office Files of Cater, LBJ Library.

7. Donovan, *The 1960's*, p. xvi.

8. Doris Kearns, *Lyndon Johnson and the Amerian Dream* (New York: Harper & Row, 1976), p. 298.

9. Letter, Miller to Vestal, 6 February 1989.

10. Cohen Oral History, p. 25, LBJ Library.

11. Hugh Davis Graham, *The Uncertain Triumph: Federal Education Policy in the Kennedy and Johnson Years* (Chapel Hill: University of North Carolina Press, 1984), p. 70.

12. Kearns, *Lyndon Johnson*, p. 218.

13. Letter, Miller to Vestal, 6 February 1989.

14. Norman C. Thomas, *Education in National Politics* (New York: David McKay, 1975), p. 104.

15. Department of Labor and HEW Appropriations for 1968, Hearings Before a Subcommittee of the Committee on Appropriations, House of Representatives, Ninetieth Congress, First Session, p. 1416; Memo, Cater to LBJ, 22 June 1967, "Memos to the President, June, 1967," Box 16, Office Files of Cater, LBJ Library.

16. Thomas, *Education in National Politics*, p. 103.

17. Letter, Miller to Vestal, 6 February 1989.

18. Letter, Miller to Vestal, 16 March 1989.

19. Frankel Oral History, p. 8, LBJ Library.

20. Letter, Bolling to Miller, 7 October 1967, "Memos to and from Paul A. Miller," Box 12, Office Files of Cater, LBJ Library.

21. Letter, Miller to Vestal, 6 February 1989.

13

Why the IEA Was Defeated: The President

From another perspective, the president's lack of continued support may have been a major cause of the IEA's failure to be funded. His willingness to commit the presidency to the cause of international education in 1965 was impressive and magnificent, but he was unable to make good on his promises. He was too busy at the time making other commitments in Southeast Asia.[1]

Miller found that the president and his staff, with the exception of Cater, "became so distracted and tired by reason of the war that the IEA just could not remain very centered in their interests." Indeed, by 1967, in the face of fiscal and political constraints imposed by the war, the Johnson administration was looking for ways to contract rather than expand its Great Society commitments. Generally, the administration's legislative efforts in education were aimed at consolidating and modifying what was already in place.

One HEW staff member remembers the period as one "of great haste, great superficiality, and political naivete of the highest order. . . . We were overextended, overtired, and our morale left a lot to be desired."[2] At that time, Gardner and Miller went to the White House to discuss the IEA but were treated instead to a lengthy presidential harangue about Vietnam.[3]

Another factor that may have diminished the president's ardor for the act may have been his love-hate relationship with intellectuals and professors. The escalation of the war in Vietnam produced an increased attack upon Johnson's policies by articulate critics from the academic community. Johnson responded with anger and rage at liberals, professors, and intellectuals. Although he continued to use selected academicians on task forces and sent his White House staff to campuses to seek new ideas from professors, Johnson's relations with the higher educational community continued to deteriorate after 1965.

The president's reactions to these scholar-critics elicited a response from Marvel and Herman Wells, former president of Indiana University, who jointly wrote Johnson in early 1967:

Substantial elements of the intellectual community feel themselves seriously alienated from the national leadership. This has resulted from disagreement over foreign policy questions. Any society depends for its progress on the constructive interaction of the intellectual community with the government. In the U.S., organized on democratic principles, it is crucially important that this relationship be maintained. Nothing is in shorter supply — not even high talent manpower — than fresh ideas that help us cope with mankind's manifold problems. The principal source of such ideas should be the scholars, the researchers, the universities — the academic world generally. It is clear that there is now an urgent need for a vast creative effort in the affairs of mankind.

The letter concluded with an appeal for conciliation between the White House and "concerned intellectuals who earn as well as claim the right to be listened to in a society of relative freedom and opportunity by filling the much-needed role of responsible citizen-critics rather than that of some kind of a professionally alienated intelligentsia."[4]

In response to the Wells-Marvel letter, the president hosted the trustees of EWA at a White House meeting on 20 January 1967. The gathering was characterized as being "useful in strengthening the relationship of the academic world with the government," but an officer of EWA remembers the meeting being dominated by the president, who carried on a dialogue about the administration's policies in Vietnam.[5]

Despite EWA's efforts for reconciliation, the president's "impossible war" made compatibility with the alienated intelligentsia increasingly impossible. It was during this time, too, that U.S. military involvement in Vietnam was hotly debated at meetings of several academic professional associations in which younger and more junior members demanded that their organizations take public stands against Johnson's policies.[6] Congressman Rooney warned the president that it was "opponents of the war to whom we were giving grants."[7] Because professors and their institutions were the main benefactors from the IEA, it is possible that Johnson, at times, lost interest in pushing for the funding of the act.

Richard Goodwin, assistant to President Johnson in 1963–65, postulates that Johnson may have been clinically paranoid during the Vietnam War era. Like many paranoids, he managed through most of his life to live with his affliction, even, at times, to use it to his own benefit, but under the strain of the presidency and the war, he began to be consumed by irrational resentments and fears of conspiracy. Goodwin found that "if the world was beginning to slip from his control, Johnson would construct a tiny inner world that he could control, barricade himself not only from disagreement, but from the need to acknowledge the very existence of disagreement except among the uninformed and the hostile."[8]

During the time the IEA was under debate, Johnson was under stress, worrying about Vietnam and the preference of Congress to cut Great Society programs rather than increase taxes. The president was going though a time of depression while being obsessed with criticism from both the left and the right. If "paranoia" were to affect his judgment at any time, the period from 1965 to 1967 would have been a prime juncture for it to occur. Perhaps this could explain his not bringing pressure to bear on Mahon and others on the appropriations committees to fund the IEA in April 1967.

On the other hand, could the "paranoid" episodes related by Goodwin be interpreted not as psychosis but as the way many powerful, insulated men blow off steam in unguarded moments?[9] Anyone who worked for Johnson had to put up with "rambling diatribes full of exaggerated grumbling, childish venom, capricious demands and other forms of rhetorical self-indulgence." These ended regularly in "brief, competent disposition of the business at hand."[10] The president's unique "Johnson style" of operations is only part of the complicated nature of the man that makes any attempt at postmortem psychoanalysis, such as Goodwin has attempted, difficult — if not impossible.

Another problem was caused by the president's grandiose rhetoric in announcing plans for the IEA in the Smithsonian address and subsequent speeches. What exactly did Johnson have in mind when he proposed the act and urged its receiving an appropriation? Did or did not the Great Society's IEA stop at the water's edge? Was the act aimed at aiding the educational efforts of developing nations, or was the IEA a purely domestic act to strengthen the international and cross-cultural capabilities of U.S. higher education — as stated so clearly by the authors of the legislation — or all of the above?

From the president's first reference to the IEA concept through his message on international education and health on 2 February 1966, his intentions were all-encompassing. During that time, he joked with Frankel by asking if the program was for Ph.D.s or for helping children "at the end of the line who can't read or write."[11] In early 1966, Johnson apparently thought the act could cover both aspects. When he made his

1967 appeal to Congress to appropriate funds for the IEA, however, Johnson made clear that he was talking about a domestic program. However, the seed of ambiguity had already been planted in the minds of those congressmen looking for a rationale to oppose the act: the IEA could be spoken of as a foreign aid program.

Miller recalls the process that produced the president's major addresses on international education: "The work of Marvel and others in the early period yielded material which speech writers put into Johnson Language, which delighted him to deliver to the Smithsonian, in Hawaii, and in Thailand." But, wrote Miller, "I'm not sure that his early understanding and resolve were as deep as his rhetoric was expansive."[12]

Perhaps the president can be forgiven for his lack of specificity in speeches. As Cater points out: "An active president is, after all, a salesman not purely a philosopher. It is understandable that certain congressmen got confused whether the Act was for money to be spent at home or abroad. In my opinion, the Act was to trigger concerted action that could accomplish worthy outcomes everywhere."[13]

There is evidence that Johnson, in his own thinking, did not tend to deal in terms of specific ingredients that give body to a policy. "The President is not conceptual," an anonymous associate reported, "but he has visions, he has dreams," meaning that Johnson knew "broadly but profoundly where he would like to head, and what he would like to do, whether in foreign or domestic policy."[14] The IEA was apparently such a conceptual dream that lacked specificity in the president's thinking. The best of Johnson's rhetoric on the subject, however, was "a description of possibility, a manifesto of intent."[15]

It is conceivable that the unpredictable Johnson may have given lower priority to additional new programs in HEW because of some ill will between him and Secretary Gardner. When Gardner resigned abruptly in 1968, a plausible rationalization was that he "quit at least in part because he could not get the necessary funds to battle the social ills which he saw growing more menacing than ever."[16] Gardner's successor at HEW, Wilbur J. Cohen, offered another explanation: "I think that they [Johnson and Gardner] got into some kind of an uneasy relationship which ended up with Gardner's resignation, and I think it would take kind of a very long explanation to completely figure it all out."[17]

Cater also may have been involved in the purported estrangement between the White House and HEW. As Cohen stated:

Although I do not know the details of the relationship between Doug Cater and John Gardner, I feel in my own heart that something about the relationship between Cater,

Gardner, and the President had a large part to do in precipitating Gardner's resignation at the time he resigned. I think he was to resign anyway, but I think the White House relationship between Cater and the President and Gardner exacerbated it or certainly didn't help it, although *the major problem was the relationship of the President and Gardner*. This third factor of the staff did not help. And although I talked to Gardner and Cater many, many times, both of them were rather reluctant to discuss it in any detail which merely confirms in my mind that something happened between Cater and Gardner and the President which I made up my mind I wouldn't let happen to me. Therefore, on several occasions I went directly to the President without telling the White House staff. This was my solution to the problem.[18]

Cohen went on to say: "Because John Gardner is a very unusual man, a great man, I enjoyed working for him, I have the highest regard for John Gardner, and yet, in this situation, all of the aspects of his final action still remain somewhat of a mystery."[19]

Cater contends that Cohen was speculating about something that he really did not understand. "John Gardner and I have remained close and intimate friends," wrote Cater. "He told me that he did not resign because of Vietnam or specific budget cuts."[20]

Any deterioration in the relations between Gardner and Cater would have been in sharp contrast to the secretary's expressed admiration of the special assistant in 1966 when he wrote the president: "I've been wanting for some time to tell you what a great help Doug Cater is to me and my Department. He's in close touch with all my top people, and we all like him and trust him. As a result, he's in a position to help us solve a lot of problems before they escalate into crises."[21]

Cater, in turn, worked to keep communications open between the president and Gardner. In autumn 1967, Cater wrote Johnson: "Gardner is not a complainer, and, in his own quiet way, I think he is doing the best he knows how in standing up for you and the Administration in the intellectual community. But he did mention to me in passing the other day that he felt he was not 'plugged in' on your thinking." Cater suggested that the president invite Gardner to "drop by for an informal talk" because it had "been a long time since he has seen you on anything except urgent business."[22]

John Roche (assistant to the president) relates an incident in the White House in which Johnson made Gardner look bad in front of administration colleagues. The occasion was a meeting of the president with Gardner, Charles Schultze of the BOB, Califano, and Roche to discuss the budget, on which Gardner would testify the next day. The president embarrassed Gardner with questions beyond Gardner's knowledge and went on to coach him on how to deal with a senator who had a bill on one of the subjects in 1956.[23] (Gardner, of course, was not unique in being ridiculed by Johnson in the presence of others.)

On another occasion, Gardner unintentionally drew the president's ire. In a cabinet meeting, "Gardner was talking along very conversationally, and he came to some item" and suddenly said, "Of course, Mr. President, you know we can't do that." The president "leaped out of his chair and leaped halfway across the table" pointing his finger at Gardner and saying: "Mr. Secretary, don't ever say that." Then Johnson "started around that room," looking everybody in the eye and pointing his finger at everyone at the table. He said: "There is nothing this country can't do. Remember that."[24]

Gardner was distinguished from most other members of Johnson's cabinet by his being a Republican and an opponent of the Vietnam War.[25] In late November 1966, as the war increasingly dominated the nation's agenda, Gardner proposed a Peace Agency, drawing together the Peace Corps, the East-West Center, the technical assistance parts of USAID, and cultural affairs from the State Department.[26] While other heads of departments were vocal in their support of the war, the secretary of HEW was proposing a peace initiative.

Nevertheless, Johnson felt a need to talk to Gardner, whom he respected,[27] and the secretary of HEW was always included in the president's elite circle of five top-level advisers.[28] Gardner, in turn, was reported to once have said that "Lyndon Johnson was one of the most intelligent men I have ever known."[29]

According to historian Hugh Davis Graham, Gardner told the president in early January 1968 that he was determined to resign. When the president sought to find out why, Gardner "stressed the message that the country was falling apart and that Johnson could not hold it together." Gardner recalled that the president responded with a "cool self-evaluation and a melancholy realism" — a response that would not have been expected from Goodwin's view.[30]

Twenty-two years later, Gardner remembered little of the IEA battle: "I do remember very well how much we wanted it — and remember that somehow we ran into substantial difficulties. But I do not remember the nature of the difficulties nor any of the discussions that went on."[31]

Miller maintains that Gardner never lost his interest in supporting the IEA and that "whatever happened in the Johnson-Gardner relationship, it did *not* sidetrack the IEA."[32]

The commitment of the president to international education, however, was questioned by Miller. He recalls meeting with the president in the

Oval Office just prior to his confirmation as assistant secretary by the
Senate. During their 30 minutes alone together, the president

Never mentioned "international education," despite the fact that I'm sure he knew that
Macy and Gardner were giving me the international portfolio. Rather, he spoke of
wanting to be known as the "education president," stressing, more than any other
topic, the provision of equal opportunity for all young people, and his feeling that
coordination and focus should come to government-wide educational innovation.

Miller contends that the president was "stirred" by international
education but that he did not make it "a shining lodestar to follow from
the very outset." Rather, "with all the Gardner, Frankel, Marvel
preparation and enthusiasm," the president said "'splendid,' and
supposed that they would take care of it."[33]

Frankel held a similar opinion: "The President was very interested
some days and forgot about it [the IEA] completely other days. When he
was reminded of it he cared, but he usually had other things on his
mind." Frankel thought that "if there had been peace the President would
have pushed this as a major part of his education in foreign policy
programs." Wrote Frankel: "He [LBJ] simply became distracted.
Samething [sic] with Rusk and Fulbright. Money got tight, and the
President's political capital went."[34]

Although Frankel felt that he "never was in a position really to find out
from him [President Johnson] how deeply interested he was in the [IEA]
program," there was "no question that he gave the people around him,
who were deeply interested, encouragement."[35]

From his perspective in the White House, Cater found the president
supportive of his efforts and maintains that "while the IEA was not
Johnson's personal brain-child, he unreservedly accepted it as a valuable
component of his education presidency and never failed to respond to
efforts by me and others to add his energy and persuasions in its
support."[36]

Johnson's enthusiasm for the IEA and other educational initiatives may
have waned, however, as his term progressed. He had strong beliefs
about the diminishing power a president has with Congress during his
four-year term. Shortly after his election, in early 1965, the president
called together some 30 people who were handling legislation in the
various departments and told them: "Now look. I've just been reelected
by the overwhelming majority. And I just want to tell you that every day
while I'm in office, I'm going to lose votes. I'm going to alienate
somebody."[37]

Johnson then spent 20 minutes tracing the history of the successful legislative efforts of Franklin Roosevelt, Woodrow Wilson, and others and warned his listeners: "The President begins to lose power fast once he has been reelected, and I'm going to do that too. It's going to be something. It's going to either be Viet Nam or it's going to be this or it's going to be that, but it's going to be something." He concluded: "We've got to get this legislation fast. You've got to get it during my honeymoon."[38]

Johnson's peptalk got results. During the following several months, the departments advanced a remarkable number of Great Society bills that were passed by the Eighty-ninth Congress. Cohen relates that Johnson knew "he was making people angry and annoyed by his rush tactics" but "he had a sense of the history of the Presidency in which he

if he didn't get it then, he probably wouldn't get it."[39]

Johnson explained his theory of the president as legislative leader in greater detail to McPherson: "You've got to give it all you can that first year. . . . Doesn't matter what kind of majority you come in with. You've got just one year when they treat you right, and before they start worrying about themselves."[40]

During the second year, Johnson said that members of his majority would "all be thinking about their reelections. I'll have made some mistakes, my polls will be down, and they'll be trying to put some distance between themselves and me. They won't want to go into the fall with their opponents calling 'em Lyndon Johnson's rubber stamps." Prophetically, the president continued: "The third year, you lose votes. If this war goes on, I'll lose a lot of 'em. A lot of our people don't belong here, they're in Republican seats, and the Republicans will get them back. The fourth year's all politics. You can't put anything through when half the Congress is thinking how to beat you. So you've got a year."[41]

Perhaps Johnson, the pragmatist and master of the legislative process, had foreseen the failure to get an appropriation for the IEA in the third year of his term and shifted his priorities elsewhere, or perhaps he believed his own theories so strongly that they became self-fulfilling prophecies. Taggart thought the president had doubts about the act's being funded.[42]

Frankel commented on the president's lack of support of the IEA before the House Appropriations Subcommittee: "We got beaten in that committee. . . . I think we would have gotten it through if the President pushed. I don't think he did. Very frankly, I think the President was always more interested in getting the legislation passed than in the follow-up in getting the funding."[43] There were few congressmen who could totally resist the influence of Johnson's personal presence, but for some reason, he chose not to exercise that power on behalf of the IEA at strategic times when it might have made a difference in getting an appropriation.

Miller offers another explanation of the president's relaxed attitude toward the act: "All the principal actors, including the President, felt the IEA and its plan were so timely in 1965–66, and the preparation so extensive, that it would simply 'sail through,' and this despite the 'Nay' votes on its initial passage." Miller thought "the President had had such success with other educational bills that, in my view, he figured that Gardner, Cater, Miller, et al. would take care of it."[44]

Shortly after the appropriation committees' hearings on the IEA, Johnson's faltering touch with the Ninetieth Congress was revealed in his tortuous struggle over the questions of taxes. The president, fearing that if Congress had a choice, it would give him the war but not the Great Society, decided to hold back on the real estimates of the cost of the war for a year. He finally asked Congress for a 6 percent surcharge in September 1967, but the price of the legislation was a crippling reduction in domestic programs.[45] As Larry Bergman expressed it, "Lyndon Johnson's greatest fault as a political leader was that *he chose* not to choose between the Great Society and the war in Vietnam."[46]

Miller recalls the ramifications for the IEA that followed from Johnson's two pronged policy:

Idealism triumphed over political acumen until one day, we (including the President) got up to find that contextual features (the war, urban riots, civil rights) had crowded IEA into a very tight corner. By that time, President Johnson (with the IEA never quite as singularly forefront in his mind as his prepared speeches imply) was spread thin, embattled, and, by his own philosophy, had lost a substantial measure of social and political capital.[47]

In the autumn of 1967, the president entered into intensive and painful negotiations with Mahon and other congressional leaders of major financial committees, bargaining a tight budget for fiscal year 1969 in order to get his tax increase. Cater noted that it was not, as journalistic cliche describes it, the choice of guns versus butter. "Guns versus social programs" was then the choice. Cater describes Johnson's last effort at that time to move Mahon to support the IEA:

We sit in the small room off the Oval Office: the President and the Chairman of the House Appropriations Committee joined by Commissioner of Education Howe and me. I have prepared the briefing paper and LBJ launches right into his pitch. He puts a proposition to Chairman Mahon: add a few million dollars for two legislative measures — the Teacher Corps and the International Education Act — and he will accept cuts of twice that size anywhere else in the budget. This is meant to convince the Chairman how deeply the President cares for these programs still aborning. But Mahon is not to be moved. A soft-spoken fellow Texan not given to bluster, he quietly tells the President that he will not budge. While he and his committee are helpless to eliminate programs already well launched because of constituency pressures to keep them going, they can and will cut off newborn ones. Commissioner Howe and I listen in awe as Mahon flatly says no to the President. For nearly an hour the two leaders go back and forth. I detect Johnson's deep sadness that he no longer has the muscle to make his persuasion credible. And so the meeting ends. Later Mahon relents a little on the Teacher Corps but many years are to pass while Congress regularly reauthorizes the International Education Act without voting a dollar to implement it.[48]

The president had told Cater that "the very instant" he asked for the surtax, the Great Society would be "put on the back burner." The IEA suffered a worse fate than that — it was taken off the stove.

Johnson must have been disappointed in his failure to get an appropriation for the act, the one major educational initiative of his administration that was not implemented. Later, during his last three months in office, the president told Cohen of his deep regret that he had been so unsuccessful in getting appropriations for his domestic programs.[49]

NOTES

1.   John C. Donovan, *The 1960's: Politics and Public Policy* (Lanham, Md.: University Press of America, 1980), p. 88.

2.   Transcript, Samuel Halperin Oral History Interview, 24 February 1969, pp. 10–11, LBJ Library.

3.   Letter, Miller to Vestal, 6 February 1989.

4.   Memo, Wells and Marvel to Board of Trustees of EWA, Memo #1, June 1966 Board of Trustees Meeting, Subject: Deterioration of the National Dialogue: How Can It Be Repaired?, pp. 2, 6, 7, quoting Professor James Billington of the History Department, Princeton University; Letter, Wells and Marvel to LBJ, 24 January 1967, Ex Ed Box 3, LBJ Library.

5.   Letter, Wells and Marvel to LBJ, 24 January 1967, Ex Ed Box 3, LBJ Library; telephone interview with Maurice Harrari, 3 April 1989.

6.   Robert A. McCaughey, "International Studies and General Education: The Alliance Yet to Be," *Liberal Education* 70 (1984): 368.

7.   Charles Frankel, *High on Foggy Bottom* (New York: Harper & Row, 1968), p. 192.

8.   Richard N. Goodwin, "President Lyndon Johnson, The War Within," *New*

York Times, 21 August 1988, p. G42; Richard N. Goodwin, *Remembering America, A Voice fom the Sixties* (Boston, Mass.: Little, Brown, 1988), p. 410.

9. Alan Brinkley, "Where Have All the Dreamers Gone?" Review of *Remembering America, New York Times,* 4 September 1988, sec. 7, pp. 7–8.

10. "The President's Wordsmith," Review of *Remembering America, Economist* 309 (29 October 1988): 94.

11. Vaughn Davis Bornet, *The Presidency of Lyndon B. Johnson* (Lawrence: University Press of Kansas, 1983), pp. 125–26.

12. Letter, Miller to Vestal, 16 March 1989.

13. Letter, Cater to Vestal, 16 May 1989.

14. Philip Geyelin, *Lyndon B. Johnson and the World* (New York: Praeger, 1966), p. 263.

15. Goodwin, *Remembering America,* p. 291.

16. Hugh Sidey, *A Very Personal Presidency* (New York: Atheneum, 1987), p. 288.

17. Cohen Oral History, p. 36, LBJ Library.

18. Ibid., p. 21.

19. Ibid., p. 36.

20. Letter, Cater to Vestal, 16 May 1989.

21. Memo, Gardner to LBJ, 8 June 1966, "Memos to the President, June 1966," Box 15, Office Files of Cater, LBJ Library.

22. Memo, Cater to LBJ, 19 September 1967, "Memos to the President, September, 1967," Box 17, Office Files of Cater, LBJ Library.

23. Transcript, John P. Roche Oral History Interview, 16 July 1970, pp. 49–50, LBJ Library.

24. Merle Miller, *Lyndon, An Oral Biography* (New York: G.P. Putnam's Sons, 1980), p. 408.

25. Doris Kearns, *Lyndon Johnson and the American Dream* (New York: Harper & Row, 1976), p. 1.

26. Memo, Cater to LBJ, 2 June 1966, "Memos to the President, June 1966;" Memo, Cater to LBJ, 26 November 1966, "Memos to the President, November 1966," Box 15, Office Files of Cater; Memo, Gardner to Cater, 27 November 1966, Ex Ed Box 3, LBJ Library.

27. Memo, Robert Kintner to LBJ, 1 August 1967 FG1 (1967), Confidential File, White House Central Files, LBJ Library.

28. Sidey, *Personal Presidency,* p. 269.

29. Jack Valenti, *A Very Human President* (New York: W. W. Norton, 1975), p. 157.

30. Hugh Davis Graham, *The Uncertain Triumph: Federal Education Policy in the Kennedy and Johnson Years* (Chapel Hill: University of North Carolina Press, 1984), p. 186.

31. Letter, Gardner to Vestal, 5 January 1989.

32. Letter, Miller to Vestal, 6 February 1989.

33. Letter, Miller to Vestal, 16 March 1989.

34. Frankel Oral History, p. 7, LBJ Library.

35. Ibid., p. 9.

36. Letter, Cater to Vestal, 16 May 1989.

37. Cohen Oral History, p. 16, LBJ Library.

38.   Ibid.

39.   Ibid., pp. 16–17.

40.   Harry McPherson, *A Political Education* (Boston: Little, Brown, 1972), p. 268.

41.   Ibid.

42.   Telephone interview with Glen Taggart, 8 May 1989.

43.   Frankel Oral History, p. 12, LBJ Library.

44.   Letter, Miller to Vestal, 16 March 1989.

45.   Kearns, *Lyndon Johnson and the American Dream*, p. 300.

46.   Larry Bergman, *Planning a Tragedy: The Americanization of the War in Vietnam* (New York: Norton, 1983), p. 150.

47.   Letter, Miller to Vestal, 16 March 1989.

48.   Cater, "Work in Progress on LBJ," enclosed in letter, Pat Smith, President's Office, Washington College, to Vestal, 15 February 1989.

49.   Cohen Oral History, p. 34, LBJ Library.

14

Why the IEA Was Defeated:
The Academic Community

The lack of political clout by spokesmen for colleges and universities and by higher education association representatives also contributed to the defeat of the appropriation for the IEA. As Rose Hayden has noted:

Lacking a strong, broadly based political constituency, let alone wide public appeal, caught between persistent isolationists on the right and domestic skeptics on the left, and inexorably enmeshed in larger controversies related to national education policies, international education programs have repeatedly faced palpable disadvantages in the federal funding marketplace.[1]

Although a few university presidents, such as Frank Rose of the University of Alabama, worked energetically on behalf of the IEA, many did nothing. Perhaps the act would have had stronger support had it been developed from demands advanced by higher education generally rather than from the work of the Johnson administration and a few individuals. Such a development would have been atypical of the usual pattern of international involvement in postsecondary institutions.

The history of international programs in U.S. universities is, for the most part, one of origins and support from off-campus sources. International studies entered U.S. higher education because of the needs of society as reflected by financial assistance from private foundations and the federal government rather than because universities found them to be inherently valuable. In developing or changing international studies, universities have generally responded to outside stimuli rather than defining the necessary changes themselves.

After the need for the IEA had been identified by the Rusk Task Force and advanced by the president, higher education, at least as it is represented by associations, organized itself in support of the program.

Although spokesmen for research universities with area study and interdisciplinary centers presented a united front, the underlying concept of the IEA — programs to expand international understanding among the rank and file of U.S. college students — never attracted strong support.[2] Where were the spokesmen for the lowly undergraduates?

There were also problems at the campus level. Within existing international education programs, turf battles and competition for sparse funding created divisiveness among the various academic groups that should have been leading the charge up Capitol Hill. Campus programs for foreign students, study abroad, area studies, technical assistance, and development research were frequently uncoordinated fiefdoms engaged in unproductive rivalries at the very time a concerted lobbying effort was needed.

Another problem was the timing of support by individual institutions. When the IEA was passed, a substantial number of colleges and universities set up international program offices in anticipation of the implementation of the act. In some instances, this created a new player in the power structure that reflected a combination of alliances among various "baronies," which were based on disciplinary and professional school interests.[3] In the competition for resources and acknowledgment within the institutional power structure, the newly created international program offices did not have sufficient maturation time to develop much campus political capability before the appropriations committees of the Ninetieth Congress began reviewing the IEA. Support of international programs by the institutions' top administrative leadership and by faculties generally awaited implementation of the IEA. Without that support from leaders of higher education, there was no groundswell of enthusiastic lobbying for funding the act.

The argument also was made that international education was already provided for by Title VI of the Higher Education Act, the successor legislation to the NDEA. Some academicians, especially those in area studies centers in universities, and government officials believed that Title VI could be refined and enlarged without the need for additional legislation. Miller remembers having trouble in explaining the differences between the IEA and Title VI "to the uninformed."[4]

Another problem was at the association level. The major higher education associations had established offices in Washington only in the early 1960s. In 1962, their executive secretaries began meetings to exchange information and ideas about federal policy and political strategy. By 1967, organized representation of postsecondary institutions had so proliferated that there was concern that Washington was "becoming filled with the babble of many voices speaking for higher education."[5] The pluralistic nature of higher learning's leadership in the nation's capital made it difficult to determine what the higher education community stood for on a particular issue.[6]

Traditionally, a small group representing the great diversification of interest found in U.S. higher education makes policy through a bargaining process of compromise and mutual adjustment within the ACE.[7] In the case of the IEA, the policy that emerged from the process seemed to favor major research universities and land-grant institutions. One subject of controversy was the proposed division of the bulk of IEA funds between graduate and undergraduate programs. When the HEW staff, at the request of Morse in the summer of 1966, prepared 50 questions and answers to questions about the IEA, the split was 50/50 between graduate and undergraduate support.[8] By the time of the request for the 1968 appropriation, the division had changed to favor graduate programs with more than twice as many funds ($13 million) as those slated for undergraduate programs ($5.95 million).

As a result of this "upstairs-downstairs" division of spoils, representatives of universities with graduate programs became active lobbyists for the act while some of the other higher education interests lost enthusiasm and became somewhat distrustful of what the ACE and HEW might do on their behalf. The AASCU played an important role in lobbying the members of the appropriation subcommittees, because there was a state college in virtually every congressional district represented. Alan Ostar, executive director of the AASCU, recalled that the IEA did not have "a full constituency-based effort" from all of higher education, however.[9]

At the same time, another struggle was going on in academic professional societies. The domination of many such groups by a relatively few members from elite universities was being challenged by the increasingly numerous members from less-prestigious institutions who were calling for a representative voice in the organizations.[10] This professional rivalry may have contributed to the erosion of ACE's consensus politics.

Whatever the cause, the funding of the IEA had generally a low order of interest and priority. As McPherson explained: "Nobody had really focused on it and had taken on the job of seeing the IEA funded. The people who are interested in educational and cultural exchange are university professors and presidents, foundations, and a number of other do-good types, who have very little political power."[11]

Efforts to recruit allies with more political strength in support of the IEA had little success. Miller recalls that the academic community "could not, or at least did not, have the capacity to mobilize a broader public interest and focus it on the funding issue." Wrote Miller: "I went to countless meetings across the U.S., and, while academics tried to bring in civic leaders, the sessions really turned out to be filled by specialists in one aspect or another of international affairs."[12]

Academic spokesmen, accustomed to an ingrown, rational, and collegial way of addressing each other, frequently make poor witnesses before Congress and less than persuasive lobbyists. During Senate hearings on the IEA, Morse had warned that spokesmen for higher education needed to do "a better job than ACE did on Higher Education Amendments of 1966 when ACE representatives were 'torn apart' by Robert Kennedy (D-NY)."[13]

Lobbyists for the IEA might have benefited from the advice of the master of the art, the president. Johnson once told Goodwin the key to successfully working with Congress: "It's not a matter of twisting arms. . . . What convinces is conviction. Logic and reasoning won't win your case for you. You just have to get full of your subject and let it fly . . . intensity of conviction is the number-one priority."[14] Records of the hearings on the IEA are replete with words of wisdom from spokesmen for higher education. In 1967, however, it would have taken more than intensity of conviction to pry funds for the IEA from the House Appropriations Subcommittee.

McPherson faulted the academic representatives for not matching their rhetoric with action. "You can get a good meeting going down here," McPherson wrote. "We had spent the entire day speaking brilliantly about the way the program ought to be run and new initiatives in the field of educational and cultural exchange, and that Congress had just cut the guts out of the appropriations bill and not one of these people had raised a voice in protest." McPherson lamented that

There is no organization in the country that buys a full page of the New York Times and says, "For Christ's sake, Mr. Rooney and Congress, you're destroying a very vital element of U.S. foreign policy." It's as if two worlds are operating and the world of the academic and foundation executive is good so far as it goes, but it goes within the State Department. It does not go into actual political power or into any attempt to influence policy at all. And it's most regrettable that's so.[15]

If the international education community had been more politically organized and if the media had been more than remotely interested in the IEA, there would have been an outcry about the decisions on appropriations. As it was, only the small group of supporters of the IEA from inside and outside of academe who had arrived at a common view of what should be done seemed to mourn its end. The IEA reports were quietly filed away for a future time.[16]

In addition to problems of support and continuing interest on the part of Congress, the president, the academic community, and the public, the IEA may have been beset by fears and suspicions of other governmental agencies. Miller found some of that uncertainty in the Federal Interagency Council on Education that he chaired in those days. He did not believe that "there were pockets of avid resistance in Washington, although other centers of international development," such as USAID and the Department of Agriculture, "could scarcely be expected to fight for the cause." Although there was no overt opposition from other agencies, "there was a certain aloofness if not suspicion over what seemed (and was) a major new effort to get into international education and development by HEW."[17] Although the BOB held a special adversarial relationship with the line agencies of government, the perfidy of the BOB could be especially noted throughout the IEA proceedings.

Miller states that the funding issue of the IEA "was then and remains to all a continuing puzzle." He believes that the defeat of the IEA came from a confluence of factors: "no one of them was singly crucial, but altogether they threw up a large barrier" to the funding of the act.[18]

By late 1967, the major proponents of the IEA had found the barrier too large to get around and had dispersed. President Johnson, the annunciator of the IEA idea, finished out his term a perplexed and disheartened leader. Frankel, who did not agree with the president's Vietnam policy, had preceded Gardner in leaving the government service, resigning in protest according to a CBS story on 27 November 1967. Frankel said that he did not intend to embarrass the administration and maintained that he had written Cater in the spring, indicating that he had planned to leave.[19] Marvel was in New York coming to grips with the reality that the raison d'être of EWA was in jeopardy. Brademas lacked leverage in dealing with the House Appropriations Committee and turned his attention to other legislative matters — especially those in education and the arts, which he continued to champion. Miller stayed on at HEW until the end of June 1968,[20] and Cater remained on the White House staff until the end of the Johnson administration, but the IEA, by necessity, was no longer a major item on their agendas.

Miller recalls:

As the funding possibility (for the IEA) cooled, and I was called by the White House into other involvements, it seemed best, since I was determined to leave government after the term, to turn to as many prospects as I could in order to use my leverage in the remaining months to accomplish as many things as possible. We kept on with the IEA funding issue, but as the matrix of Vietnam and urban and racial tension ramified, and then the President announced that he would not run again, this turning to other projects seemed all the more necessary.[21]

NOTES

1. Rose L. Hayden, *Federal Support for International Education: Assessing the Options* (Washington, D.C.: National Council on Foreign Studies, August 1985), p. 1.

2. Norman C. Thomas, *Education in National Politics* (New York: David McKay, 1975), pp. 103, 231.

3. Ralph Smuckler, Dean of International Studies and Programs, Michigan State University, quoted in Barbara B. Burn, *Expanding the International Dimension* (San Francisco, Calif.: Jossey-Bass, 1980), p. 144.

4. Letter, Miller to Vestal, 6 February 1989. In 1990, directors of Title VI Centers still were concerned with protecting their turf in the face of other international education initiatives. See National Association of State Universities and Land Grant Colleges, Division of International Affairs, "Workshop on the Reauthorization of Title VI of the Higher Education Act," University of Pittsburgh, 2–3 March 1990.

5. Allan W. Ostar, "Higher Education and National Policy," in *Agony and Promise*, ed. G. Kerry Smith (San Francisco, Calif.: Jossey-Bass, 1969), p. 29.

6. Lawrence E. Gladieux and Thomas R. Wolanin, *Congress and the Colleges* (Lexington, Mass.: Lexington Books, 1976), p. 44.

7. Thomas, *Education in National Politics*, p. 231.

8. "Notebook Concerning International Education and Health, 1966," Questions and Answers, p. 22, Box 44, Office Files of Cater, LBJ Library.

9. Coalition for the Advancement of Foreign Languages and International Studies, "CAFLIS Update; Consensus Reached," 14 July 1989, p. 3.

10. Robert A. McCaughey, "International Studies and General Education: The Alliance Yet to Be," *Liberal Education* 70 (1984): 368.

11. McPherson, Oral History, AC 74-210, Interview 2, 19 December 1968, pp. 10–11, LBJ Library.

12. Letter, Miller to Vestal, 6 February 1989.

13. Memo, Huitt to Cater, Wilson, and Manatos, 12 September 1966, HEW Subject Files, PL 89-698, Microfilm #59, LBJ Library.

14. Richard N. Goodwin, *Remembering America, A Voice from the Sixties* (Boston, Mass.: Little, Brown, 1988), p. 258.

15. McPherson, Oral History, AC 74-210, Interview 2, 19 December 1968, pp. 10–11, LBJ Library.

16. Harry McPherson, *A Political Education* (Boston: Little, Brown, 1972), p. 268.

17. Letter, Miller to Vestal, 6 February 1989.

18. Ibid.

19.   Memo for the Record, Cater, 27 November 1967; Letter, Frankel to Cater, 17 January 1967, "Memos to the President, November, 1967," Box 17, Office Files of Cater, LBJ Library; Letter, Cater to Vestal, 16 May 1989.

20.   The president accepted Miller's resignation effective 30 June 1968. Letter, LBJ to Miller, 17 June 1968, Name File, "Miller, Paul A-E," LBJ Library.

21.   Letter, Miller to Vestal, 6 February 1989.

15

The Legacy of the IEA in the Office of Education

The IEA was comatose but still alive for a few more years. In 1968 it was included as an amendment to the Higher Education Act, and after Gardner's resignation, Acting HEW Secretary Cohen, Miller, and Commissioner of Education Harold Howe again requested initial funding of the act, including $100,000 to establish the NACIS. Their efforts were of no avail. Despite this setback, Howe maintained that the IEA should "be kept alive, and appropriations for it should be a high priority matter."[1] So it was to be within HEW — for another year.

The appropriations hearings for HEW in fiscal year 1968 did produce a significant document for international education. In response to a congressional directive, Cohen appointed OE veteran Ralph C. M. Flynt as deputy assistant secretary for international education in the office of the assistant secretary for education, to direct "study of all Federal activities related to international education or cooperation." Flynt's work described 159 programs in 31 different agencies and was a thorough analysis of the national government's efforts in the field.[2]

Meanwhile, Miller bolstered his staff to carry forward the IEA effort and in the process strengthen ties among the Departments of HEW and State and OE. Dr. Robert Leestma, an international education policy adviser to Frankel in the Department of State, was chosen by Miller to be his senior associate for IEA matters. With the departure from government service of Miller, Frankel, and Howe, it was Leestma's challenge to provide leadership for the international education initiative symbolized by the IEA.

After the unsuccessful effort to get funding for the IEA in 1968, Miller spent "considerable time" with Howe and Cohen "working out and 'planting' an Institute of International Studies (IIS) in the Office of Education" to administer authorized international education programs and keep the idea of the IEA alive.[3] Cohen formally established the IIS in March 1968 "to bring together international activities of HEW," and Leestma was appointed director of the IIS.[4] He shaped its vision and guided OE's international programs for the next dozen years.

In this role, Leestma presided over the last efforts to get an appropriation for the IEA. In 1969, after the election of President Richard Nixon, Robert Finch became the third secretary of HEW to back the IEA, which had survived the department's rigorous budgetary review that had cut $1 billion from the HEW budget. On 13 May 1969, officers of HEW and OE again appeared before the House Appropriations Subcommittee. Flood was still chairman, and the only change in the committee membership was the replacement of Laird (who had become secretary of defense) by Charlotte T. Reid (R-IL).

OE sought appropriations for "Education in Foreign Languages and World Affairs" that included $2 million of initial funding of the IEA. These funds would have provided planning for the development of a comprehensive international dimension in 64 undergraduate programs, 10 regional consortia, and 20 graduate centers for advanced international studies.[5]

The hearings provoked an extensive discussion of the IEA. In his testimony, Leestma continued the tradition of forceful eloquence of departmental spokesmen in pointing out the compelling national need for the act: "I believe that you have before you in the International Education Act as significant a piece of legislation for higher education as any that has come before you." Testified Leestma:

I think we have something here that will help higher education cope with a world in which there is a growing interdependence of all countries, and a weaving together of economies. We are faced with the situation in which, whether we like it or not, the world is growing smaller and our role in it will remain a major one simply because of our economic heft, our technological capability, and our various political relationships. This is distinctly not a world we can opt out of. We are in it, and the nature of it is not reflected in higher education; it simply is not. . . . I think we have here before us the opening of a door to the modernization of higher education that is desperately needed.[6]

Although the committee members did not offer strong encouragement about the possibility of funding the IEA, the tone of the hearings was far less hostile than had been the case only two years before. Committee members showed a better understanding of the objectives of the IEA, and Leestma's carefully worded answers to their questions seemed to satisfy them.

Congressman Michel's response to Leestma's remarks was indicative of the committee's attitude: "I cannot quarrel at all with some of the good points you make, but it is so true we are under such pressure to retrench or scale back ongoing, proven programs that we have to hesitate even more than usual before getting involved in something that is new."[7] Mrs. Reid found it frustrating to have to set priorities that made it difficult to fund a new program because she agreed "in essence with everything" Leestma had said.[8]

The hearings built to what Leestma described as "quite an emotional climax on both sides of the table."[9] Mrs. Reid even expressed appreciation for the associate commissioner's sincerity.

In his concluding statement, Leestma stressed the importance that the Nixon administration, "like the last administration," put upon the international dimension of higher education.[10] Unfortunately, this support was short lived, and the administration dropped the IEA item from the budget after the House hearing and before Senate Appropriations Committee hearings began.[11] Thus, the IEA stayed on the books until 1970, but it never received an appropriation. However, thanks to Miller's initiation, Howe's cooperation, and Cohen's support, a fresh institutional base, a new bureau, was in place to keep alive the ideas of the IEA in the circumscribed programs authorized in the OE.

The scale of federal involvement in international education declined rapidly during the Nixon and Ford administrations. In the early 1970s, Nixon initiated the first of several attempts to reduce the Title VI budget substantially and ultimately to phase out the program. Each time, Congress came to the rescue. The relatively stagnant appropriations levels for Title VI programs during this era created a competitive environment in which the universities that had NDEA programs were reluctant to admit new clienteles. The "haves" were also disinclined to promote new federal initiatives out of fear of losing programs already in place.[12]

Despite this discouraging milieu, the IIS, as Miller had hoped, became a CEC-like office that provided "consultant, clearinghouse, and catalytic relationships with the educational community at home and abroad."[13] The IIS had, as its mission, to communicate to an ever-widening audience the concept that the national interest in education includes an international dimension; to increase Americans' knowledge of the world and its people; to infuse an appropriate international dimension throughout the domestic educational program; to stimulate or support research and development projects designed to improve methods and materials for international education; to educate more specialists for international studies and services; and to promote international understanding and cooperation.[14]

Under Leestma's leadership, the IIS, with meager resources and little agency interest or support, carried on a remarkable range of international education activities that helped maintain and even expand the field despite the budget constraints of the times. The IIS served as a national rallying point for fostering international education during the dark days of the 1970s, more so than is generally known.

While important OE staff functions and programs such as teacher exchanges with USIA funding and studies of education in other countries were carried forward, the IIS instituted major changes in the Title VI and Fulbright-funded programs through a redirection of the NDEA program in the early 1970s. For example, two new programs corresponding to those included in the IEA were developed and implemented. The first assisted primarily four-year institutions, including the historically black colleges, and two-year community colleges to strengthen the international dimensions of general education at the undergraduate level. These institutions previously had not been players in the NDEA Title VI centers program. The second assisted development of international problem-, issue-, or topic-centered programs at the master's degree level. Directors of NDEA area studies centers were not pleased at having to share the limited funding available with the expanded range of institutional partners.

In the NDEA centers program, modest funding was made available for centers concerned with Canadian studies, contemporary Western Europe, and international studies more broadly conceived. An outreach program was developed that was aimed primarily at having the centers use their expertise to assist the development of international dimensions in elementary and secondary education. This move was resisted by most centers initially but in time came to be seen as mutually beneficial and helped expand the international education constituency at the pre-c9llegiate level, as the new kind of undergraduate and graduate programs did at the post secondary level.[15]

In programs abroad, OE opportunities under Fulbright and PL-480 auspices were recast into more functional categories to ensure balanced coverage with available resources (for example, Faculty Research Abroad, Doctoral Dissertation Research Abroad, Group Projects Abroad, and Foreign Curriculum Consultants). Also, international perspectives were developed among chief state school officers through field seminars abroad and other activities.

Further, the NDEA research program was broadened to include more attention to non-foreign language material needs, particularly in elementary and secondary education and in general education at the post secondary level. Basic studies of status, needs, and priorities in international education continued to receive appropriate attention.[16]

In addition to budget problems and lack of agency program priority during this period, a major policy problem further complicated matters for the OE international education program. In the 1970s, OE policies reflected those of the parent HEw and other fedearl education programs. The main concerns were equal acces and serving the unmet needs of special populations previously neglected by states and localities.

The NDEA programs had been launched in the wake of Sputnik with excellence as the objective and standard. The IIS sought to broaden the scope with programs of excellence for all students in the full range of institutions and levels, not just in the major research universities and the top tier of liberal arts colleges. The tradition and continuing concern with excellence were out of synch with the times. By the late 1980s, federal policy had shifted and was concerned with excellence as well as access, but agency program priorities still lagged where international studies were concerned. Thus, the IIS with its continuing emphasis on excellence had its hands full in an agency whose institutional priorities were focused on access and entitlement programs on other than international themes throughout most of the period.

There was a resurgence of interest in international education, however, during the Carter administration. Ernest Boyer, Carter's commissioner of education, repeatedly asserted that global education was one of his priorities, and a task force was organized in his office to investigate the subject.[17] Carter also appointed the Commission on Foreign Language and International Studies in 1978 that found the state of international studies to be in "scandalous condition" and "unlikely to survive, let alone maintain its quality."[18] The task force and commission, like their predecessors, produced useful studies of what had been done and what should be done in international studies, but the recommendations developed from their work had limited impact on U.S. higher education.

President Carter's science advisor, Frank Press, created a national task force (that included Miller and Taggart in its membership) that recommended the establishment of an Institute for Scientific and Technological Cooperation (ISTC) to strengthen U.S. relationships in science and technology essentially with developing nations.[19] Miller described the Institute as "a kind of remake of the CEC and an attempt to concentrate certain of the educational and long-term development aspects of AID in a removed and distinct agency." The ISTC suffered the same fate as the IEA, being approved by Congress but never receiving an appropriation.[20]

Another Carter administration initiative was the authorization in 1980 of the International Communications Agency to assume responsibilities formerly exercised by USIA and the Department of State's CU to increase U.S. citizens' knowledge of other countries. The last appropriations bill passed during Carter's tenure provided a significant increase in the budgets of Title VI programs. All of these Carter-era plans and programs came to an end with the election of President Reagan. Although a new cabinet-level ED was created, international education received little support from the administration. Indeed, Congress, stimulated by an active international studies constituency lobbying effort, had to rescue several programs that were to be greatly reduced or eliminated under President Reagan's proposed budgets.

One of the first publications of the new ED was an updated inventory of international programs in federal departments and agencies prepared at Leestma's initiative and produced under the sponsorship of the Federal Interagency Council on Education. The inventory listed 181 programs in 28 federal departments and agencies as of mid-1979 and included brief descriptions of what occurred in each program, participants and beneficiaries, legislative authority, funding, countries involved, and contacts within the administration.[21]

During his first year in office, President Bush declared his interest in being another "education president." International education, however, was never a high priority. Prior to the enactment of the NSEA of 1991, federal support for international studies was limited primarily to programs under Title VI of the Higher Education Act and the Fulbright-Hays Act. By fiscal year 1990, ED's appropriation for these programs was just under $40 million, an amount equal to only $13.4 million in inflation-adjusted dollars — approximately $2 million less than Congress had appropriated for NDEA centers, research, and fellowships in fiscal year 1967. Although the need for the scholarly products of these programs had increased since the time of the Vietnam War, the purchasing power of federal expenditures had actually declined. The One Hundred Second Congress began to remedy this situation in fiscal year 1992.[22]

Title VI and Fulbright-Hays programs now are administered by the ED's Center for International Education (CIE).[23] Seven programs described in new terminology authorized under Title VI are conducted primarily in the United States:

1. The National Resource Centers program provides grants to higher education institutions to strengthen centers focusing on a foreign country or a region of the world or on general,

worldwide topics. The centers are expected to offer appropriate foreign language instruction and to conduct research related to the particular world area or topic. About 100 National Resource Centers offer instruction in a variety of disciplines throughout the nation.

2. The Foreign Language and Area Studies Fellowships (FLAS) program offers academic-year and summer awards for advanced students in foreign language and either area or international studies. Allocations of fellowships are made to selected U.S. higher education institutions, which, in turn, award FLAS grants to individual students.

3. The Research program provides grants to institutions of higher education, public and private organizations, and individuals to support surveys, studies, and the development of specialized instructional materials for foreign languages, foreign areas, and related studies.

4. The Language Resource Center program is designed to improve the nation's capacity to teach and learn foreign languages effectively. The program supports research and development of new materials for teaching foreign languages and for proficiency testing and disseminates its research results, teaching materials, and improved pedagogical strategies to colleges and universities.

5. The Undergraduate International Studies and Foreign Language program awards grants to higher education institutions to plan, develop, and carry on a program to strengthen and improve undergraduate instruction in international studies and foreign languages.

6. The Business and International Education program, a relatively new and important addition, provides matching grants to colleges and universities to promote linkages between them and the U.S. business community engaged in international economic activity. Such projects are designed to both enhance the international academic programs in higher education and provide appropriate services to the business community to expand its capacity to engage in commerce abroad.

7. The Centers for International Business Education program, another recent and significant addition, provides grants to colleges and universities that will be national resources for the teaching of improved business techniques, strategies, and methodologies; provide instruction in critical foreign languages and international fields; provide research and training in the

international aspects of trade, commerce, and other fields of study; provide training to students; and serve as regional resources to businesses by offering programs and providing research designed to meet their international training needs.

The CIE also funds and administers four programs, all carried over from the OE era, for study overseas under the Fulbright-Hays Act:

1. the Doctoral Dissertation Research Abroad program, which assists graduate students in Ph.D. dissertation work in modern foreign language and area studies;
2. the Faculty Research Abroad program, designed to improve foreign language training and area studies in the United States by providing scholars with fellowships of 3 to 12 months' duration;
3. the Group Projects Abroad program, by which institutions of higher education may conduct summer seminars for faculty, school administrators, and teachers, designed to improve their knowledge and skills in international subjects; and
4. the Seminars Abroad Program/Special Bilateral Projects, which provide three- to eight-week summer seminars for U.S. educators to improve their knowledge and understanding of the people and cultures of another country.

The CIE also administers the International Visitors (IV) program and serves as the main point of contact for visits to the ED by international educators.

Despite recent budget increases, the magnitude of the present-day ED programs suffer by comparison with those planned under the IEA. The CIE's appropriation of $54.1 million for fiscal year 1993 is composed of $48.3 million (about 90 percent) for programs under Title VI of the Higher Education Act, the present-day descendants of Title VI of the NDEA, and $6 million for Fulbright-Hays Act programs. While the addition of NSEA funds in the DOD meaningfully augments the international education mix available from federal funds, the amount available from ED remains woefully inadequate.

Directors of university-based Title VI programs point to two weaknesses in their efforts to lobby for larger appropriations: international studies are marginal to the Higher Education Act, because Title VI forms such a small part of the act's budget, and Title VI programs are perceived as marginal to their "own universities in some cases." Program directors, thus, find that they cannot count on strong lobbying by university officials charged with the task of seeking increased funding from Congress.[24]

With the federal government's support limited during the Reagan-Bush years, some state governments took a more aggressive role in promoting international studies. The National Governors' Association prepared a series of reports outlining what "steps Governors and their states can take to lead the nation into the 21st century."[25] Almost all of the states have established active programs to promote exports to other nations and to encourage foreign investments in new industries within their borders. Several states have set up offices overseas to foster direct international trade, and many governors have traveled abroad on official visits to assist these efforts. Indeed, an increased awareness of the global economy and the internationalization of attitudes of governmental leaders was a marked change in the 50 states during the 1980s. The connections between the political and economic global transitions, the competitiveness of the U.S. economy, and the international aspects of U.S. higher education have been the subject matters of a number of state-sponsored research studies.[26] In addition, in fiscal year 1993, Congress appropriated almost $11 million in grants to states for Foreign Languages Assistance, a new ED program to bolster language instruction in the schools.

Concurrent with the activities of the IIS and the states was the growth of international programs in universities. In anticipation of the funding of the IEA, international program offices were established on many campuses. Parkinson's law may have been at work, and when there were no appropriations for the IEA, these offices had to produce to survive. Thus, universities and colleges became resourceful in finding ways to finance international studies. Funds came in various guises, but the result was the survival of the ideas of the IEA in substance if not in form. Figures on such expenditures are sketchy, but possibly billions of dollars, far more than would have been available under the IEA over the years, have been spent to accomplish some of the same things authorized under the act. Most major universities have benefited from a farrago of programs sponsored by government agencies and requiring matching funds from local sources (for example, Title VI and Fulbright-Hays programs, Fulbright and other teacher exchanges, International Research Exchange Board [IREX] programs, and USAID contracts). Such federal "carrots" have encouraged university and private financial support through gifts and grants that, in some cases, exceed the federal funds. Spokesmen for the international education enterprise argue, however, that the combined federal, state, and campus programs have produced a hodgepodge of contradictions, overlaps, and gaps that fail to meet the nation's needs.[27]

To meet those needs, another legacy of the IEA, a plan for a nation-wide international education program, is relevant. The deliberations of the Rusk Task Force, the published record of the splendid seminar on international education conducted by the Brademas Task Force and its subsequent publication of readings, "International Education: Past, Present, Problems and Prospects," and the House Committee on Education and Labor report on the IEA provide a philosophical as well as a legislative background for the program. A plan of action for implementing the IEA was formulated by Miller and his staff in collaboration with representatives of higher education and other client groups. The experience of the IIS under Leestma (with the help of a determined, effective lobbying effort by the Title Vi and Fulbright-Hays constituencies and related associations) in keeping international education alive in OE and the ED through tough times during both Republican and Democratic administrations presents a practical lesson in implementing IEA programs on a smaller scale within a large bureaucracy. These plans and lessons need only a fine tuning to make them applicable to current conditions.

NOTES

1.   Interview with Harold Howe, II, Commissioner, OE, ACm66-1, 12 July 1968, "The Federal Government's Remaining Role in Education," by Jack Broudy, Appendices: The History of the Office of Education, LBJ Library.

2.   U.S. Office of Education, Institute of International Studies, *Inventory of Federal Programs Involving Educational Activities Concerned with Improving International Understanding and Cooperation: An Interagency Survey Conducted for the Congress of the United States by the Department of Health, Education, and Welfare* (Washington, D.C.: U.S. Government Printing Office, 1969).

3.   Letter, Miller to Vestal, 16 March 1989.

4.   Memo, Cohen to Howe, 7 March 1968, HEW Subject Files, PL 89-698 (Senate Hearings) Dup. 60; Administrative History of Department of HEW, Vol. I, Part I, Box 1, p. 5; Part VIII, "International Education," Box 3, p. 798, LBJ Library. Leestma has served on the faculty of the University of Michigan and worked abroad for USAID and ICA. He headed OE's IIS until the end of the Carter administration. In the ED, he held senior positions in the Office of Educational Research and Improvement.

5.   Department of Labor and Health, Education, and Welfare Appropriations for 1970, Hearings before a Subcommittee of the Committee on Appropriations, House of Representatives, Ninety-First Congress, First Session, pp. 970–1022.

6.   Ibid., p. 985.

7.   Ibid., p. 1000

8.   Ibid., p. 1002.

9.   Letter, Leestma to Vestal, 2 August 1989.

10.   Department of Labor and Health, Education, and Welfare Appropriations for 1970, Hearings before a Subcommittee of the Committee on Appropriations, House of

Representatives, Ninety-First Congress, First Session, p. 1001.

11. Letter, Leestma to Vestal, 2 August 1989.

12. Rose L. Hayden, *Federal Support for International Education: Assessing the Options* (Washington, D.C.: National Council on Foreign Studies, August 1985), pp. 2–9.

13. Letter, Miller to Vestal, 16 March 1989; Robert Leestma, "OE's Institute of International Studies," *American Education*, May 1969, USOE, Washington, D.C., p. 8.

14. Leestma, "OE's Institute of International Studies," p. 8.

15. See, for example, Lewis W. Pike, *Other Nations, Other Peoples* (Washington, D.C.: U.S. Government Printing Office, 1979); Thomas Barrows, John Clark, and Stephen Klein, "What Students Know about Their World," *Change* 12 (May–June 1980): 10.

16. See, for example, Audrey W. Gray, *International and Intercultural Education in Selected State Colleges and Universities: An Overview and Five Cases* (Washington, D.C.: American Association of State Colleges and Universities, 1977); William G. Shannon, *A Survey of International/Intercultural Education in Two Year Colleges — 1976* (La Plata, Md.: Charles County Community College, 1978).

17. Barbara B. Burn, *Expanding the International Dimension* (San Francisco, Calif.: Jossey-Bass, 1980), pp. xxxv, 31.

18. *Strength through Wisdom: A Critique of U.S. Capability*, A Report to the President from the President's Commission on Foreign Language and International Studies (Washington, D.C.: U.S. Government Printing Office, 1979), pp. 1–2, 7–8.

19. Letter, Ralph H. Smuckler, dean of International Studies and Programs and assistant to the president, Michigan State University, to Vestal, 25 November 1987; letter, Philip M. Smith, executive officer, National Research Council, to Vestal, 2 November 1987.

20. Letter, Miller to Vestal, 14 November 1987.

21. International Education Task Force, Federal Interagency Committee on Education, Robert Leestma, Chairman, *International Education Programs of the U.S. Government, an Inventory Compiled by Helen R. Wiprud* (Washington, D.C.: U.S. Department of Education, 1980).

22. See *International Exchange Policy Monitor*, Washington, D.C., Liaison Group for International Educational Exchange, 15 October 1992, pp. 1–8.

23. *Center for International Education (CIE)*, Description of Programs, Washington, D.C., U.S. Department of Education, May 1990.

24. National Association of State Universities and Land Grant Colleges, Division of International Affairs, "Workshop on the Reauthorization of Title VI of the Higher Education Act," University of Pittsburgh, 2–3 March 1990, p. 5.

25. Gerald L. Baliles, "Chairman's Overview," *America in Transition, the International Frontier* (Washington, D.C.: National Governors' Association, 1989), p. 6.

26. See, for example, Commonwealth of Virginia, Commission on the University of the 21st Century, *The Case for Change*, "III. Global Perspectives and Literacies," pp. 4–6; Sven Groennings, *Economic Competitiveness and International Knowledge*, New England Board of Higher Education, Staff Paper II, October 1987.

27. See, for example, Richard D. Lambert, *Points of Leverage: An Agenda for a National Foundation for International Studies* (New York: Social Science Research Council, 1986), pp. 1–7.

16

The Role of
Private Foundations

The private foundations, especially the Ford Foundation, helped build nonpareil language and area studies centers in several of the nation's universities before that era of philanthropic enterprise ended. In doing so, the foundations set the stage for federal funding of international training and research through the NDEA when the Soviets threw up their Sputnik challenge to U.S. science. Between 1953 and 1966, when its International Training and Research (ITR) program was terminated, the Ford Foundation made grants exceeding $270 million to some 34 universities, specifically and exclusively for international studies.[1] The ITR made a transforming difference, not only in the development of international studies during the 1950s and 1960s but also since.[2]

The foundations retreated from the field of international education in the 1960s, when it appeared that the IEA would take over the major responsibility.[3] Testifying before the Brademas Task Force, Champion Ward, deputy vice president for international programs of the Ford Foundation, indicated the direction the foundations were headed. "When foundations find the Government moving into areas in which they have been working for a long period of time," said Ward, "we feel this gives us freedom to move into new areas of experience; to have the flexibility to experiment; and to demonstrate the vitality and visibility of new approaches to human problems."[4]

The foundations moved quickly into other fields. A study by Education and World Affairs revealed that $58 million of external financing was expended for international studies in 36 major U.S. universities in 1966–67. Of that amount, $32 million came from the federal government and $24.6 million from private foundations. The Ford Foundation provided $21.3 million of the foundation total.[5]

By 1969 the Ford Foundation had reduced its budget for international studies to less than half of the 1966 amount.[6] By the early 1970s the foundation's sharply eroded capital base prompted substantial cutbacks in overall expenditure levels and made inconceivable any revival of its international education programs.

The efforts of the foundations had been most successful in making international studies an estimable and perdurable academic enterprise. According to Robert McCaughey, the foundations also provided the wherewithal to aid in the enterprise's academic enclosure, the isolating of area centers from academic departments with their mundane teaching and from nonacademic constituencies and nonprofessional audiences.[7] The fortunate few university centers, treated by foundations in a manner to which they quickly became accustomed, have provided elegiac laments over a lost academic style of life and demands for stronger outside support of international studies to restore their lost elegance ever since the withdrawal of the private benevolence. Until the passage of the Boren initiative in 1991, their jeremiads fell on deaf federal ears — or at least on the hearing challenged in Congress.

In 1993, foundation support of international studies, although significant where it exists, is of narrow scale and scope. Reports published by the Ford Foundation and the Rockefeller Foundation expressed concern about the doleful state of international education.[8] Nevertheless, the void created by the retreat of private foundations from the field in the late 1960s remains unfilled. Cater expressed the sentiments of many who regretted the course followed by the foundations in 1969: "I continue to bleed when I recognize that the private foundations reduced their funding devoted to international education projects in anticipation of federal government involvement which did not follow. There are times when it might have been better to have stayed in bed."[9]

NOTES

1. Richard D. Lambert with Elinor G. Barbar, Eleanor Jorden, Margaret B. Merrill, and Leon I. Twarog, *Beyond Growth: The Next Stage in Language and Area Studies* (Washington, D.C.: Association of American Universities, 1984), pp. 8–9.

2. Robert McCaughey, *International Studies and Academic Enterprise: A Chapter in the Enclosure of American Learning* (New York: Columbia University Press, 1984), p. 198.

3. For Leestma's analysis in 1969 of the financial crisis that resulted in foundations withdrawing support of external funding of international studies in 36 leading universities and colleges, see Department of Labor and Health, Education, and

Welfare Appropriations for 1970, Hearings before a Subcommittee of the Committee on Appropriations, House of Representatives, Ninety-First Congress, First Session, pp. 982–84.

4.   Hearings before the Task Force on International Education of the Committee on Education and Labor, "International Education," 30 March–7 April 1966, U.S. House of Representatives, Eighty-Ninth Congress, Second Session, p. 274.

5.   *A Crisis of Dollars: The Funding Threat to International Affairs in U.S. Higher Education* (New York: EWA, 1968), p. 46.

6.   Department of Labor and Health, Education, and Welfare Appropriations for 1970, Hearings before a Subcommittee of the Committee on Appropriations, House of Representatives, Ninety-First Congress, First Session, pp. 982–84.

7.   McCaughey, *International Studies*, pp. 220–21, 253–55.

8.   Elinor G. Barber and Warren Ilchman, *International Studies Review* (New York: Ford Foundation, 1979); Edwin A. Deagle, Jr., *A Survey of United States Institutions Engaged in International Relations Research and Related Activities* (New York: Rockefeller Foundation, 1981).

9.   Letter, Cater to Vestal, 16 May 1989. Cater continued: "But it is surprising how many worthy enterprises, including the international center [the Woodrow Wilson Center] now located in the Smithsonian Castle, did get launched in that final dismal year when Johnson decided not to run again."

17

What the IEA
Might Have Accomplished

By the mid-1960s the United States, as the leader of the Free World, had rebuilt the war-devastated economies of Western Europe and Japan, which flourished while protected under the umbrella of U.S. military might from the aggressive, expansionist tendencies of the USSR. In retrospect it now can be seen that the West was winning the Cold War as the demand economies of the Communist Bloc nations rotted in the miasma of supply and demand failures, environmental degradation, and the stifling of individual initiative. The United States, the world's number one economic power, was poised to reinvest its enormous and unprecedented surplus capital in education, health, and the general welfare of its citizenry — to create a Great Society. President Johnson had an overwhelming electoral mandate and congressional majorities in both houses to begin such an effort.

Unfortunately, the administration chose to divert a major part of the national bounty into an unpopular war in Southeast Asia that divided the public and squandered the opportunity to further improve domestic institutions and infrastructures. The mighty U.S. dollar fell in jungles and rice paddies on the other side of the globe and on world money markets. The results were national wounds that were slow to heal and lost opportunities to improve the lives of our people.

Twenty-five years ago, higher education in the United States had failed to keep pace with the global leadership role assumed by the United States in foreign affairs. Two only partially distinguishable national needs in higher education stood out: timely and adequate new knowledge of international affairs and relations, in the widest sense of those terms, and a much larger measure and higher quality of instruction in international studies at all levels in our educational system, from elementary through postsecondary to adult.[1] The IEA, as we have seen, was an attempt to address these needs. Without the impetus of federal financial support until 1991, however, international studies failed to reach the takeoff stage to fully serve the national interest.

Although the whole world changed, our universities and colleges remained largely the same. Nationwide growth of international studies, although cumulative, was glacial. Despite the admonitions of scholars such as Edwin O. Reischauer that education "is not moving rapidly enough in the right direction to produce knowledge about the outside world and the attitudes toward other peoples that may be essential for human survival,"[2] most universities did their least-impressive work on the very subjects in which society's need for greater knowledge and better education was most acute. Maurice Harari's chiding that "a system of education which ignores the major problems of most of mankind is not acceptable" generally went unheeded.[3]

One can but speculate what the state of international education in higher education in the United States would be today had the IEA been funded in 1966 or 1967. Without doubt, the addition of federal dollars in international education would have had a revolutionary impact on the provincialism of U.S. universities and colleges and would have brought changes in scale, quality, opportunities, and procedures. International program offices on individual campuses would have had the financial strength to gain access to the power centers of the university and to assert institutional leverage. As a result, an entire generation of Americans would have been exposed to more global information, and they probably would have been better informed about other countries, cultures, and peoples.

Perhaps a more knowledgeable public would have influenced U.S. foreign policy decisions in directions other than those in which the nation's policy makers have operated during the 1970s and 1980s. Perhaps we as a nation would have been far better prepared to deal with the problems we have suffered in Asia, the Middle East, Latin America, Africa, and elsewhere.[4] Perhaps the United States would have lost less of its competitive advantage in world markets and the balance of payments deficit would today be smaller had U.S. business people had a more sophisticated appreciation of how the world works, greater sensitivity to cultural differences, and an understanding of the contribution of international trade to the national interest.

What the IEA might have accomplished can be seen through the impact of the more narrowly focused NDEA programs. Beginning in 1958, first through Title VI of the NDEA and, since 1980, through Title VI of the Higher Education Act, the federal government has spent about $0.5 billion to enhance the international capabilities of U.S. higher education.

This federal contribution to colleges and universities has been a catalyst that has provided prestige, the margin of excellence, and the drawing power for other funding. NDEA grants have assisted in funding some 100 campus-based graduate centers, most of which focus on geographic area studies; and the FLAS program has provided almost 30,000 grants to graduate students, most of whom are teaching in colleges and universities. There have also been more than 200 awards to advance undergraduate international education at a variety of institutions.[5] These accomplishments have come about with a very modest investment of federal funds.

NDEA centers constitute an unprecedented national pool of competence in language and area teaching and research. The United States is instructing more students and producing more research concerning the lands and peoples of Asia, Africa, Latin America, and Eastern and Central Europe than is any other nation,[6] but the area approach is limited in scope to basically a small proportion of U.S. education, primarily at the graduate level in humanistic and social science disciplines. As Taggart points out, the language and area studies centers do not emphasize processes in international affairs, and centers focusing on international trade and agriculture and international political forces are badly needed (a broadening of the scope of substantive fields of NDEA centers was one of the proposed programs of the IEA).[7]

Joseph F. Belmonte, deputy director of the U.S. ED's CIE, has observed the changes in the NDEA and its progeny programs during the 1960s, 1970s, and 1980s and notes that proposals under the IEA have had a serendipitous effect on undergraduate programs in international studies — especially through outreach activities of Title VI international studies centers. "A law that was never funded," said Belmonte, "can have a history — and an impact."[8] If such good could come from a fiscally failed act, what could have been accomplished with a fully funded IEA?

Three different scenarios are helpful in speculating on what might have been accomplished under the IEA had funds been appropriated. The worst-case scenario would have limited federal expenditures to annual $2 million appropriations for planning grants to colleges and universities as requested for fiscal year 1970. Under this request, $300,000 would have been divided among 20 graduate institutions and $1.7 million would have provided planning grants for 164 undergraduate programs (100 colleges and universities in consortia and 64 individual institutions). Had the same number of postsecondary institutions received funds for planning grants in subsequent years, by 1985, virtually all of the nation's 2,500 colleges and universities would have had the stimulus of a planning grant, as would have 300 graduate centers. Through 1990, the total appropriations would have been $40 million in 1970 dollars. Had the appropriation kept up with inflation, the $2 million of 1970 would now be $4.5 million and the appropriations total for 20 years would have equaled $64.31 million. Even the modest funding of this worst-case scenario would have provided money for administrators and faculty on individual campuses throughout the country to attempt to restructure curricula and bring greater international awareness to their students and communities.

A middle-level scenario would have had the IEA funded at the requested $40 million level for fiscal year 1968 and continued at that level through 1990. Such a scheme would have provided $800 million in 1968 dollars (worth over $1.5 billion now) to be invested in a broad spectrum of the international aspects of higher education. If the annual appropriation were divided equally between graduate and undergraduate programs, $400 million would have gone into undergraduate project grants — an amount well above the $300 million that Ward Morehouse had told the Brademas Task Force would be needed to have "any pervasive impact on colleges and universities in this country."[9] An additional $400 million would have been used to develop or improve graduate centers of excellence — a sum sufficient to reach virtually all graduate programs in the United States.

The third and most optimistic scenario would have provided appropriations for the IEA as authorized under the original act: $40 million in fiscal year 1968 and $90 million in subsequent years. By 1990, over $2 billion in 1968 dollars would have been spent to improve all aspects of international studies and research in U.S. colleges and universities. Taking inflation into account, the $90 million annual appropriation would today equal more than $200 million and the total appropriation would have been over $3.342 billion. Such an amount would have had a profound impact on higher education in the United States. Graduate centers of research and training for area studies and for particular subject matters or issues in world affairs could have been funded in every doctoral-granting institution. Parochialism in higher learning could have been strongly combatted by improved and expanded undergraduate instruction in international studies and foreign languages. Increased numbers of faculty could have been trained in foreign countries, and a much larger percentage of the 5.7 million students enrolled in baccalaureate programs in the United States could have participated in college-sponsored work-study-travel programs. Visiting scholars programs could have improved the network of learning in international studies. Teacher training with a stronger international component might have brought an added dimension to elementary and secondary school instruction throughout the country. More foreign teachers and students might have had the opportunity to study English.

Had the impact of IEA grants been of the same quality as that brought about by the NDEA program, a salient shortcoming of U.S. education would have been substantially remedied and a series of performance gaps closed. By failing to fund the IEA, the United States lost two decades of such qualitative improvements. Some educational leaders of the time mourned the loss.

Shortly before he retired as president of Harvard University in 1992, Derek Bok observed that in advanced education and research, regional and international centers were probably no stronger, and might be even less so, than they were at the time of the passage of the IEA. Bok noted that very few of those centers had joint programs with business schools or with other professional faculties as envisioned under the 1966 act.[10]

Bok also perceived a serious erosion in the numbers of first-rate faculty who specialize in different areas of the world or work on global problems such as economic development, international security, foreign trade, and international law. Of all the needs in international studies, Bok believed this the most crucial.[11]

Ernest Boyer, commissioner of education in the Carter administration, writing in the late 1980s, was concerned about another legacy of the failed IEA — a dangerous parochialism pervading many higher learning institutions. "While some students have a global perspective," wrote Boyer, "the vast majority, although vaguely concerned, are inadequately informed about the interdependent world in which they live." Boyer warned that if colleges cannot help students "see beyond themselves and better understand the interdependent nature of our world, each new generation will remain ignorant, and its capacity to live confidently and responsibly will be dangerously diminished."[12]

If the level of awareness of international events remains low on campuses, there are signs that the citizens of the country at large have learned something about global connections from experience during the past quarter of a century. Jobs lost to foreign competition and, in the 1970s, long waits in lines to buy higher priced gasoline resulting from Organization of Petroleum Exporting Countries (OPEC)-induced energy shocks have made the average citizen painfully cognizant of worldwide interdependence. The man in the street has very practical pocketbook concerns about the nation's debtor status and balance of trade deficits. In addition, the ethnic diversity of the United States is much more evident, because millions of immigrants have come to this country during the 1970s and 1980s. The bitter lessons of the Vietnam War also have colored U.S. perceptions of global politics, as seen in the cautious response of the public and of government to U.S. military initiatives in the world's "hot spots" of the 1990s. Ubiquitous cable television brings scenes of other nations and cultures into U.S. homes throughout the day. News of diplomatic and military activities of the United States sharpen citizens' knowledge of world geography, and awareness of such nations as Kuwait, Somalia, Bosnia, and Herzegovina has been heightened by the well-reported presence of Americans there. In short, our people know more about the world scene in general terms than they did 25 years ago.

In 1966 the president and the other policy makers who had a vision of the IEA saw further than they knew. They were right in what they proposed, but they were too early, too premature. Most of the nation had not grasped the concept of an interdependent world and had little understanding of the need for programs of education in foreign languages and world affairs.

Today, the public consciousness of this need is higher, and the demand for such a program comes from the internationally enlightened of the academy, government, and business. Furthermore, the United States has greater capacities, resources, and skills in the 1990s than it had in the 1960s. With these changes in mind, Congress in 1991 set about addressing the concerns of Bok and Boyer and other   advocates of an expanded federal role in international education.

NOTES

1.   Robert E. Ward, *National Needs for International Education*, CSIS Monograph, Center for Strategic and International Studies, Georgetown University, Washington, D.C., 1977, p. 8.

2.   Edwin O. Reischauer, *Toward the 21st Century: Education for a Changing World* (New York: Alfred A. Knopf, 1973), p. 3.

3.   Maurice Harari, *Global Dimensions in U.S. Education: The University* (New York: Center for War/Peace Studies, 1972), p. 9.

4.   John Brademas with Lynne P. Brown, *The Politics of Education: Conflict and Consensus on Capitol Hill* (Norman: University of Oklahoma Press, 1987), p. 110.

5.   Sven Groennings, "Higher Education, International Education and the Academic Disciplines," in *Group Portrait: International Education in the Academic Disciplines* (New York: American Forum for Education in a Global Age, 1989).

6.   "Notebook Concerning International Education and Health, 1966," Letter, W. Norman Brown, director, South Asia Language and Area Center, University of Pennsylvania, to Gardner, 28 October 1965, Box 44, Office Files of Cater, LBJ Library.

7. Telephone interview with Glen Taggart, 8 May 1989.

8. Interview with Joseph F. Belmonte, 7 August 1990; see also Robert Leestma, "U.S. Office of Education Programs Abroad," *International Educational and Cultural Exchange* 8 (Fall 1972): 32–45; Robert Leestma, "Comparative and International Education in the U.S. Office of Education: A Bibliography of Studies and Publications, 1968–1980," *Comparative Education Review* 25 (June 1981): 272–288.

9. Hearings before the Task Force on International Education of the Committee on Education and Labor, "International Education," 30 March–7 April 1966, U.S. House of Representatives, Eighty-Ninth Congress, Second Session, p. 329.

10. Derek Bok, *Universities and the Future of America* (Durham, N.C.: Duke University Press, 1990), p. 37. See also, Derek Bok, *Higher Learning* (Cambridge, Mass.: Harvard University Press, 1986), p. 170.

11. Bok, *Universities*, p. 37.

12. Ernest L. Boyer, *College: The Undergraduate Experience in America* (New York: Harper & Row, 1987), pp. 281–82.

LBJ signs the International Education Act into law at Chulalongkorn University, Bangkok, Thailand, 29 October 1966. (Photograph by Frank Wolfe)

LBJ after the International Education Act signing ceremony at Chulalongkorn University, Bangkok, Thailand, 29 October 1966. (Photograph by Frank Wolfe)

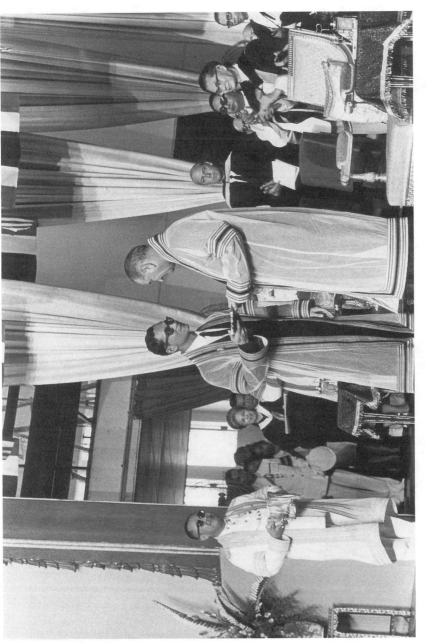

LBJ receiving an honorary degree at Chulalongkorn University in Bangkok, Thailand, 29 October 1966. (Photograph by Yoichi R. Okamoto)

Paul A. Miller, Assistant Secretary of Education, Department of Health, Education, and Welfare with LBJ. (Photographer unknown)

William W. Marvel, President of Education and World Affairs, with Secretary Rusk, Secretary McNamara, and Douglass Cater, 20 January 1967. (Photograph by Yoichi R. Okamoto)

LBJ and the Ad Hoc Task Force of the National Advisory Committee on International Education, 20 February 1967. (Photograph by Yoichi R. Okamoto)

Congressman George H. Mahon, Chairman of the Appropriations Committee of the House of Representatives. (Photograph by Yoichi R. Okamoto)

III

INTERNATIONAL EDUCATION IN THE POST–COLD WAR ERA

18

The National Security Education Act of 1991

Senator David Boren (D-OK), first elected to the Senate in 1978, emerged as a champion of international education only in 1990, when, in a series of speeches and op-ed pieces, he began to stress the importance of international   competence in the United States' new leadership role.[1] Until that time, Boren, a trustee of Yale University and a former Rhodes scholar, was principally known for his chairing of the Intelligence Committee, his work on the Agriculture Committee and Finance Committee, and his efforts to reform congressional campaign finance.[2] The senator from Oklahoma brought global perspectives to his committee assignments — backing bipartisan cooperation in foreign policy, strengthening export programs to promote farm products overseas, and advancing the competitive position of the United States in the world marketplace — but the armorial bearing of international education was not yet engraved on his escutcheon.

This changed when Boren and Senator Claiborne Pell (D-RI), chairman of the Foreign Relations Committee, wrote President Bush urging him to explore a significant new exchange agreement with the USSR during the 1989 Malta Summit Meeting with President Gorbachev. The senators proposed an annual two-way exchange of 20,000 students paid for by the United States, with a possible Soviet contribution of ruble costs charged against lend-lease debts still owed the United States.[3] From this initiative, the thousand-thousand agreement announced by the two nations' leaders at the summit enlarged USIA exchange programs. This led Boren and Pell to sponsor the Educational Exchanges Enhancement Act (EEEA) of 1990 that expanded programs to send U.S. students, including undergraduates, to nations with limited contact with the United States (the new democracies of Eastern Europe, the former Soviet Union, and non-Western European countries) and to bring students from those countries to the United States.[4] Boren thought the EEEA "an important step, a signal of a larger intention" by the United States to assume "a different kind of leadership role, one based on talent and training, not military might."[5] Boren and Pell, however, were able to mobilize only limited resources in the foreign assistance budget for such exchanges.

In the summer of 1991, members of Boren's staff contacted Jack Vaughn, senior federal relations officer of the Association of American Universities, about the activities of the CAFLIS. This contact was the precursor of a mid-July meeting of a few scholars and higher education association representatives with Rebecca Cooper and John Deekin of Boren's office that was the first indication that the senator was developing a major international education initiative in the Intelligence Committee. The nascent NSEA presented at the meeting contained most of the provisions that were to become law, although Boren envisioned it as a larger, $180 million program to be administered by the DE. The senator and his staff did the lobbying for the proposal because it was considered "semi-controversial." Of special significance were Boren's frequent communications with General Brent Scowcroft of the White House staff and with Senator Robert C. Byrd (D-WV), chairman of the Senate Appropriations Committee and an important ally.

The first obstacle Boren encountered was from the president's Office of Management and Budget (OMB). Under the Budget Enforcement Act of 1990, overall spending limits were placed on three appropriations categories: defense, domestic, and international.[6] The OMB, Bush's faithful Cerberus, with a snarling head for each category, discourages forays into the nether abode of budgets beyond the West Wing of the White House. The OMB ruled that if the DE were to run the NSEA, funds would have to come from the domestic education budget rather than from the intelligence (defense) budget. This would have killed the proposal due to the lack of funding in the domestic education category.

Boren considered proposing a Senate "override" of the Budget Enforcement Act to get intelligence funds reallocated to the domestic budget. Such action requires a two-thirds vote of the Senate membership. Senator Jim Sasser (D-TN), chairman of the Budget Committee, dissuaded Boren from this plan, noting that the number of senators opposed to reallocating funds precluded his getting the 66 votes needed for an override.[7]

Thus, Boren found his only funding source inexorably linked to the defense budget. Confronted with the OMB ruling that, to qualify as a defense budget-supported program under the budget agreement, the NSEA would have to be housed in the Department of Defense (DOD),

Boren settled on the Defense Intelligence College (DIC), an accredited, postsecondary education institution in Washington, D.C., as the agency through which to administer NSEA programs. Even after moving the program to the DOD, however, OBM only grudgingly conferred a defense classification for the NSEA just before the Senate intelligence bill went to the Senate floor.[8]

Because of the complex budgeting process for intelligence programs, Boren had to shepherd the legislation through six congressional committees: the Armed Services Committees, the Intelligence Committees, and the Appropriations Committees of both Houses. Considering the size and scope of the NSEA, the act moved through the legislative process in nearly record time. This was accomplished primarily due to the persuasion, dedication, and clout of the senior senator from Oklahoma.[9]

At a Capitol Hill press conference on 18 July 1991, Boren and his co-sponsors, Senators Sam Nunn (D-GA), chairman of the Armed Services Committee, and John Warner (R-VA), ranking minority member of the Armed Services Committee, publicly announced their proposed NSEA that was contained in the 1992 Intelligence Authorization Act. The senators cited a number of statistics documenting the United States' glaring deficiency in foreign languages and area studies and highlighting the need to catch up to the high level of international training in Europe and Japan. Boren noted that ideas on the importance of international education to U.S. national security had been endorsed by a draft report of the CIA director's Task Force on Reorganization and by some of the most prominent founding fathers of the U.S. intelligence services.[10]

In negotiations behind the closed doors of the Senate Intelligence Committee, Senator John Glenn (R-OH) opposed the enactment of the NSEA. Glenn did not believe the bill to be the right stuff for inclusion in the intelligence budget, and he expressed his concern about utilizing "increasingly scarce intelligence resources to fund educational programs at a time when we are terminating important intelligence systems and programs."[11] The dissent of Glenn, however, was the exception in the Senate, where the NSEA received generally strong support.

On the House side, the Boren Bill had no champion, and reaction to the program and its funding was less favorable. In both the authorization and appropriations conferences, NSEA encountered sharp, bipartisan opposition by House conferees who saw the Boren initiative as taking away money produced by intelligence cuts for a Senate program that they had no role in creating.[12]

In the House Select Committee on Intelligence, objections centered on the large cost of the program (amounting to 0.005 percent of the intelligence budget, estimated at that time to be about $30 billion a year) and its contribution to U.S. security interests. Critics complained that there was no requirement for students receiving support to work for intelligence agencies when they finished their studies, an idea strongly opposed by Boren.[13] Representative Bud Shuster (R-PA), the ranking Republican on the House committee, called the program a diversion of funds from intelligence to education and said that "U.S. intelligence will reap little tangible dividend, if any."[14] Subsequently, all House Republican Intelligence conferees withheld support of the conference agreement on NSEA.

Chairman of the House committee Dave McCurdy (D-OK) had earlier introduced a $33 million package specifically for language training for CIA agents in a newly created Center for the Advancement of Language Learning (CALL), and he drove a hard bargain with Boren to lower the authorization level of the program. McCurdy was joined by the other House Democratic conferees in signing the conference agreement, but their support was generally weak. House conferees made some nine modifications in the Senate proposals, the most important of which was reducing the authorization of the NSEA from $180 million to $150 million, of which $35 million might be spent on programs in the initial year.[15]

In the House Appropriations Subcommittee on Defense, Representative Norman D. Dicks (D-WA) argued against providing any funding for the NSEA, which he characterized as wasteful and a disguised intrusion of education into the intelligence budget. Only the forceful intervention of Senator Byrd saved the appropriation. Byrd sent word to House subcommittee chair John P. Murtha (D-PA) that the NSEA was his top priority and a "must-have" item. Murtha then announced that the House receded.[16] In the end, the proposal survived very much intact on the basis of Boren's influence and that of Senator Byrd. Senate staff contended, however, that House critics would have to be convinced about the importance of the program during annual congressional authorization and appropriations hearings or its future might be in jeopardy.[17]

CONTENT OF NSEA

The NSEA, as passed in 1991, created three new international education programs: one to provide undergraduate scholarships for study abroad, one to fund graduate fellowships in international studies in the United States, and one to award grants to strengthen international programs in U.S. colleges and universities. A funding allocation goal was set, with each of the programs receiving one-third of the funds annually allocated from the National Security Trust Fund.

The objectives of the act are to meet broad national security education needs as they change over time; to strengthen teaching and scholarship in language, area, and international studies; to interest more people in working for the government; to broaden the nation's international perspective; and to strengthen the federal government's advocacy and support for international education.

The act establishes a National Security Education Board (NSEB), with the secretary of defense as chairman, to govern the program. Board members include the secretaries of commerce, education, and state and the directors of USIA and the CIA, or their designated representatives, plus four presidential appointees with expertise in international education. The NSEB will set qualifications for eligibility of students and institutions for funding, establish criteria for selecting recipients, disseminate information about program activities, and recommend critical countries and academic areas to receive priority attention. The NSEB is not assigned responsibility for management of the program, nor is it given a direct role in making awards.

Undergraduate scholarship recipients, who may be called "International Exchange Scholars," must be U.S. citizens planning to study abroad for at least one academic semester in foreign countries deemed "critical" by the NSEB. The NSEB will identify critical countries that are not emphasized in other study-abroad programs or in which few U.S. students are studying.

House conferees added a provision requiring all undergraduates supported for a calendar year or longer to serve in the federal government or in higher education upon completion of their studies. The duration of service is to be no longer than the period of scholarship assistance. Students who fail to fulfill their service will be subject to repayment provisions. Representative McCurdy, who earlier had sponsored legislation linking federal college student assistance to national service, may have added this requirement.[18] Few International Exchange Scholars will be affected, however, because most undergraduates study overseas for an academic year or less.

The NSEA originally provided graduate fellowships to U.S. citizens for graduate education *in the United States*. Graduate fellowships will be awarded in foreign languages, area studies, and other international fields judged critical by the NSEB. Recipients, who may be called "International Graduate Fellows," will be required to fulfill service requirements in the federal government or in education for a period one to three times longer than the duration of their fellowships — or face reimbursement obligations.

A program of grants to U.S. universities and colleges will be set up under the NSEA to establish, operate, and improve programs in foreign languages, area studies, or other international fields identified as critical by the NSEB. All NSEA scholarships, fellowships, and grants will be awarded on the basis of merit review to recipients reflecting the geographic, cultural, racial, and ethnic diversity of the nation.

Responding to concerns that host countries may think that those receiving NSEA support are involved in intelligence-gathering activities, Boren insisted in conference on an express prohibition of intelligence agency involvement with NSEA recipients during their period of sponsorship. In answer to critics' disdain of perceived ties between universities and the CIA, Boren replied: "The choice was to begin the program in this way or to not begin it at all, because none of the other [Congressional] committees up here — while their members might be very supportive of these goals — had any funds to do anything like this."[19]

The organizational arrangements for making NSEA awards may help diffuse criticism of potential intelligence community intrusions into the academy. The act authorizes the secretary of defense to enter into contracts with private national organizations having expertise in international studies for the awarding of scholarships, fellowships, and grants. The wording of the contract authority is significant: "the Secretary *may*," not "the Secretary *shall*." This proviso also frees the secretary from legal requirements to use competitive procedures in awarding such contracts.

The secretary, thus, could contract with national scholarly organizations such as the Social Science Research Council (SSRC) or the American Council of Learned Societies (ACLS) to act as "regrant" or "pass-through" agencies for NSEA awards. The SSRC, ACLS, and similar organizations have the capacity to hold competitions for grants and make awards on the basis of meritorious peer review. Such private organizations could serve as buffers between higher education and the original source of the trust fund, the moneyed DOD. A comparable two-step allocation procedure has been used in making awards under Title VIII of the Higher Education Act. The State Department receives an annual appropriation for Slavic studies, but awards are made by pass-through organizations (for example, ACLS, International Research Exchange Board) on the basis of national competitions. This procedure, using regrant organization boards that include members representing higher education, is thought to allay some professorial unease about State Department administration of the program.[20]

1992 "PERFECTING AMENDMENTS"

In Senate Intelligence Committee markup of the fiscal year 1993 intelligence bill, a $30 million increase in the ceiling of the trust fund (from $150 million to $180 million) was authorized. This was accomplished before any money had been spent under the original appropriation. The NSEA called for the creation of a trust fund in the U.S. Treasury, resources for which were to be drawn from $150 million of funds authorized and appropriated from cuts to be made in intelligence programs for fiscal year 1992. The legislation failed to indicate any line items for the funds, however, a technical error that delayed implementation of the program and cost the NSEA trust fund some $6 million in interest. Protracted and complex negotiations among the relevant authorizing and appropriating committees and subcommittees of both houses and the DOD as to which intelligence line items in the defense budget were to provide the money for the trust fund delayed the start of the program until close to the end of the 1992 fiscal year. Finally, on 24 August 1992, $140 million was deposited in the NSEA trust fund, with the remaining $10 million transferred on 4 September.

During Senate floor debate, the name of the act was officially changed to the "David L. Boren National Security Education Act of 1991," in honor of the work Senator Boren had done in initiating the program.[21] Other "minor" or "perfecting" amendments to the NSEA were made by Senate and House conferees in September 1992. These included:

1. Expanding the size of the NSEB from 10 to 13, by adding the chairperson of the National Endowment for the Humanities as an ex officio member and two private members appointed by the president. This action would help diffuse the impact of DOD and Director of Central Intelligence representation on the board.
2. Changing the minimum period for an undergraduate scholarship abroad to "one academic semester or equivalent term." The purpose of this provision was to take into account the variety of academic terms other than the semester used in many institutions abroad and in the United States.
3. Permitting the award of graduate fellowships to study abroad if such study is part of a graduate degree program of a U.S. institute of higher learning. The requirement that graduate study

abroad be directed toward a degree program from a U.S. institution was intended to prevent any perceived overlap between the NSEA program and the Fulbright exchange program. By allowing International Graduate Fellows to study abroad, the NSEA creates a new type of fellowship that will facilitate students' pursuit of the demanding training required for scholarly international expertise: knowledge of an area, a language, and a discipline, plus overseas experience.[22]

4. Authorizing the secretary of defense to enter into up to ten personal service contracts for a period up to one year in order to administer the program. This authority frees the program administrator from relying solely on full-time government employees and makes it possible for him or her to employ international education and area studies specialists when needed.

5. Removing the requirement that the act be administered through the DIC. The Senate bill also provided for the establishment of an independent center for international studies to administer the program. It was thought that the new center would better facilitate interaction between the program and members of the education community and the public, especially if it were in a location accessible to the public without the need for security screening or visitor controls. An independent center would also separate the program more distinctly from the field of intelligence. The DOD successfully lobbied against this provision as a congressional intrusion into the department's administrative authority. Instead, conferees emphasized in report language that the board retains authority to establish NSEA policy and the DOD is obliged to carry out the program in accordance with policies approved by the NSEB. The program administrator intends to establish a center to run the program that will be outside the Pentagon.

During the first week of October, House and Senate conferees of the Appropriations Committees convened to consider the DOD budget requests, purported to have been overappropriated by $6 billion. The conference looked to the intelligence budget as a likely source from which to make cuts, and among the deletions was Senator Boren's $30 million increase to the NSEA trust fund. Senator John McCain (R-AZ) spoke against any additional funds for the NSEA, and the House conferees again demonstrated no enthusiasm for the act. This time, Senator Byrd did not come to the rescue of the NSEA. The amended act was duly passed by both houses and signed into law by President Bush on 24 October.

The deletion of more money for the trust fund must have been disappointing to Boren, who was serving in his last year as chair of the Intelligence Committee and was attempting to build up a larger sustainable basis for NSEA. Boren and Byrd have indicated that their long-range goal is to increase the trust fund of $300 million to $350 million, so that annual appropriations for the NSEA would have more impact on higher education. In the future, appropriations committees will be requested to provide annual increases to the trust fund to work toward that goal.[23] The $29 billion intelligence budget from which requests will be made is roughly the equivalent of what the federal government is spending on education and the environment combined in 1993.[24]

NOTES

1. See, for example, David L. Boren, "...For a Model Nation," *Washington Post*, 2 May 1990; "Ignorance of World Puts America at Risk," *Atlanta Constitution*, 19 September 1991; "The New Isolationism; A Threat to National Security," Commencement Address, The American University, Washington, D.C., 26 January 1992; "A New U.S. Foreign Policy for a Changed World," Lecture, Conference on After 1992: A New European Order?, University of Tulsa, 21 February 1992; "The Intelligence Community: How Crucial?" *Foreign Affairs* 17 (Summer 1992): 52–62.

2. "United States Senator David L. Boren Biography," March 1991, Photocopy.

3. Memo, Peter Galbraith to Boren, 1 June 1989, with draft letter to President Bush.

4. S. 517, Educational Exchanges Enhancement Act of 1991; Statement by Senator David L. Boren, "Educational Exchanges Enhancement Act of 1991." The EEEA was enacted into law in 1991 with an authorization of $10 million under the Senate's Foreign Operations Authorization for 1992–93.

5. David L. Boren and Claiborne Pell, "Give Students the World," *St. Louis Post Dispatch*, 31 August 1990.

6. *Congressional Quarterly*, 21 December 1991, pp. 3728–29.

7. Telephone interview with Jack Vaughn, Association of American Universities, 16 January 1992.

8. Memo, Vaughn to Council on Federal Relations, 16 July 1992, p. 2.

9. Liaison Group for International Educational Exchange, "Congress Approves $150 Million International Education Trust Fund," *International Exchange Policy Monitor*, Washington, D.C., 4 December 1991; see also *Defense Intelligence College 1991–92 Catalog*, Washington, D.C. The DIC, chartered by a DOD directive and a Joint Chiefs of Staff memorandum, provides education for military and civilian intelligence personnel and conducts research on topics of significance to the intelligence community. Among DIC programs is a nine-month resident postgraduate course leading to Master of Science of Strategic Intelligence degrees. Martin Hurwitz stressed that the DIC's sole function under the original NSEA was to provide

administrative support for the administrator's office. Interview, Stillwater, Oklahoma, 30 March 1992.

10.   "Boren, Nunn, Warner Introduce National Security Education Act," Press Release, U.S. Senator David Boren, 18 July 1991.

11.   Senate Select Committee on Intelligence authorizing appropriations for fiscal year 1993 for Intelligence Activities of the U.S. Government, Report 102-324, One Hundred Second Congress, Second Session, 21 July 1992, "Additional Views," pp. 46–48

12.   Memo, Vaughn, p. 3.

13.   *Congressional Quarterly*, 23 November 1991, p. 3470.

14.   *Congressional Quarterly*, 20 November 1991, p. H10628–29.

15.   House Permanent Select Committee on Intelligence, Intelligence Authorization Act, Fiscal Year 1992, Conference Report, H.R. 2038, Report 102-327, One Hundred Second Congress, First Session, 18 November 1991.

16.   Telephone interview with C. Richard D'Amato, 4 May 1992.

17.   Liaison Group for International Educational Exchange, "Congress Approves $150 Million International Education Trust Fund," *International Exchange Policy Monitor*, Washington, D.C., 4 December 1991. Critics on the House Intelligence Committee demonstrated their displeasure with Boren's "independence" in not always supporting President Clinton's economic programs. To punish Boren, on 17 June 1993, the committee voted to eliminate the NSEA trust fund as part of a broader cost-cutting effort. "Tribute, a Political Casualty, Is Taken Back," *New York Times*, 18 June 1993, p. A20.

18.   Dave McCurdy, "A Quid Pro Quo for Youth," *New York Times*, 26 June 1989.

19.   Paul Desruisseaux, "Congress Approves Program to Support Overseas Study," *Chronicle of Higher Education*, 4 December 1991, pp. A53, A55.

20.   Telephone interview with Jack Vaughn, Association of American Universities, 16 January 1992.

21.   The change of name was proposed by Senator Frank Murkowski (R-AR).

22.   Richard D. Lambert, *Points of Leverage* (New York: Social Science Research Council, 1986), pp. 62–63.

23.   Memo, Vaughn, p. 6.

24.   Douglas Jehl, "Campaign Is Begun to Protect Money for Intelligence," *New York Times*, 14 March 1993, pp. 1, 15. Private experts have published authoritative accounts of how the $29 billion is now divided: the CIA receives about 10 percent; most of the rest is spent on satellites, eavesdropping operations, and other technical systems; about $10 billion is devoted to military intelligence. The best financed single agency is the National Reconnaissance Office, which receives $5.2 billion and builds the imagery satellites on which the United States relied to monitor Soviet missile sites.

19

Administration of the National Security Education Act

In April 1992, Secretary of Defense Richard Cheney officially established the National Security Education Program Office (NSEPO) in the Pentagon. Implementation of the NSEA was delegated to Dwane P. Andrews, assistant secretary for command, control, communications, and intelligence (ASD [C3I]), who reported directly to Cheney. Martin Hurwitz, a veteran of the DOD, was appointed administrator of the NSEPO on 12 May 1992, and Charlene King, a former staff member of the Senate Intelligence Committee and professor, was named director of external affairs and was to serve as executive secretary for the NSEB when the board was formally constituted. An interim office was set up in the Pentagon with six staff assigned from the Defense Intelligence Agency.

In its first year, the NSEPO widely publicized the NSEA, established its bona fides with the U.S. academic community, and secured requisite documents, approvals, and clearances to set up the NSEB and begin the grants program. These efforts were hindered by the technical flaws in appropriations legislation and by President Bush's dalliance in nominating board members. The administration did not give initial strong support to the "Boren initiative," and when the presidential election heated up, the NSEA received little notice. Nevertheless, Hurwitz and King proceeded to plan for the implementation of the act, preparing the pieces of the NSEA puzzle for the day when they could be put together in a systematic way and the grants programs launched.

From the beginning, "national security" has been given a broad definition by NSEPO executives. King speaks of the concept "reaching out to every aspect of society" and including new sensibilities to cultural, demographic, economic, and environmental factors.[1] President Bush's National Security Strategy of August 1991 spoke of security needs in similarly fresh conceptualizations. The strategy dealt with intelligence requirements through the end of the century and advocated a thorough examination of the mission, role, and priorities of the national security community.[2] Three closely related areas were emphasized: economics, foreign affairs, and defense.

With the "new" national security as a mandate, Hurwitz and his staff, in consultation with higher education associations, began writing regulations for the NSEA. When the regulations are completed, they must be submitted for a 30-day congressional review period.

Since its inception, the NSEPO has been besieged with inquiries about the program. During the first year of operations, the NSEPO staff made some 3,000 formal written responses to inquiries and participated in over 270 symposia, meetings, and conferences on the "Boren initiative." Hurwitz and King met regularly with a group of advisors from the academic community, known as the "Breakfast Club," which became a useful forum of communications for both the government and the academy.[3]

The NSEB, technically an advisory committee, was required to have a charter by the Federal Advisory Committee Act. The board could not meet or take any action until such a charter was filed with Cheney and "with standing committees of Senate and House having legislative jurisdiction" over defense. The charter was approved by the Office of the Secretary of Defense (OSD) on 23 June and notice of the establishment of the board appeared in the *Federal Register* on 2 July 1992.[4]

Governmental representatives of the NSEB will be at the assistant secretary level and will be joined by six public members, "experts in the fields of international, language, and area studies education," to be named by the president.[5] Constituting the board has not been easy. Shortly before the end of his term, on 7 January 1993, President Bush named the four public members of the NSEB authorized under the original act. These recess appointments were to be valid only for the first session of the One Hundred Third Congress, about one year, and did not require confirmation by the Senate.[6] The commissions of these Bush recess appointees were never tendered, however, and during the first year (1993) of the new democratic administration, President Clinton named no one to the board. Finally, in January 1994, the president nominated six public members for the NSEB. Timely confirmation of the Clinton nominees by the Senate will enable the NSEB to meet in early 1994 to begin making recommendations on qualifications, criteria, and critical areas for grants.

Recommendations to the NSEB will come from at least two other organizations authorized in the charter to assist in implementing the act:

the working group and the advisory panel. King chairs a senior-level working group of representatives of the governmental agencies of the NSEB. When funds are available, nongovernmental members of the working group will be appointed as consultants. The working group, which meets at the call of the chairman, will coordinate board activities and select members of the advisory panel.

Under the charter, advisory subgroups may be constituted to provide advice, guidance, and recommendations to the board.[7] The first such subgroup will be the advisory panel, which will be composed of some 20 consultants representing major fields of international education. Principal educational associations have been asked to recommend possible members for the advisory panel, which will play a prominent role in developing program alternatives and in determining critical areas, priorities, national security needs, and shortfalls in fields of academic study. In addition, the program director may appoint individual consultants to advise and support the board.

The advisory panel will serve two principal purposes: to provide expertise and advice to the NSEB and program staff concerning all elements of the NSEA and to facilitate communication between the NSEB and the higher education community.

To assist in getting pilot programs started, Hurwitz envisioned six preliminary studies to be conducted by his staff in consultation with educators to determine national needs in international education:

1. An "ethno-linguistic baseline, an ethnic, cultural and linguistic atlas of the world (in contrast to an atlas of political boundaries) to identify cultures and languages that might be studied."[8] The Federal Research Division of the Library of Congress, assisted by the Smithsonian Institution, has been selected to carry on this research.
2. An academic baseline that shows higher education's language and area teaching and research capacity.
3. A survey of where students study abroad — both ethnocultural areas and countries.
4. An assessment by the intelligence community of commerce, foreign affairs, and defense during the next three to five years to ascertain the most likely areas to generate problems, crises, and dangers to the world community.
5. A survey of academic deficiencies in languages, area studies, and international education. A brief survey of this type was conducted in March 1992 by the National Endowment for the

Humanities. Hurwitz envisioned a subsequent "full-blown study."

6. Assessments by government agencies and educators of their personnel needs during the next five to ten years and of the international study skills they will look for in new employees.[9]

These proposed studies will provide justification for the board's recommendations of critical areas. In addition, they will help lay the foundation for a strategy of NSEA investment for the combined efforts of the federal sector and colleges and universities in significant fields of international education.

Plans for a nationwide survey of higher education's resources in international education already exist. Included among a substantial number of useful publications and materials about the IEA are detailed strategies to conduct a national baseline study to assess the status of international education and to evaluate progress made over time in various international fields. These plans need only a fine tuning by the NSEPO staff to make them applicable to the NSEA.

The National Endowment for the Humanities (NEH) Preliminary Survey included a review of data from the Modern Language Association, the National Foreign Language Center, the CIE, and the Intelligence Community Foreign Language Committee in identifying shortfalls in language and area studies "that reasonable people would agree were real."[10] The NEH recommended that NSEA pilot programs be limited to nine critical language and area groups: Chinese (all widely spoken dialects), Japanese, East and Southeast Asian (emphasis on Korean, Indonesian, Vietnamese, Thai, Tibetan), South Asian (emphasis on Hindi, Urdu, Bengali), Russian, Other European (emphasis on Polish, Serbo-Croatian, Czech, Ukrainian, Bulgarian, Romanian, Hungarian), Arabic, other Near Eastern (emphasis on modern Hebrew, Turkish, Persian), and African (emphasis on Swahili, Hausa, Yoruba).[11]

Within the parameters of the critical language and area groups, Hurwitz foresaw grants focusing on "developing capacity to overcome shortfalls and on increasing the numbers of institutions that teach international and area studies." He also anticipated grants being approved to set up programs for intensive language instruction and for critical areas now covered poorly or not covered at all; expand and strengthen fragile programs; maintain and expand the skills of international study experts; form academic-business teams to develop strategies to open foreign markets to U.S. products; and focus on secondary school teachers and their most promising students.[12]

THE NSEA IN THE CLINTON ADMINISTRATION

The reorganization of the DOD by the Clinton administration produced significant changes in philosophy and personnel for the implementation of the NSEA. The new secretary of defense, former Congressman Les Aspin (D-WI), is a friend of Senator Boren. The two worked closely together during the "Irangate" hearings when A pin,was chairman of the House Armed Services Committee. When Aspin took his oath of office as secretary, Boren was present to congratulate him and to remind him of

One of Aspen's first acts was to issue a Decision Memorandum delegating authority for the NSEA program to the under secretary of policy. This action removed implementation of the act from the intelligence part of the defense hierarchy, ASD (C3I), and transferred it to the assistant secretary for democracy and peace keeping (ASD [D&P]) — a move reassuring to academics. The OMB earlier had "scored" the NSEA as a defense budget line.

On 1 April 1993, Charlene King was named acting administration, and on 1 May she was appointed director of the National Security Education Program. Bob Slater, a political scientist formerly at the Defense Intelligence College, became the deputy director. Shortly after King's appointment the NSEPO was moved to a new location in Roslyn, Virginia, and she commissioned a number of systematic statistical studies to aid the work of the NSEB. She also disseminated a formal working paper on pilot program models and guidelines to the higher education community after extensive reviews and requests for comments from a broadly representative group of educators. With the imminent appointment and confirmation of Clinton appointees to the board, King foresees NSEA grants being made for pilot programs during the 1994–95 academic year.[13]

King was to report directly to Morton Halperin, the ASD (D&P) nominee, who served in the late 1960s in the Pentagon and on the staff of the National Security Council. Halperin, with a Ph.D. from Yale, is a respected author and professor whose experience as a senior fellow at the Brookings Institution, director of the Washington office of the American Civil Liberties Union, and MacArthur Foundation Fellow should have highly qualified him to provide policy leadership to the NSEA. These plans changed on 10 January 1994 when Halperin withdrew from consideration by the Senate.

The new lines of authority have legislative ramifications for the NSEA. The Armed Services Committees, bodies probably more favorably disposed to the act than the not-always-friendly Intelligence Committees, now will vet budget and related financial matters of them NSEA. Any legislative changes in the act still will go through the Intelligence Committees, but NSEPO officials are optimistic that the NSEA will fare better on Capitol Hill.

The first annual report on the status of the NSEA programs during fiscal year 1992 was submitted to President Clinton and to the Congress on 7 April 1993. In addition, an irritating burr under the NSEA saddle was removed during the first session of the One Hundred Third Congress. A 3 December 1992 DOD General Counsel staff officer opinion had stated that the secretary of defense needed a provision in an appropriation act in order to obligate money from the National Security Education Trust Fund. Language granting authority to obligate $10 million from the trust fund was included in the supplemental appropri-ations act for 1993. The House approved the bill containing this provision in May 1993 and the Senate approved a similar bill containing the same provision in June. This bill was enacted by Congress and signed by the president on 2 July 1993.

The Clinton White House appears to give a higher priority to the implementation of the NSEA than did the Bush regime. The support of the new administration can be demonstrated by its dispatch in appointing and lobbying for Senate confirmation of the six public members to the NSEB.

PROBLEMS OF NSEA

Three interrelated problems, none of which are insurmountable, becloud the future of the NSEA: higher education's perceptions of the ties of government intelligence agencies to the act, the commitment of the academy to international studies during the nascence of the NSEA and the building of its trust fund, and the dilemma caused by the 1990 budget agreement that will keep a potentially opulent source of support for international education locked in the "defense" category. Each of these problems needs to be addressed during the first year of the implemen-tation of the NSEA.

Even though the CIA is in the throes of reorganization and is seeking acceptance as a benign arm of the government bureaucracy, its legacy of covert activities and infiltration of the academic world will be difficult for some academicians to forget. These concerns surfaced during the initial meeting on the proposed NSEA in July 1991 and were articulated by Jack Egle, president of the Council for International Educational Exchange, and by the presidents of three scholarly organizations in letters to Boren.[14]

Some area studies groups argue that any connection, real or perceived, between the academic community — particularly students and faculty working overseas — and defense and intelligence agencies could compromise the reputations of researchers at home and abroad, close off access to overseas research sites, and threaten the safety of faculty, students, and colleagues with whom they work.[15]

In the past, the credibility of U.S. scholars in a number of countries was undermined by programs through which the intelligence community co-opted scholars to contribute to intelligence collection or covert action goals. In other countries, credibility has been undermined by unfounded rumors or allegations of such co-optation.[16]

During House floor debate on the act, Representative Don Edwards (D-CA) said suspicions are likely to persist. He recalled that "great damage was done" to the CIA by its efforts to gain "influence in universities" through covert funding in the 1960s and 1970s.[17]

As a result, the intelligence card will have to be dealt deftly. A cordon sanitaire between the CIA and higher education may have to be maintained until stereotypes are torn down and the bona fides of a kindlier, more gentle intelligence community are established. On the other hand, the DOD, as the third-largest supporter of scientific research in higher education, is a familiar government partner on major university campuses (perhaps too familiar to those charging overhead expenses). Open-mindedness and flexibility on the part of all parties to the NSEA will be required.

The source of appropriations for the trust fund should be made clear: money comes from cuts that Congress made in the intelligence budget. Some of the funds came from reductions or deletions of classified intelligence projects, but such dollars are thoroughly cleansed of stains of secrecy before being deposited in a Treasury trust fund that may be used only for higher education. Hurwitz further explained that the funds are not defense monies; the DOD only handles deposits, withdrawals, and investments.

In response to concerns of the academic community about intelligence and DOD influences on the NSEA, Hurwitz made the point that no intelligence agency will have a role in making awards. All decisions on academic awards will be made by independent institutions, panels, and peer groups. Most academicians would agree that the use of regrant or other peer review mechanisms should enable the program to operate in a manner acceptable to the academic community. Such intermediary organizations will allocate funding, provide a buffer between defense and intelligence sectors of government and academic recipients of NSEA support, and assess merit in NSEA competitions.[18]

Merit review is widely used to allocate grant funds in the academic community. It provides for the appointment of independent panels of specialists who can make judgments on academic and scholarly merit of proposals and individuals. Such a review separates the selection process from the institutional interest and biases of the sponsoring and administering institutions with respect to specific cases.[19]

Another concern of the academic sector is that the NSEA board, in defining critical world areas based on intelligence projections, might prescribe too narrowly the criteria for allocating funds. Such action could compromise the independence of academic scholarship by replacing scholarly judgments about the research and educational needs of the various academic disciplines with judgments based on national security objectives. International studies involves mainly basic research, providing a general understanding of other societies, and only rarely does it focus on a specific problem with findings aimed at direct policy relevance. The use of intermediary organizations, such as the NEH, the Library of Congress, and the Smithsonian Institution, in making studies to define critical areas should help alleviate such anxieties of academicians.

Representatives of area studies groups expressed specific concerns about the presence of the director of the CIA in the oversight of NSEA programs and the designation of the DIC as the agency responsible for administering the program under the original legislation. The inclusion of the director of central intelligence on the board was probably required by skeptical senators to lend credibility to Boren's claim that the program would serve national security needs. The addition of three more board members as part of the 1992 amendments to NSEA should lessen the perceived significance of the CIA director's oversight role. The DIC's administrative role was eliminated by the 1992 amendments to the act.

Although government can stimulate, give shape and direction, and provide large-scale financing, the ideas and activities that make up international education are mainly the province of colleges and universities. The responsibility is fully upon higher education to make a decisive contribution to the further shaping of the NSEA initiatives in international education. What happens in the years ahead may well depend significantly on how the academic community now responds.

That response should not be to abandon international programs and projects in the squeeze of tight university budgets during a recession.

Yet, that is precisely a current concern voiced by Robert H. Atwell, president of the ACE. Atwell warns that it is more important than ever to preserve and even expand international activities in the face of neo-isolationism and anxiety about domestic problems.[20] It would be most inauspicious for universities to be infirm of purpose — to cut back on international studies just as the NSEA reaches take-off stage. Opponents of the bill will be watching for such signs of weakness.

The 1990 budget summit agreement that set strict limits on new spending tied Congress' hands to an unprecedented degree. Defense spending was locked away, unavailable for redirection to needy domestic programs even after the collapse of the USSR. Any change had to be mutually agreed to by the Congress and the president.

During 1991, Senator Byrd wrote President Bush, asking the White House to work with Congress to change the budget agreement to shift defense funds to domestic programs. The administration would not break the deal.[21] The deadlock ended, however, and the so-called firewalls between budget categories came tumbling down with the adjournment of the One Hundred Second Congress followed soon afterward by Bush's departure. The Clinton administration, faced with mounting pressures to cut taxes and shift defense spending to home-front programs, will inevitably develop some new patterns of spending. The president now will have more latitude in making budget choices. One such choice might be to join the NSEA with other international education programs in a domestic budget category administered by the ED, as originally proposed by Boren.

NOTES

1. Telephone interview with Charlene King, 3 March 1992.

2. See also President Bush's National Security Directive No. 29, issued November 1991; Elaine Sciolino, "C.I.A. Casting About for New Missions," *New York Times*, 4 February 1992, pp. A1, A4; Stansfield Turner, "Intelligence for a New World Order," *Foreign Affairs* 70 (Fall 1991): 150–66. In Congress, Boren and McCurdy have offered their own sweeping restructuring plan for all intelligence operations. See "Spying a New Game," *Tulsa Tribune*, 5 February 1992, p. 1.

3. Members of the "Breakfast Club" were Richard Brecht, National Foreign Language Center; John Deupree, The College Board; David Edwards, Joint National Committee on Languages; John Hammer, National Humanities Alliance; Kay King, Association of Professional Schools of International Affairs; Norman Peterson, Liaison Group for International Education Exchange; Cassandra Pyle, Council for International Exchange of Scholars; and John Vaughn, Association of American Universities.

4. 57 Fed Reg 29475, 2 July 1992.

5. House Permanent Select Committee on Intelligence, Intelligence Authorization Act, Fiscal Year 1992, Conference Report, H.R. 2038, Report 102-327, One Hundred Second Congress, First Session (18 November 1991), p. 15.

6. It took President Bush 13 months from the passage of the NDEA on 6 December 1991 until he announced his four nominees to the NSEB on 7 January 1993: Steven Muller, chairman of the 21st Century Foundation in Washington, D.C., and the former president of Johns Hopkins University; S. William Pattis, president of NTC Publishing Group of Illinois; John P. Roche, professor of civilization and foreign affairs at the Fletcher School of Law at Tufts University; and Richard F. Stolz, a consultant from Bethesda, Maryland, and former director of operations at the CIA. The president's dawdling created a situation analogous to that of President John Adams' appointment of the "midnight judges" in the closing hours of his administration in 1801. The commissions of the Bush Four were never tendered before the Republican administration came to an end — circumstances similar to those in the cases of William Marbury and other Adams appointees whose commissions were not delivered by the Jefferson administration. The Clinton White House did not tender the commissions to the NSEB nominees. Two of the Bush appointees had connections to the IEA. John P. Roche served on President Lyndon Johnson's staff during the time of the passage of the IEA, and Steven Muller, while on the faculty of Cornell University, worked with the author in coordinating a one-day regional conference on the IEA in 1967.

7. Charter of the NSEB, p. 3.

8. Telephone interview with Martin Hurwitz, 23 January 1992.

9. "Presentation: Overview of the National Security Act of 1991," 1 February 1993, pp. 14–16. The Library of Congress proposal, "A Global Ethnocultural-Linguistic Baseline," was submitted to the NSEPO by Louis R. Mortimer, chief, Federal Research Division, on 17 September 1992.

10. NEH, Summary, National Endowment for the Humanities Preliminary Survey, 29 January 1993.

11. Letter, Celeste Colgan, deputy chairman, NEH, to Hurwitz, 16 March 1992.

12. "Presentation," p. 19.

13. Telephone interview with Charlene King, 4 May 1993.

14. Paul Desruisseaux, "Congress Approves Program to Support Overseas Study," *Chronicle of Higher Education*, 4 December 1991, p. A55; "Dispatch Case," *Chronicle of Higher Education*, 25 March 1992, p. A35. The presidents of the three groups were Edmund Keller of the African Studies Association, Lars Schoultz of the Latin American Studies Association, and Barbara Aswad of the Middle East Studies Association of North America. In 1993, Professor David Wiley of Michigan State University continued to express concerns about the deleterious effect of ties between intelligence agencies and the academic enterprise in overseas African studies. See also David MacMichael, "Spooks on Campus," *Nation* 254: 780 (8 June 1992).

15. Memo, Vaughn, p. 3.

16. Stanley J. Heginbotham, *The National Security Education Program: A Review and Analysis* (New York: SSRC, 1992), p. 12.

17. *Congressional Record*, 20 November 1991, p. H10629.

18. Memo, Vaughn, pp. 3–4.

19. Heginbotham, *The National Security Education Program*, p. 7.

20. Paul Desruisseaux, "President of American Council Urges Colleges Not to Let Economic Strains Cause Cutbacks in International Programs," *Chronicle of Higher Education*, 29 January 1992, pp. A38, A40.

21. *Congressional Quarterly*, 21 December 1991, pp. 3728–29; see also Jim Sasser, "Recycle the Budget Agreement," *New York Times*, 5 January 1992, p. E13.

20

The Magnanimous One Hundred Second Congress

The One Hundred Second Congress, disparaged by some political commentators as the ineffective and unproductive epitome of governmental gridlock in the final years of the Bush administration, may be more fondly remembered by the international education community, because during its two sessions in 1991 and 1992, the One Hundred Second Congress terminated a quarter century's constriction of federal support of international education and spawned a national revival of interest in foreign studies and exchange programs. The capstone of the One Hundred Second's remarkable accomplishments was the passage of the NSEA, one of the most significant expansions of federal international education programs since the establishment of the Fulbright Program in 1946 and the Title VI program of the NDEA in 1958. In addition to the Boren initiative, the One Hundred Second Congress provided substantial funding increases for USIA's exchange programs and amended the Higher Education Act to strengthen the DE's role in international education. Altogether, the One Hundred Second Congress appropriated over $256 million in new funds for international education.

In its first session, Congress provided $150 million to establish the NSEA. In addition, funding for USIA's educational and cultural exchanges was increased by more than $21 million (or 10.8 percent), from $173.151 million in fiscal year 1991 to $194.232 million for fiscal year 1992. This pattern of unprecedented support continued into the second session, when Congress appropriated over $80 million in new funds for international education and exchange. Most significant was a $50 million exchange program that was included as part of a technical assistance package for the former republics of the Soviet Union. Funding for USIA exchanges also was increased by approximately $30 million.[1]

Much of the impetus for the new and expanded exchange programs came from the collapse of the USSR. The U.S. State Department saw unprecedented opportunities to encourage peaceful change and democratic reform in the newly independent nations of the former Soviet Union. Central to this strategy was public diplomacy with its emphasis on educational exchanges. As a result, tens of millions of dollars of international affairs funds were redirected by Congress to democracy-building educational and cultural exchange programs. Most of the redirected funds increased appropriations for USIA and USAID.

A $50 million exchange program with the former states of the Soviet Union was approved by Congress as part of the Freedom Support Act, a package of technical assistance to the former USSR, funded under foreign operations appropriations. The exchange program, proposed originally by Senator Bill Bradley (D-NJ), a former Rhodes scholar, and Representative Jim Leach (R-IA) as the Freedom Exchange Act, is intended to provide the citizens of the former Soviet Union, particularly the younger generations, with exposure to democratic institutions and to the U.S. way of life.

The $50 million approved for exchanges is one of the largest such initiatives for a specific world region in U.S. history. Of the total appropriation, $20 million will provide for secondary school exchanges and the remaining $30 million will be divided among exchanges of undergraduate and graduate students, farmers and other agricultural practitioners, and local and regional government officials.

Most of the funds will be used to bring students to the United States, but about 15 percent of exchange money will provide opportunities for Americans to study abroad. The appropriations conference report "strongly recommends" that no less than 40 percent of the available scholarships go to women. USIA has been designated to administer all of the educational and cultural exchanges included in this package. Although a very large initiative, the final outcome represents only a portion of the original Bradley-Leach proposal, which was to have been funded at over $1 billion over a period of five years.

On 6 October 1992, President Bush signed the fiscal year 1993 appropriation for the USIA, including a total appropriation for exchange programs of just over $223 million — an increase of more than $29 million (or 15 percent) over previous year funding. Combined with the $30–$40 million coming to USIA exchanges from the USAID appropriation to fund the Bradley exchange initiative for the former USSR, USIA's exchange programs will have an overall increase of between $60 and $70 million, the largest single-year increase in the history of USIA's exchange programs.

Within the $29 million increase, $16 million is for the Fulbright and other academic exchange programs, $3 million for the Near and Middle East Research and Training Program, and $9.25 million for a general enhancement to be distributed among USIA's exchange programs at the agency's discretion; other individual programs received incremental increases.

Much of the credit for the increase goes to Senator Ernest Hollings (D-SC), chairman of the Senate appropriations subcommittee, which funds USIA. Hollings originally proposed an increase of almost $40 million above fiscal year 1992 funding, of which $30 million was to go to the Fulbright program to expand exchanges with the former Soviet Union and to respond to a recommendation included in the Board of Foreign Scholarship's White Paper to restore the number of graduate fellowships, a number that has eroded since the program's inception.[2] Still, an increase of more than $100 million in educational and cultural exchanges over a two-year period was an enviable accomplishment for Hollings and his colleagues.

Over the same time frame, the ED's international education programs received a 16 percent increase of $6.7 million (from $34.7 million in fiscal year 1991 to $41.376 million in fiscal year 1993). In addition, Congress in 1992 appropriated $2.5 million for an important new pilot exchange program with the European Community (EC) based on the EC's innovative European Community Action Scheme for the Mobility of University Students (ERASMUS). The program will be administered through the Fund for the Improvement of Postsecondary Education (FIPSE) at the ED and will support joint curricular development between academic departments at participating institutions in the United States and the EC, which will ensure that students will receive credit for their study-abroad program at these institutions. This will be particularly useful for students in nontra-ditional fields of study abroad, such as business and sciences, who often do not receive credit for study abroad and, therefore, have to lengthen their program of study. The additional time and money involved in doing this has been seen to be one of the major inhibitions to study abroad for students in these types of disciplines.[3]

Title VI and Fulbright programs of ED's CIE, after getting a $5 million increase during the first session, received little more in fiscal year 1993. Domestic international education and foreign language programs were augmented by $1.6 million, most of which was earmarked for specific programs. Funding for the FLAS fellowships and for the component of Fulbright-Hays administered by ED were cut by approximately 2 percent each (down to $12.767 million and $5.843 million, respectively).

Within the firewalls of the Budget Enforcement Act, the One Hundred Second Congress, with Senators Boren, Bradley, and Hollings leading the way, had been kind to international education. Appropriations from the defense and foreign categories were generous, and even the compressed domestic category yielded increased funding for programs of the ED's CIE.

In addition to boosting appropriations, Congress authorized major revisions to the Higher Education Act that extend authority for ED higher education programs for five years. Among provisions relating to international education are changes in federal financial aid programs authorized under Title IV that will enable many more students to use their financial aid to study abroad on programs approved by their home institutions. Extensive changes also were made to Title VI that now allow the ED to support development and enrichment of study abroad programs and U.S. overseas research centers that provide facilities for U.S. researchers in many parts of the world. On 24 July 1992, President Bush signed into law the revisions to the Higher Education Act.[4]

Another accomplishment of the One Hundred Second Congress was the mandating of a new inventory of international education programs in the national government. "Reaganization" and changes during the Bush administration altered organization and operating arrangements in the federal bureaucracy since 1980, when Leestma's office published its last catalogue of governmental programs in international education. As a result, responsibility for programs and policies related to international studies of considerable importance to colleges and universities is strewn across many units of the federal government. To determine where duplication or overlap may exist in programs, the House Committee on Foreign Affairs initiated a study by the General Accounting Office (GAO) of all educational, cultural, and training programs currently being administered through federal agencies. The GAO inventory was submitted to congress in mid-1993.

NOTES

1. *International Exchange Policy Monitor*, Washington, D.C., Liaison Group for International Educational Exchange, 17 August 1992, pp. 2–4.

2. *International Exchange Policy Monitor*, Washington, D.C., Liaison Group for International Educational Exchange, 15 October 1992, pp. 4–5.

3. Paul Desruisseaux, "U.S. and European Community Agree to Try New Types of Collaboration and Exchange," *Chronicle of Higher Education*, 12 May 1993, pp. A43, A45; U.S. Department of Education, Fund for the Improvement of Postsecondary Education (FIPSE), Information and Application Procedures for the Special Focus Project: Higher Education Collaboration between the United States and the European Community, Application Deadline: July 20, 1993; Charles H. Karelis, "The New Europe: Replace U.S. Indifference with Collaboration," *Chronicle of Higher Education*, 16 October 1991, pp. B1–B2.

4. Higher Education Amendments of 1992, Pub. L. 102-325, Title VI — International Education Programs, 106 Stat. 720-737 (23 July 1992); see also Miriam A. Kazanjian, "Section by Section Summary of Final Amendments to HEA-Title VI, International Education Programs, Higher Education Amendments of 1992" (8 July 1992).

21

The Future and the Three Streams

At the beginning of the 1990s, the topography of international studies in the United States appeared little changed since the days of the IEA in 1966. From the myriad rivers, tributaries, branches, and creeks that rise from the federal headspring in Washington, D.C., meandered two streams of international education: the sluggish affluent of exchange, a tributary of the stately river of diplomacy; and the dammed narrow stream of the CIE, a channel of the ED water system. Both international education streams receded during the drought years of the Reagan and Bush administrations, and in following their course, many observers thought they were up a creek.

Nevertheless, the faithful of the academy made annual pilgrimages to the streams in a rough semblance to the Hindu festival of Kumbh Mela. Although thousands of fakirs and sadhus from universities and colleges throughout the land thronged the banks, the federal brahmins dispensed the holy waters of the streams to only a chosen few. Obese sadhus from national resource centers, most of whom had gotten fat from the handouts of patron foundations when generosity was in vogue, carried more weight in the crush to reach the banks of the stream, and they pushed aside worthy devout who were overlooked by the brahmins. Although the corpulent complained that they were losing weight each year, they were rotund compared with their famished colleagues who never received the federal nectar. Proceedings turned ugly when push came to shove at the Mela. Noted one guru: "Never have so many squabbled over so little." Said another, "The smaller the stakes, the meaner the political battles."[1] Meanwhile, the benefactors in Congress watched the annual debacle, wrung their hands, and murmured "'tis a pity." And so it went until 1991.

During the same era that federal waters remained stagnant, there was a third stream, a subterranean river developing underground. Under the impetus of the IEA, hydrologists in the nation's universities and colleges began to channel their international brooks, burns, and rills into institutional waterways. Some new springs were uncovered and their flow directed into local bayous. Fed by contributions from state and private sources and frequently by institutional funds, the international waterworks were submerged in the general campus milieu. As a result, the incremental growth of underground streams was so gradual and so widespread that few were aware of the magnitude of the developing nationwide watercourse. Connections between the new bourns are tenuous, sometimes amounting to no more than irrigation ditches cared for by a single field hand. Taken together, however, the international flow of the nation's universities and colleges create a mighty subterranean river. The stream needs direction to be used to its best effect. With some master planning, coordinating, and crosscutting of channels by the national equivalent of the U.S. Corps of Engineers, the subterranean river might emerge as a rapidly flowing stream with the power to engage in widespread downcutting of the banks and shoals of international ineptitude.

The tectonic shifts brought about by the appropriations of the One Hundred Second Congress in 1991–92 altered the topography of international education. David Boren, the Moses of the lost children of international education, struck the rock of the CIA with his staff and loosed the flow of aspirations of international studies long pent up behind the floodgate of domestic budgets into a new stream. Though yet a trickle considering its titan source, the NSEA stream was of sufficient size to ease the pressure at the ED Kumbh Mela. The previously spurned faithful of the academy gathered at the River Boren and prepared to make libations.

Meanwhile, Congress authorized a greater flow into the dammed stream of the ED, and portly mendicants from national resource centers found more room at the water's edge, with some competitors seeking to take the waters elsewhere. The banks of the affluent of exchange were expanded and currents from the river of diplomacy diverted to it to transform the once-sluggish affluence into a mighty stream. Bill Bradley redirected torrents from foreign operations into the same exchange stream to make it the most affluent of the federal tides of international education. Ernest Hollings could take pride in restoring the exchange affluence to a magnitude similar to that created by master hydrologist William Fulbright in 1946.

The challenge to international education in the 1990s is to make sense of the new patterns of waterways. Three federal streams, those of the NSEA, those of Title VI of the Higher Education Act and other older international programs administered by the ED, and those of public diplomacy and related exchange activities of the Department of State flow parallel out of Washington, where the fountains of the great rivers lie. Where and how they will connect with the subterranean river of universities and colleges must be carefully thought out. The need for coordination in channeling the federal streams to avoid duplication of effort is obvious. The sums of the impressive but disjointed parts need to add up to a larger national interest.

Three streams, although currently required by budget constraints, are not necessarily better than one over the long haul. Ultimately, it will make more sense to have direction or at least coordination of all international education streams in a single office. The establishment of a center for international studies to administer the NSEA outside the Pentagon may be the catalyst needed to bring about the consolidation of coordination of all federal international programs, including those identified in GAO's 1993 inventory. With the secretaries of the Departments of Defense, State, and Education and the director of USIA serving on the NSEB, that board offers a sterling opportunity to coordinate the diverse programs. An expanded NSEA center could "lead and support an integrated, comprehensive and con-certed effort to meet the nation's international needs."[2] The studies and assessments being carried on by the NSEPO could create a grid of information with which the federal government and higher education could plan adjustments to cover the uneven distribution of disciplines, area studies, exchanges, and specialties resulting from the laissez-faire system that has so far existed.

The NSEB could support new programs designed to fill existing gaps, provide for needed partnerships, and promote creative responses to new international challenges. It could complement and expand existing capacity, creating important competence in critical functions now receiving little support. Under such leadership, a new mosaic of international education — one better conceived and executed — might begin to take shape.

Again, a model from the IEA of 1966 may be useful. The IEA's CEC was to serve as the focal point for leadership in international education. Governed by a presidentially appointed National Advisory Committee, the center was to have three main functions: to channel communications between missions abroad and the U.S. educational community, to direct authorized federal programs, and to assist public and private agencies conducting international education programs.[3]

Once (if ever?) major funding for international studies comes from a single source or budget category, the creation of a new CEC would reduce duplication, increase efficiency, and save money. A CEC separated from controls by the DOD or Department of State also would do much to remove possible suspicions at home or abroad that U.S. institutions and scholars in foreign lands are mere extensions of U.S. policy, or, perhaps, such suspicions will fade away under the new world order.

More importantly, a CEC could coordinate a long-term strategy of investment for the combined efforts of the federal sector and colleges and universities in significant fields of international education. *A national strategy* for international education would provide more lasting benefit to the country than an assortment of programs with short-term political objectives. A decade-long investment would bring more order to the contemporary haphazard mosaic of international studies in the United States and would have a profound impact on the provincialism of U.S. campuses.

The magnitude of the investment is significant. Twenty-five years ago it was thought that an annual appropriation of $90 million starting in the third year of the IEA would be needed to make "any pervasive impact" on colleges and universities in this country.[4] Taking inflation into account, the $90 million annual appropriation would today equal more than $200 million. The 1993 combined budgets of the NSEA, ED programs, and USIA's public diplomacy have increased to $350 million, a sum greater than the international education goals of a quarter of a century ago. Expenditures for international programs on the individual campuses have also grown significantly since the 1960s.

Under these circumstances, if federal appropriations for international education can be maintained at the 1993 level during the next decade, international education may play the significant role foreseen for it by the supporters of the IEA. The new NSEA, the 1992 amendments to the Higher Education Act, and the revised programs of educational and cultural exchange provide the mechanisms to realize most of the goals enunciated in the IEA. The NSEB can coordinate the distribution of funds to the most-needed programs. If the NSEA Trust Fund can be brought up, over time, to the $350 million level envisioned by Boren and Byrd, the annual appropriation from the fund could address national security education needs as well as bring new strength to undergraduate, graduate, and international programs on the campuses. Funding of Higher Education Act Title VI International and Foreign Language Studies programs at the fiscal year 1993 authorization of $80 million, an increase of $31.7 million, would provide adequate support for graduate and undergraduate national centers. Relatively small increases in appropriations for Title VI Business and International Education programs would engender an expanded global perspective in many of the nation's colleges of business. A ten-year sustenance approximating the 1993 level of support for educational and cultural exchanges would have a profound impact on the international "mix" of students and faculty on many U.S. campuses.

The good news for the international education enterprise is that the logjam of federal funding is broken. Although financial support will not extend to all institutions of higher education or be distributed in amounts deemed sufficient by some recipients, federal grants will be available, as they never have been before, to assist many colleges and universities. Compared with the prospects of only a few years ago, international education is in a new age, perhaps a golden one. The onus is on the higher education community to react responsibly to the new federal initiatives.

In light of President Clinton's comprehensive program of tax increases and spending cuts designed to trim the federal deficit and to revitalize the nation's economy,[5] it is incumbent upon the international studies enterprise to justify the importance of its programs. An annual assessment of results from federal expenditures for international programs takes on added significance in a time of budget cuts at the federal level and of reduced appropriations for higher education in many states. The time is no longer right (if it ever was) for the traditional "international education is in a state of crisis" lament or for arguments that "the national interest" requires exponential growth of academic international studies. President Clinton's plea for painful sacrifice has knocked over the bottomless trough of demand. Now it is the turn of trustees, academic senates, deans, presidents, chancellors, provosts, department chairmen, and curriculum committees to utilize well the available grants and to press for the maintenance of a long-term federal investment in international education of such magnitude as to make a difference on U.S. campuses.

If this is done, the laudable goals of the IEA of 1966 may at last be realized in the 1990s. Those goals remain salient in the post–Cold War world, where still

A knowledge of other countries is of the utmost importance in promoting mutual understanding and cooperation between nations;

strong American educational resources are a necessary base for strengthening our relations with other countries;

this and future generations of Americans should be assured ample opportunity to develop to the fullest extent possible their intellectual capacities in all areas of knowledge pertaining to other countries, peoples, and cultures;

it is both necessary and appropriate for the Federal Government to assist in the development of resources for international studies and research, to assist in the development of resources and trained personnel in academic and professional fields, and to coordinate the existing and future programs of the Federal Government in international education, to meet the requirements of world leadership.[6]

In the post–Cold War world of great peril and promise, international education, as John Gardner has observed, "will help us to lessen the peril and to increase the promise — not only for our Nation but for people all over the world."[7]

NOTES

1. Rose L. Hayden, *Federal Support for International Education: Assessing the Options* (Washington, D.C.: National Council on Foreign Studies, August 1985), p. 106.

2. CAFLIS, "International Competence: A Key to America's Future," Executive Summary of the Plan of Action, December 1989; see also "CAFLIS Update: The Final Stretch," 7 April 1989; "CAFLIS Update: Consensus Reached," 14 July 1989; "Proposal for a New National Endowment for International Education and Competence as Presented by Working Group I of CAFLIS," no date, enclosed in Letter, Smuckler to Vestal, 11 August 1989.

3. Center for Educational Cooperation, Draft OMP-OS, 25 March 1966, "Notebook Concerning International Education and Health, 1966," LBJ Library.

4. Hearings before the Task Force on International Education of the Committee on Education and Labor, "International Education," 30 March–7 April 1966, U.S. House of Representatives, Eighty-ninth Congress, Second Session, p. 330.

5. R. W. Apple, Jr., "Clinton Plan to Remake the Economy Seeks to Tax Energy and Big Incomes," *New York Times*, 18 February 1993, pp. 1, 11–14.

6. 20 U.S.C. sec. 1171 et seq.; 80 Stat. 1066–1073 (1966).

7. Testimony of John Gardner, Hearings before the Task Force on International Education of the Committee on Education and Labor, "International Education," 30 March–7 April 1966, U.S. House of Representatives, Eighty-ninth Congress, Second Session, p. 19.

Appendix I:
Public Papers of President Lyndon B. Johnson about the International Education Act of 1966

Remarks at the Smithson Bicentennial Celebration, September 16, 1965

Mr. Chief Justice, Secretary Ripley, Dr. Carmichael, Bishop Moore, Reverend Campbell, ladies and gentlemen, distinguished scholars from 80 nations:

Amid this pomp and pageantry we have gathered to celebrate a man about whom we know very little but to whom we owe very much. James Smithson was a scientist who achieved no great distinction. He was an Englishman who never visited the United States. He never even expressed a desire to do so.

But this man became our Nation's first great benefactor. He gave his entire fortune to establish this Institution which would serve for the increase and diffusion of knowledge among men.

He had a vision which lifted him ahead of his time — or at least of some politicians of his time. One illustrious United States Senator argued that it was beneath the dignity of the country to accept such gifts from foreigners. Congress debated 8 long years before deciding to receive Smithson's bequest.

JAMES SMITHSON'S LEGACY

Yet James Smithson's life and legacy brought meaning to three ideas more powerful than anyone at that time ever dreamed.

The first idea was that learning respects no geographic boundaries. The Institution bearing his name became the first agency in the United States to promote scientific and scholarly exchange with all the nations of the world.

The second idea was that partnership between Government and private enterprise can serve the greater good of both. The Smithsonian Institution started a new kind of venture in this country, chartered by act of

Congress, maintained by both public funds and private contributions. It inspired a relationship which has grown and flowered in a thousand different ways.

Finally, the Institution financed by Smithson breathed life in the idea that the growth and the spread of learning must be the first work of a nation that seeks to be free.

These ideas have not always gained easy acceptance among those employed in my line of work. The Government official must cope with the daily disorder that he finds in the world around him.

But today, the official, the scholar, and the scientist cannot settle for limited objectives. We must pursue knowledge no matter what the consequences. We must value the tried less than the true.

To split the atom, to launch the rocket, to explore the innermost mysteries and the outermost reaches of the universe these are your God-given chores. And even when you risk bringing fresh disorder to the politics of men and nations, these explorations still must go on.

IDEAS, NOT ARMAMENTS

The men who founded our country were passionate believers in the revolutionary power of ideas.

They knew that once a nation commits itself to the increase and diffusion of knowledge, the real revolution begins. It can never be stopped.

In my own life, I have had cause again and again to bless the chance events which started me as a teacher. In our country and in our time we have recognized, with new passion, that learning is basic to our hopes for America. It is the taproot which gave sustaining life to all of our purposes. And whatever we seek to do to wage the war on poverty or to set new goals for health and happiness, to curb crime or try to bring beauty to our cities and our countryside — all of these, and more, depend on education.

But the legacy we inherit from Smithson cannot be limited to these shores. He called for the increase and diffusion of knowledge among men, not just Americans, not just Anglo-Saxons, and not just the citizens of the Western World — but all men everywhere.

The world we face on his bicentennial anniversary makes that mandate much more urgent than it ever was. For we know today that certain truths are self-evident in every nation on this earth; that ideas, not armaments, will shape our lasting prospects for peace; that the conduct of our foreign policy will advance no faster than the curriculum of our classrooms; that the knowledge of our citizens is the one treasure which grows only when it is shared.

It would profit us little to limit the world's exchange to those who can afford it. We must extend the treasure to those lands where learning is still a luxury for the few.

Today, more than 700 million adults — 4 out of 10 of the world's population — dwell in darkness where they cannot read or write. Almost half the nations of this globe suffer from illiteracy among half or more of their people. And unless the world can find a way to extend the light, the force of that darkness may ultimately engulf us all.

A NEW BEGINNING

For our part, this Government and this Nation are prepared to join in finding the way. During recent years we have made many hopeful beginnings. But we can and we must do more. That is why I have directed a special task force within my administration to recommend a broad and long range plan of worldwide educational endeavor.

Secretary of State Dean Rusk has accepted my request to chair this task force. Secretary John Gardner of the Department of Health, Education, and Welfare has agreed to serve on it. Both these men have proved, in their past careers, how great is their devotion to international education.

I intend to call on leaders in both public and private enterprise to join with us in mapping this effort.

We must move ahead on every front and at every level of learning. We can support Secretary Ripley's dream of creating a center here at the Smithsonian where great scholars from every nation will come and collaborate. At a more junior level, we can promote the growth of the school-to-school program started under Peace Corps auspices so that our children may learn about — and care about each other.

AN INTERNATIONAL EFFORT

We mean to show that this Nation's dream of a Great Society does not stop at the water's edge: and that it is not just an American dream. All are welcome to share in it. All are invited to contribute to it.

Together we must embark on a new and a noble adventure:

First, to assist the education efforts of the developing nations and the developing regions.

Second, to help our schools and universities increase their knowledge of the world and the people who inhabit it.

Third, to advance the exchange of students and teachers who travel and work outside their native lands.

Fourth, to increase the free flow of books and ideas and art, of works of science and imagination.

And, fifth, to assemble meetings of men and women from every discipline and every culture to ponder the common problems of mankind.

In all these endeavors, I pledge that the United States will play its full role. By January, I intend to present such a program to the Congress.

Despite the noise of daily events, history is made by men and the ideas of men. We — and only we — can generate growing light in our universe, or we can allow the darkness to gather.

DeTocqueville challenged us more than a century ago: "Men cannot remain strangers to each other, or be ignorant of what is taking place in any corner of the globe." We must banish the strangeness and the ignorance.

In all we do toward one another, we must try — and try again — to live the words of the prophet: "I shall light a candle of understanding in thine heart which shall not be put out."

NOTE: The President spoke at 4:33 P.M. on the south side of the Mall in front of the Smithsonian Institution. In his opening words he referred to Earl Warren, chief justice of the United States, Dr. S. Dillon Ripley, secretary of the Smithsonian Institution, Dr. Leonard Carmichael, vice president of the National Geographic Society and former secretary of the Smithsonian Institution, the Right Reverend Paul Moore, Jr., suffragan bishop of Washington (Episcopal), and the Very Reverend Gerard J. Campbell, president of Georgetown University.

The group was composed of more than 500 scholars and scientists representing 90 countries. After the president's remarks, they moved in formal academic procession across the Mall to an area behind the Museum of Natural History, where some 3,000 spectators listened to other speeches and to music provided by the U.S. Marine Band.

The ceremony marked the beginning of the celebration of the two hundredth anniversary of the birth of James Smithson, for whom the institution is named.

Special Message to the Congress Proposing International Education and Health Programs, February 2, 1966

To the Congress of the United States:

Last year the Congress by its action declared: the nation's number one task is to improve the education and health of our people.

Today I call upon Congress to add a world dimension to this task.

I urge the passage of the International Education and Health Acts of 1966.

We would be shortsighted to confine our vision to this nation's shore lines. The same rewards we count at home will flow from sharing in a worldwide effort to rid mankind of the slavery of ignorance and the scourge of disease.

We bear a special role in this liberating mission. Our resources will be wasted in defending freedom's frontiers if we neglect the spirit that makes men want to be free.

Half a century ago, the philosopher William James declared that mankind must seek "a moral equivalent of war."

The search continues — more urgent today than ever before in man's history.

Ours is the great opportunity to challenge all nations, friend and foe alike, to join this battle.

We have made hopeful beginnings. Many of the programs described in this message have been tested in practice. I have directed our agencies of government to improve and enlarge the programs already authorized by Congress.

Now I am requesting Congress to give new purpose and new power to our efforts by declaring that:

— programs to advance education and health are basic building blocks to lasting peace.

— they represent a long-term commitment in the national interest.
— the Department of Health, Education and Welfare is charged
with a broad authority to help strengthen our country's capacity
to carry on this noble adventure.

EDUCATION

Education lies at the heart of every nation's hopes and purposes. It
must be at the heart of our international relations.

We have long supported UNESCO and other multilateral and
international agencies. We propose to continue these efforts with renewed
vigor.

Schooled in the grief of war, we know certain truths are self-evident in
every nation on this earth:

— Ideas, not armaments, will shape our lasting prospects for
peace.
— The conduct of our foreign policy will advance no faster than the
curriculum of our classrooms.
— The knowledge of our citizens is one treasure which grows only
when it is shared.

International education cannot be the work of one country. It is the
responsibility and promise of all nations. It calls for free exchange and
full collaboration. We expect to receive as much as we give, to learn as
well as to teach.

Let this nation play its part. To this end, I propose:

— to strengthen our capacity for international educational
cooperation.
— to stimulate exchange with students and teachers of other
lands.
— to assist the progress of education in developing nations.
— to build new bridges of international understanding.

I. To Strengthen Our Capacity for
International Educational Cooperation

Our education base in this country is strong. Our desire to work with
other nations is great. But we must review and renew the purpose of our

programs for international education. I propose to:

1. Direct the Secretary of Health, Education, and Welfare to establish within his Department a Center for Educational Cooperation

This Center will be a focal point for leadership in international education. While it will not supplant other governmental agencies already conducting programs in this field, it will:

— Act as a channel for communication between our missions abroad and the U.S. educational community;
— Direct programs assigned to the Department of Health, Education, and Welfare;
— Assist public and private agencies conducting international education programs.

2. Appoint a Council on International Education

Our commitment to international education must draw on the wisdom, experience, and energy of many people. This Council, to be composed of outstanding leaders of American education, business, labor, the professions, and philanthropy, will advise the Center for Educational Cooperation.

3. Create a Corps of Education Officers to serve in the United States Foreign Service.

As education's representatives abroad, they will give sharper direction to our programs. Recruited from the ranks of outstanding educators, they will report directly to the Ambassador when serving in foreign missions.

4. Stimulate New Programs in International Studies for Elementary and Secondary Schools

No child should grow to manhood in America without realizing the promise and the peril of the world beyond our borders. Progress in teaching about world affairs must not lag behind progress made in other areas of American education.

I am directing the Secretary of Health, Education, and Welfare to earmark funds from Title IV of the Elementary and Secondary Education Act of 1965, so that our regional education laboratories can enrich the international curricula of our elementary and secondary schools.

5. Support Programs of International Scope in Smaller and Developing Colleges

Many of our nation's institutions have been unable to share fully in international projects. By a new program of incentive grants administered through HEW these institutions will be encouraged to play a more active role.

6. Strengthen Centers of Special Competence in International Research and Training

Over the past two decades, our universities have been a major resource in carrying on development programs around the world. We have made heavy demands upon them. But we have not supported them adequately.

I recommend to the Congress a program of incentive grants administered by HEW for universities and groups of universities —

(a) to promote centers of excellence in dealing with particular problems and particular regions of the world,
(b) to develop administrative staff and faculties adequate to maintain long-term commitments to overseas educational enterprises.

In addition, I propose that AID be given authority to provide support to American research and educational institutions, for increasing their capacity to deal with programs of economic and social development abroad.

II. To Stimulate Exchange with the Students and Teachers of Other Lands

Only when people know about — and care about — each other will nations learn to live together in harmony. I therefore propose that we:

1. Encourage the Growth of School-to-School Partnerships

Through such partnerships, already pioneered on a small scale, a U.S. school may assist the brick-and-mortar construction of a sister school in less developed nations. The exchange can grow to include books and equipment, teacher and student visits.

To children, it can bring deep understanding and lasting friendships.

I recommend a goal of 1,000 school-to-school partnerships.

This program will be administered by the Peace Corps, in cooperation with AID, particularly its Partners of the Alliance Program. The chief cost will be borne by the voluntary contributions of the participating schools.

2. Establish an Exchange Peace Corps

Our nation has no better ambassadors than the young volunteers who serve in 46 countries in the Peace Corps. I propose that we welcome similar ambassadors to our shores. We need their special skills and understanding, just as they need ours.

These "Volunteers to America" will teach their own language and culture in our schools and colleges. They will serve in community programs alongside VISTA Volunteers. As our Peace Corps Volunteers learn while they serve, those coming to the United States will be helped to gain training to prepare them for further service when they return home.

I propose an initial goal of 5,000 volunteers.

3. Establish an American Education Placement Service

We have in the United States a reservoir of talent and good will not yet fully tapped:

— school and college teachers eager to serve abroad;
— professors and administrators who are retired or on sabbatical leave;
— Peace Corps volunteers who desire further foreign service.

To encourage these men and women to assist in the developing nations and elsewhere, I recommend that we establish an American Education Placement Service in HEW.

It will act as an international recruitment bureau for American teachers, and will provide supplemental assistance for those going to areas of special hardship.

In time, I hope this Service will lead to the development of a World Teacher Exchange — in which all nations may join to bring their classrooms into closer relationship with one another.

III. To Assist the Progress of Education in Developing Nations

To provide direct support for those countries struggling to improve their education standards, I propose that we:

1. Enlarge AID programs of education assistance

In my message on Foreign Assistance, I directed AID to make a major effort in programs of direct educational benefit. These will emphasize teacher training — vocational and scientific education — construction of education facilities — specialized training in the U.S. for foreign students — and help in publishing badly needed textbooks.

2. Develop new Techniques for Teaching Basic Education and Fighting Illiteracy

Our own research and development in the learning process can be adapted to fit the needs of other countries. Modern technology and new communications techniques have the power to multiply the resources available to a school system.

I am calling on HEW to support basic education research of value to the developing nations.

I am requesting AID to conduct studies and assist pilot projects for applying technology to meet critical education shortages.

3. Expand U.S. Summer Teaching Corps

The Agency for International Development now administers programs for American teachers and professors who participate in summer workshops in less developed countries. They serve effectively to support teacher-training in these countries. They also enrich their own teaching experience.

I propose this year that AID double the number of U.S. participants in the Summer Teaching Corps.

4. Assist the Teaching of English Abroad

Many of the newer nations have a vital need to maintain English as the language of international communication and national development. We must help meet this demand even as we extend the teaching of foreign languages in our own schools.

I have directed AID, supported by other agencies, to intensify its efforts for those countries which seek our help.

5. Establish Bi-National Educational Foundations

We have at our disposal excess foreign currencies in a number of developing nations. Where conditions are favorable, I propose that significant amounts of these currencies be used to support Bi-National Educational Foundations. Governed by leading citizens from the two nations, they would have opportunities much like those afforded major foundations in the United States to invest in basic educational development.

To the extent further currencies are created by our sales of agricultural commodities abroad, I propose that a portion be earmarked for educational uses, particularly to assist technical training in food production.

IV. To Build New Bridges of International Understanding

The job of international education must extend beyond the classroom. Conferences of experts from many nations, the free flow of books and ideas, the exchange of works of science and imagination can enrich every citizen. I propose steps to:

1. Stimulate Conferences of Leaders and Experts

I have directed every department and agency to support a series of seminars for representatives from every discipline and every culture to seek answers to the common problems of mankind.

We are ready to serve as host to international gatherings. I have therefore called on the Secretary of State and the Attorney General to explore ways to remove unnecessary hindrances in granting visas to guests invited from abroad.

2. Increase the Flow of Books and Other Educational Material

I recommend prompt passage of legislation to implement the Florence Agreement and thus stimulate the movement of books and other educational material between nations. This Agreement was signed by representatives of the U.S. Government in 1959 and ratified by the Senate in 1960. This necessary Congressional action is long overdue to eliminate duties and remove barriers for the importation of educational materials.

I also recommend that Congress implement the Beirut Agreement to permit duty-free entry of visual and auditory materials of an educational, scientific or cultural nature.

Finally, we must encourage American private enterprise to participate actively in educational exchange. I urge the Congress to amend the United States Information and Educational Exchange Act of 1948 to permit improvements in the Informational Media Guarantee Program.

3. *Improve the Quality of U.S. Schools and Colleges Abroad*

We have a potentially rich resource in the American elementary and secondary schools and colleges overseas assisted by the Department of State and AID.

They should be showcases for excellence in education.

They should help make overseas service attractive to our own citizens.

They should provide close contact with students and teachers of the host country.

I request additional support to assist those institutions which meet these standards.

4. *Create Special Programs for Future Leaders Studying in the United States*

There are some 90,000 foreign students now enrolled in U.S. institutions. Many of them will someday play leading roles in their own countries. We must identify and assist these potential leaders.

I recommend that HEW and AID provide grants to enrich their educational experience through special courses and summer institutes.

HEALTH

The well-being of any nation rests fundamentally upon the health of its people.

If they are cursed by disease, their hopes grow dim.

If they are plagued by hunger, even the blessings of liberty give little comfort.

We have committed ourselves for many years to relieving human suffering. Today our effort must keep pace with a growing world and with growing problems. . . .

THE CHOICE WE MUST MAKE

We call on rich nations and poor nations to join with us — to help each other and to help themselves. This must be the first work of the world for generations to come.

For our part, the programs in International Education and Health I am recommending this year will total $524 million:

— $354 million in the foreign assistance program.

— $103 million in the Health, Education, and Welfare Department program.
— $11 million in the Peace Corps program.
— $56 million in the State Department cultural and education program.

As I indicated in my message on Foreign Assistance yesterday, these programs will be conducted in a manner consistent with our balance of payments policy.

Last Fall, speaking to a gathering of the world's scholars at the Smithsonian Institution, I said: ". . . We can generate growing light in our universe — or we can allow the darkness to gather." In the few months since then, forty-four million more children have come in the world. With them come more hunger — and more hope.

Since that time the gross national produce of our nation has passed the $700 billion mark.

The choice between light and darkness, between health and sickness, between knowledge and ignorance, is not one that we can ignore.

The light we generate can be the brightest hope of history. It can illuminate the way toward a better life for all. But the darkness — if we let it gather — can become the final, terrible midnight of mankind.

The International Education and Health Acts of 1966 present an opportunity to begin a great shared adventure with other nations.

I urge the Congress to act swiftly for passage of both measures.

Our national interest warrants it. The work of peace demands it.

Lyndon B. Johnson
The White House
February 2, 1966

NOTE: The International Education Act of 1966 was approved by the president on 29 October 1966. The proposed International Health Act was not adopted by the Eighty-ninth Congress.

Statement by the President on the Message on International Education and Health, February 2, 1966

LAST YEAR Congress, by its acts, declared this Nation's number one task is to now improve the education and health of our people.

Today I call upon Congress to add a world dimension to this task. The International Education Act of 1966 marks our commitment to help others to rid themselves of the slavery of illiteracy and ignorance. . . .

Appendix II:
The International Education Act of 1966 and David L. Boren National Security Education Act of 1991

The International Education Act of 1966

(Public Law 89-698, approved October 29, 1966)

TEXT OF THE LAW

Following is the text of Public Law 89-698.

AN ACT to provide for the strengthening of American educational resources for international studies and research.

Be it enacted by the Senate and House of Representatives of the United States of America in Congress assembled, That this Act may be cited as the "International Education Act of 1966"

FINDINGS AND DECLARATIONS

Sec. 2. The Congress hereby finds and declares that a knowledge of other countries is of the utmost importance in promoting mutual understanding and cooperation between nations; that strong American educational resources are a necessary base for strengthening our relations with other countries; that this and future generations of Americans should be assured ample opportunity to develop to the fullest extent possible their intellectual capacities in all areas of knowledge pertaining to other countries, peoples, and cultures; and that it is therefore both necessary and appropriate for the Federal Government to assist in the development of resources for international study and research, to assist in the development of resources and trained personnel in academic and professional fields, and to coordinate the existing and future programs of the Federal Government in international education, to meet the requirements of world leadership.

TITLE I—GRANT PROGRAMS FOR ADVANCED AND UNDERGRADUATE INTERNATIONAL STUDIES

CENTERS FOR ADVANCED INTERNATIONAL STUDIES

Sec. 101. (a) The Secretary of Health, Education, and Welfare (hereinafter referred to as the "Secretary") is authorized to arrange through grants to institutions of higher education, or combinations of such institutions, for the establishment, strengthening, and operation by them of graduate centers which will be national and international resources for research and training in international studies and the international aspects of professional and other fields of study. Activities carried on in such centers may be concentrated either on specific geographical areas of the world or on particular fields or issues in world affairs which concern one or more countries, or on both. The Secretary may also make grants to public and private nonprofit agencies and organizations, including professional and scholarly associations, when such grants will make an especially significant contribution to attaining the objectives of this section.

(b) Grants under this section may be used to cover part or all of the cost of establishing, strengthening, equipping, and operating research and training centers, including the cost of teaching and research materials and resources, the cost of programs for bringing visiting scholars and faculty to the center, and the cost of training, improvement, and travel of the staff for the purpose of carrying out the objectives of this section. Such grants may also include funds for stipends (in such amounts as may be determined in accordance with regulations of the Secretary) to individuals undergoing training in such centers, including allowances for dependents and for travel for research and study here and abroad. Grants under this section shall be made on such conditions as the Secretary finds necessary to carry out its purposes.

GRANTS TO STRENGTHEN UNDERGRADUATE PROGRAMS IN INTERNATIONAL STUDIES

Sec. 102. (a) The Secretary is authorized to make grants to institutions of higher education, or combinations of such institutions, to assist them in planning, developing, and carrying out a comprehensive program to strengthen and improve undergraduate instruction in international studies. Grants made under this section may be for projects and activities which are an integral part of such a comprehensive program such as—

(1) planning for the development and expansion of undergraduate programs in international studies;

(2) teaching, research, curriculum development, and other related activities;

(3) training of faculty members in foreign countries;

(4) expansion of foreign language courses;

(5) planned and supervised student work-study-travel program;

(6) programs under which foreign teachers and scholars may visit institutions as visiting faculty; and

(7) programs of English language training for foreign teachers, scholars, and students.

The Secretary may also make grants to public and private nonprofit agencies and organizations, including professional and scholarly associations, when such grants will make an especially significant contribution to attaining the objectives of this section.

(b) A grant may be made under this section only upon application to the Secretary at such time or times and containing such information as he deems necessary. The Secretary shall not approve an application unless it—

(1) sets forth a program for carrying out one or more projects or activities for which a grant is authorized under subsection (a);

(2) sets forth policies and procedures which assure that Federal funds made available under this section for any fiscal year will be so used as to supplement and, to the extent practical, increase the level of funds that would, in the absence of such Federal funds, be made available for purposes which meet the requirements of subsection (a), and in no case supplant such funds;

(3) provides for such fiscal control and fund accounting procedures as may be necessary to assure proper disbursement of and accounting for Federal funds paid to the applicant under this section; and

(4) provides for making such report, in such form and containing such information, as the Secretary may require to carry out his functions under this section, and for keeping such records and for affording such access thereto as the Secretary may find necessary to assure the correctness and verification of such reports.

(c) The Secretary shall allocate grants to institutions of higher education under this section in such manner and according to such plan as will most nearly provide an equitable distribution of the grants throughout the States while at the same time giving a preference to those institutions which are most in need of funds for programs in international studies and which show real promise of being able to use funds effectively.

METHOD OF PAYMENT; FEDERAL ADMINISTRATION

Sec. 103. (a) Payments under this title may be made in installments, and in advance or by way of reimbursement with necessary adjustments on account of overpayments or underpayments.

(b) In administering the provisions of this title, the Secretary is authorized to utilize the services and facilities of any agency of the Federal Government and of any other public or nonprofit agency or institution, in accordance with written agreements between the Secretary and the head thereof published in the Federal Register three weeks prior to the date on which any such agreement is to become effective.

FEDERAL CONTROL OF EDUCATION PROHIBITED

Sec. 104. Nothing contained in this Act shall be construed to authorize any department, agency, officer, or employee of the United States to exercise any direction, supervision, or control over the curriculum, program of instruction, administration, or personnel of any educational institution, or the selection of library resources by any educational institution or over the content of any material developed or published under any program assisted pursuant to this Act.

AUTHORIZATION AND REPORTS

Sec. 105. (a) There is authorized to be appropriated $1,000,000 for the fiscal year ending June 30, 1967, which shall be available only for the purpose of preparing the report provided for in subsection (b) of this section. There are authorized to be appropriated $40,000,000 for the fiscal year ending June 30, 1968, and $90,000,000 for the fiscal year ending June 30, 1969, for the purpose of carrying out the provisions of this title. For the fiscal years thereafter there shall be appropriated for the purpose of carrying out the provisions of this title only such amounts as the Congress may hereafter authorize by law.

(b) The Secretary shall prepare, with the advice of the Advisory Committee appointed pursuant to section 106, a report containing specific recommendations for carrying out the provisions of this title, including any recommendations for amendments to this title and to portions of other laws amended by this Act, and shall submit such report to the President and the Congress not later than April 30, 1967.

(c)   Prior to January 31, 1968, and prior to January 31 in each year thereafter, the Secretary shall make a report to the Congress which reviews and evaluates activities carried on under the authority of this Act and which reviews other activities of the Federal Government drawing upon or strengthening American resources for international study and research and any existing activities and plans to coordinate and improve the efforts of the Federal Government in international education.

NATIONAL ADVISORY COMMITTEE ON INTERNATIONAL STUDIES

Sec. 106. (a) The President is authorized to establish in the Department of Health, Education, and Welfare a National Advisory Committee on International Studies, consisting of the Assistant Secretary of Health, Education, and Welfare for Education who shall be chairman, and not more than fifteen additional members appointed by the President so that a majority shall constitute a broad representation of higher education in the United States and the remainder shall include representatives of the general public and individuals experienced in foreign affairs.

(b)   The Advisory Committee shall advise the Secretary in the preparation of the report provided for in section 105(b) of this Act, and thereafter shall advise the Secretary in carrying out the provisions of this Act. The recommendations of the Advisory Committee shall be included in the report provided for in section 105(b) of this Act and in the annual reports provided for in section 105(c) of this Act.

(c)   Members of the Advisory Committee who are not regular full-time employees of the United States shall, while serving on business of the Committee be entitled to receive compensation at rates fixed by the President, but not exceeding $100 per day, including travel time; and while so serving away from their homes or regular places of business, they may be allowed travel expenses, including per diem in lieu of subsistence, as authorized by section 5703 of title 5 of the United States Code for persons in Government service employed intermittently.

(d)   The Advisory Committee is authorized to appoint without regard to the provisions of title 5, United States Code, covering appointment in the competitive service, and fix the compensation of, without regard to chapter 51 and subchapter III of chapter 53 of such title, such professional and technical personnel as may be necessary to enable it to carry out its duties.

TITLE II—AMENDMENTS TO OTHER LAWS

AMENDMENTS TO STRENGTHEN TITLE VI OF THE NATIONAL DEFENSE EDUCATION ACT OF 1958

Removing Requirement for Area Centers That Adequate Language Instruction Not Be Readily Available

Sec. 201. (a)(1) The first sentence of section 601(a) of the National Defense Education Act of 1958 is amended by striking out "(1)" and by striking out ", and (2) that adequate instruction in such language is not readily available in the United States".

(2) The first sentence of section 601(b) of such Act is amended by striking out "(with respect to which he makes the determination under clause (1) of subsection (a))" and inserting in lieu therefor "(with respect to which he makes the determination under subsection (a))".

Removing 50 Per Centum Ceiling on Federal Participation

(b) The third sentence of section 601(a) of such Act is amended by striking out "not more than 50 per centum" and inserting "all or part" in lieu thereof.

Authorizing Grants as Well as Contracts for Language and Area Centers

(c) Section 601(a) of such Act is amended further by inserting "grants to or" after "arrange through" in the first sentence, and by inserting "grant or" before "contract" each time that it appears in the second and third sentences.

Vesting Authority for Language and Area Programs in Secretary

(d) Section 601 of such Act is further amended by striking out "Commissioner" each time such term occurs therein and inserting in lieu thereof "Secretary".

AMENDMENTS TO STRENGTHEN TITLE XI OF THE NATIONAL DEFENSE EDUCATION ACT OF 1958

Sec. 202. Title XI of the National Defense Education Act of 1958 is amended—

(1) by inserting after the title the following: "PART I—GENERAL";

(2) by striking out the word "title" in section 1102 and inserting in lieu thereof the word "part"; and

(3) by adding at the end thereof a new part as follows:

"PART II—INTERNATIONAL AFFAIRS

"INTERNATIONAL AFFAIRS INSTITUTES FOR SECONDARY SCHOOL TEACHERS

"Sec. 1111. There are authorized to be appropriated $3,500,000 for the fiscal year ending June 30, 1967, and $6,000,000 for the fiscal year ending June 30, 1968, to enable the Commissioner to arrange through contracts with institutions of higher education for the establishment and operation of short-term or regular-session institutes for teachers in secondary schools in order to give them a broader understanding of international affairs. Any such arrangement may cover the cost of the establishment and operation of the institute with respect to which it is made, including the cost of grants to the staff of travel in the foreign areas, regions, or countries with which the subject matter of the field or fields in which they are or will be working is concerned, and the cost of travel of foreign scholars to enable them to teach or assist in teaching in such institute and the cost of their return, and shall be made on such conditions as the Commissioner finds necessary to carry out the purposes of this section.

"STIPENDS

"Sec. 1112. The Commissioner is authorized to pay stipends to any individual to study in a program assisted under the provisions of this part upon determining that assisting such individual in such studies will promote the purpose of this part. Stipends under the provisions of this section may include allowances for dependents and for travel to and from the place of residence."

AMENDMENTS TO MUTUAL EDUCATION AND CULTURAL EXCHANGE ACT OF 1961

Sec. 203. (a) Section 102(a) of the Mutual Educational and Cultural Exchange Act of 1961 (22 U.S.C. 2452) is amended (1) by striking the period at the end of clause (9) and substituting a semicolon and the word "and"; and (2) by adding at the end thereof a new clause as follows:

"(10) promoting studies, research, instruction, and other educational activities of citizens and nationals of foreign countries in American schools, colleges, and universities located in the United States by making available to citizens and nationals of less developed friendly foreign countries for exchange for currencies of their respective countries (other than excess foreign currencies), at United States embassies, United States dollars in such amounts as may be necessary to enable such foreign citizens or nationals who are coming temporarily to the United States as students, trainees, teachers, instructors, or professors to meet expenses of the kind described in section 104(e)(1) of this Act."

(b)   Section 104 of the Mutual Educational and Cultural Exchange Act of 1961 is amended by adding at the end thereof a new subsection as follows:

"(g)(1) For the purpose of performing functions authorized by section 102(b)(10) of this Act, the President is authorized to establish the exchange rates at which all foreign currencies may be acquired through operations under such section, and shall issue regulations binding upon all embassies with respect to the exchange rates to be applicable in each of the respective countries where currency exchanges are authorized under such section.

"(2) In performing the functions authorized under section 102(b)(10) of this Act, the President shall make suitable arrangements for protecting the interests of the United States Government in connection with the ownership, use, and disposition of all foreign currencies acquired pursuant to exchanges made under such section.

"(3) The total amount of United States dollars acquired by any individual through currency exchanges under the authority of section 102(b)(10) of this Act shall in no event exceed $3,000 during any academic year.

"(4) An individual shall be eligible to exchange foreign currency for United States dollars at United States embassies under section 102(b)(10) of this Act only if he gives satisfactory assurances that (A) he will devote essentially full time to his proposed educational activity in the United States and will maintain good standing in relation to such program; (B) he will return to the country of his citizenship or nationality prior to coming to the United States and will render such public service as is determined acceptable for a period of time determined reasonable and necessary by the government of such country; and (C) he will not apply for an immigrant visa or for permanent residence or for a nonimmigrant visa under the Immigration and Nationality Act after having received any benefits under such section for a period of time equal to the period of study, research, instruction, or other educational activity he performed pursuant to such section.

"(5) As used in section 102(b)(10) of this Act, the term 'excess foreign currencies' means foreign currencies, which if acquired by the United States (A) would be in excess of the normal requirements of departments, agencies, and embassies of the United States for such currencies, as determined by the President, and (B) would be available for the use of the United States Government under applicable agreements with the foreign country concerned."

(c) Section 105 of the Mutual Educational and Cultural Exchange Act of 1961 is amended by adding at the end thereof a new subsection as follows:

"(g) Notwithstanding any other provision of this Act, there are authorized to be appropriated for the purposes of making currency exchanges under section 102(b)(10) of this Act, not to exceed $10,000,000 for the fiscal year ending June 30, 1968, and not to exceed $15,000,000 for the fiscal year ending June 30, 1969."

EXTENDING THE BENEFITS OF THE LOAN INSURANCE PROGRAM UNDER TITLE IV-B OF THE HIGHER EDUCATION ACT OF 1965 TO STUDENTS STUDYING ABROAD

Sec. 204. The second sentence of section 435(a) of the Higher Education Act of 1965 is amended by inserting after "Such term" the following: "includes any institution outside the States which is comparable to an institution described in the preceding sentence and which has been approved by the Commissioner for the purposes of this title, and".

TITLE III—STUDY BY THE SECRETARY OF HEALTH, EDUCATION, AND WELFARE

AUTHORIZATION FOR A STUDY ON WAYS TO REDUCE THE DRAIN FROM DEVELOPING COUNTRIES OF PROFESSIONAL PERSONS AND SKILLED SPECIALISTS WHOSE SKILLS ARE URGENTLY NEEDED

Sec. 301. (a) The Secretary of Health, Education, and Welfare shall conduct a study and investigation to determine (1) the total number of individuals who enter the United States from developing countries annually to further their education, and who remain in the United States; (2) the reasons for their failure to return to their home countries; and (3) means of encouraging the return of such individuals to the countries of their last residence or nationality, so they may put their education and training to work in the service of their homelands.

(b) The Secretary of Health, Education, and Welfare shall report to the President and to the Congress as soon as practicable on his findings and conclusions together with such recommendations for any legislation he deems desirable to encourage the return of such individuals to such countries.

(c) It is hereby authorized to be appropriated the sum of $50,000 for the purpose of carrying out this study.

David L. Boren National Security Education Act of 1991, Signed by the President December 4, 1991

(Public Law 102-183, as amended*)

TITLE VIII–NATIONAL SECURITY SCHOLARSHIPS, FELLOW-SHIPS, AND GRANTS

SEC. 801. SHORT TITLE, FINDINGS, AND PURPOSES.

(a)   SHORT TITLE.—This title may be cited as the "David L. Boren National Security Education Act of 1991."

(b)   FINDINGS.—The Congress makes the following findings:

(1)   The security of the United States is and will continue to depend on the ability of the United States to exercise international leadership.

(2)   The ability of the United States to exercise international leadership is, and will increasingly continue to be, based on the political and economic strength of the United States, as well as on United States military strength around the world.

(3)   Recent changes in the world pose threats of a new kind to international stability as Cold War tensions continue to decline while economic competition, regional conflicts, terrorist activities, and weapon proliferation have dramatically increased.

(4)   The future national security and economic well-being of the United States will depend substantially on the ability of its citizens to communicate and compete by knowing the languages and cultures of other countries.

(5)   The Federal Government has an interest in ensuring that the employees of its departments and agencies with national security

---

*Amendments in P.L. 102-496, signed by the President on October 24, 1992, are incorporated.

responsibilities are prepared to meet the challenges of this changing international environment.

(6) The Federal Government also has an interest in taking actions to alleviate the problem of American undergraduate and graduate students being inadequately prepared to meet the challenges posed by increasing global interaction among nations.

(7) American colleges and universities must place a new emphasis on improving the teaching of foreign languages, area studies, and other international fields to help meet those challenges.

(c) PURPOSES.—The purposes of this title are as follows:

(1) To provide the necessary resources, accountability, and flexibility to meet the national security education needs of the United States, especially as such needs change over time.

(2) To increase the quantity, diversity, and quality of the teaching and learning of subjects in the fields of foreign languages, area studies, and other international fields that are critical to the Nation's interest.

(3) To produce an increased pool of applicants for work in the departments and agencies of the United States Government with national security responsibilities.

(4) To expand, in conjunction with other Federal programs, the international experience, knowledge base, and perspectives on which the United States citizenry, Government employees, and leaders rely.

(5) To permit the Federal Government to advocate the cause of international education.

SEC. 802. SCHOLARSHIP, FELLOWSHIP, AND GRANT PROGRAM.

(a) PROGRAM REQUIRED.—

(1) IN GENERAL.—The Secretary of Defense shall carry out a program for—

(A) awarding scholarships to undergraduate students who are United States citizens in order to enable such students to study, for at least one academic semester or equivalent term, in foreign countries that are critical countries (as determined under section 803(d)(4)(A));

(B) awarding fellowships to graduate students who—

(i) are United States citizens to enable such students to pursue education as part of a graduate degree program of a United States institution of higher education in the disciplines of foreign languages, area studies, and other international fields that are critical areas of those disciplines (as determined under section 803(d)(4)(B)); and

(ii) pursuant to subsection (b)(2), enter into an agreement to work for an agency or office of the Federal Government or in the field of education in the area of study for which the fellowship was awarded; and

(C) awarding grants to institutions of higher education to enable such institutions to establish, operate, or improve programs in foreign languages, area studies, and other international fields that are critical areas of those disciplines (as determined under section 803(d)(4)(C)).

(2) FUNDING ALLOCATIONS.—Of the amount available for obligation out of the National Security Education Trust Fund for any fiscal year for the purposes stated in paragraph (1), the Secretary shall have a goal of allocating—

(A) -1/3- of such amount for the awarding of scholarships pursuant to paragraph (1)(A);

(B) -1/3- of such amount for the awarding of fellowships pursuant to paragraph (1)(B); and

(C) -1/3- of such amount for the awarding of grants pursuant to paragraph (1)(C).

(3) CONSULTATION WITH NATIONAL SECURITY EDUCATION BOARD.—The program required under this title shall be carried out in consultation with the National Security Education Board established under section 803.

(4) CONTRACT AUTHORITY.—The Secretary may enter into one or more contracts, with private national organizations having an expertise in foreign languages, area studies, and other international fields, for the awarding of the scholarships, fellowships, and grants described in paragraph (1) in accordance with the provisions of this title. The Secretary may enter into such contracts without regard to section 3709 of the Revised Statutes (41 U.S.C. 5) or any other provision of law that requires the use of competitive procedures. In addition, the Secretary may enter into personal service contracts for periods up to one year for program administration, except that not more than 10 such contracts may be in effect at any one time.

(b) SERVICE AGREEMENT.—In awarding a scholarship or fellowship under the program, the Secretary or contract organization referred to in subsection (a)(4), as the case may be, shall require a recipient of any fellowship, or of scholarships that provide assistance for periods that aggregate 12 months or more, to enter into an agreement that, in return for such assistance, the recipient—

(1) will maintain satisfactory academic progress, as determined in accordance with regulations issued by the Secretary, and agrees that failure to maintain such progress shall constitute grounds upon which the Secretary or contract organization referred to in subsection (a)(4) may terminate such assistance;

(2) will, upon completion of such recipient's baccalaureate degree or education under the program, as the case may be, and in accordance with regulations issued by the Secretary, work for the Federal Government or in the field of education in the area of study for which the scholarship or fellowship was awarded for a period specified by the Secretary, which period for the recipients of scholarships shall be no more than the same period for which scholarship assistance was provided and for the recipients of fellowships shall be not less than one and not more than three times the period for which the fellowship assistance was provided: and

(3) if the recipient fails to meet either of the obligations set forth in paragraph (1) or (2), will reimburse the United States Government for the amount of the assistance provided the recipient under the program, together with interest at a rate determined in accordance with regulations issued by the Secretary.

(c) DISTRIBUTION OF ASSISTANCE.—In selecting the recipients for awards of scholarships, fellowships, or grants pursuant to this title, the Secretary or a contract organization referred to in subsection (a)(4), as the case may be, shall take into consideration (1) the extent to which the selections will result in there being an equitable geographic distribution of such scholarships, fellowships, or grants (as the case may be) among the various regions of the United States, and (2) the extent to which the distribution of scholarships and fellowships to individuals reflects the cultural, racial, and ethnic diversity of the population of the United States.

(d) MERIT REVIEW.—The Secretary shall award scholarships, fellowships, and grants under the program based upon a merit review process.

(e) LIMITATION ON USE OF PROGRAM PARTICIPANTS.—No person who receives a grant, scholarship, or fellowship or any other type of assistance under this title shall, as a condition of receiving such assistance or under any other circumstances, be used by any department, agency, or entity of the United States Government engaged in intelligence activities to undertake any activity on its behalf during the period such person is pursuing a program of education for which funds are provided under the program carried out under this title.

SEC. 803. NATIONAL SECURITY EDUCATION BOARD.

(a) ESTABLISHMENT.—The Secretary of Defense shall establish a National Security Education Board.

(b) COMPOSITION.—The Board shall be composed of the following individuals or the representatives of such individuals:

(1) The Secretary of Defense, who shall serve as the chairman of the Board.

(2) The Secretary of Education.

(3) The Secretary of State.

(4) The Secretary of Commerce.

(5) The Director of Central Intelligence.

(6) The Director of the United States Information Agency.

(7) The Chairperson of the National Endowment for the Humanities.

(8) Six individuals appointed by the President, by and with the advice and consent of the Senate, who shall be experts in the fields of international, language, and area studies education and who may not be officers or employees of the Federal Government.

(c) TERM OF APPOINTEES.—Each individual appointed to the Board pursuant to subsection (b)(7) shall be appointed for a period specified by the President at the time of the appointment, but not to exceed four years. Such individuals shall receive no compensation for service on the Board but may receive reimbursement for travel and other necessary expenses.

(d) FUNCTIONS.—The Board shall perform the following functions:

(1) Develop criteria for awarding scholarships, fellowships, and grants under this title.

(2) Provide for wide dissemination of information regarding the activities assisted under this title.

(3) Establish qualifications for students desiring scholarships or fellowships, and institutions of higher education desiring grants under this title, including, in the case of students desiring a scholarship or fellowship, a requirement that the student have a demonstrated commitment to the study of the discipline for which the scholarship or fellowship is to be awarded.

(4) Make recommendations to the Secretary regarding—

(A) which countries are not emphasized in other United States study abroad programs, such as countries in which few United States students are studying, and are, therefore, critical countries for the purposes of section 802(a)(1)(A);

(B) which areas within the disciplines described in section 802(a)(1)(B) are areas of study in which United States students are deficient in learning and are, therefore, critical areas within those disciplines for the purposes of that section;

(C) which areas within the disciplines described in section 802(a)(1)(C) are areas in which United States students, educators, and Government employees are deficient in learning and in which insubstantial numbers of United States institutions of higher education provide training and are, therefore, critical areas within those disciplines for the purposes of that section; and

(D) how students desiring scholarships or fellowships can be encouraged to work for an agency or office of the Federal Government involved in national security affairs or national security policy upon completion of their education.

(5) Review the administration of the program required under this title.

SEC. 804. NATIONAL SECURITY EDUCATION TRUST FUND.

(a) ESTABLISHMENT OF FUND.—There is established in the Treasury of the United States a trust fund to be known as the "National Security Education Trust Fund." The assets of the Fund consist of amounts appropriated to the Fund and amounts credited to the Fund under subsection (e).

(b) AVAILABILITY OF SUMS IN THE FUND.—

(1) Sums in the Fund shall, to the extent provided in appropriations Acts, be available—

(A) for awarding scholarships, fellowships, and grants in accordance with the provisions of this title; and

(B) for properly allocable costs of the Federal Government for the administration of the program under this title.

(2) No amount may be appropriated to the Fund, or obligated from the Fund, unless authorized by law.

(c) INVESTMENT OF FUND ASSETS.—The Secretary of the Treasury shall invest in full the amount in the Fund that is not immediately necessary for expenditure. Such investments may be made only in interest-bearing obligations of the United States or in obligations guaranteed as to both principal and interest by the United States. For such purpose, such obligations may be acquired on original issue at the issue price or by purchase of outstanding obligations at the market price. The purposes for which obligations of the United States may be issued under chapter 31 of title 31, United States Code, are hereby extended to authorize the issuance at par of special obligations exclusively to the Fund. Such special obligations shall bear interest at a rate equal to the average rate of interest, computed as to the end of the calendar month next preceding the date of such issue, borne by all marketable interest-bearing obligations of the United States then forming a part of the public debt, except that where such average rate is not a multiple of -1/8- of 1 percent, the rate of interest of such special obligations shall be the multiple of -1/8- of 1 percent next lower than such average rate. Such special obligations shall be issued only if the Secretary of the Treasury determines that the purchases of other interest-bearing obligations of the United States, or of obligations guaranteed as to both principal and interest by the United States or original issue or at the market price, is not in the public interest.

(d) AUTHORITY TO SELL OBLIGATIONS.—Any obligation acquired by the Fund (except special obligations issued exclusively to the Fund) may be sold by the Secretary of the Treasury at the market price, and such special obligations may be redeemed at par plus accrued interest.

(e) AMOUNTS CREDITED TO FUND.—

(1) The interest on, and the proceeds from the sale or redemption of, any obligations held in the Fund shall be credited to and form a part of the Fund.

(2) Any amount paid to the United States under section 802(b)(3) shall be credited to and form a part of the Fund.

SEC. 805. REGULATIONS AND ADMINISTRATIVE PROVISIONS.

(a) REGULATIONS.—The Secretary may prescribe regulations to carry out the program required by this title. Before prescribing any such regulations, the Secretary shall submit a copy of the proposed regulations to the Select Committee on Intelligence of the Senate and the Permanent Select Committee on Intelligence of the House of Representatives. Such proposed regulations may not take effect until 30 days after the date on which they are submitted to those committees.

(b) ACCEPTANCE AND USE OF GIFTS.—In order to conduct the program required by this title, the Secretary may—

(1) receive money and other property donated, bequeathed, or devised, without condition or restriction other than that it be used for the purpose of conducting the program required by this title; and

(2) may use, sell, or otherwise dispose of such property for that purpose.

(c) VOLUNTARY SERVICES.—In order to conduct the program required by this title, the Secretary may accept and use the services of voluntary and noncompensated personnel.

(d) NECESSARY EXPENDITURES.—Expenditures necessary to conduct the program required by this title shall be paid from the Fund, subject to section 804(b).

SEC. 806. ANNUAL REPORT.

(a) ANNUAL REPORT.—The Secretary shall submit to the President and to the Congress an annual report of the conduct of the program required by this title. The report shall be submitted each year at the time that the President's budget for the next fiscal year is submitted to Congress pursuant to section 1105 of title 31, United States Code.

(b) CONTENTS OF REPORT.—Each such report shall contain—

(1) an analysis of the trends within language, international, and area studies, along with a survey of such areas as the Secretary determines are receiving inadequate attention;

(2) the effect on those trends of activities under the program required by this title;

(3) an analysis of the assistance provided under the program for the previous fiscal year, to include the subject areas being addressed and the nature of the assistance provided;

(4) an analysis of the performance of the individuals who received assistance under the program during the previous fiscal year, to include the degree to which assistance was terminated under the program and the extent to which individual recipients failed to meet their obligations under the program;

(5) an analysis of the results of the program for the previous fiscal year, and cumulatively, to include, at a minimum—

(A) the percentage of individuals who have received assistance under the program who subsequently became employees of the United States Government;

(B) in the case of individuals who did not subsequently become employees of the United States Government, an analysis of the reasons why they did not become employees and an explanation as to what use, if any, was made of the assistance by those recipients; and

(C) the uses made of grants to educational institutions; and

(6) any legislative changes recommended by the Secretary to facilitate the administration of the program or otherwise to enhance its objectives.

(c) SUBMISSION OF INITIAL REPORT.—The first report under this section shall be submitted at the time the budget for fiscal year 1994 is submitted to Congress.

SEC. 807. GENERAL ACCOUNTING OFFICE AUDITS.

The conduct of the program required by this title may be audited by the General Accounting Office under such rules and regulations as may be prescribed by the Comptroller General of the United States. Representatives of the General Accounting Office shall have access to all books, accounts, records, reports, and files and all other papers, things, or property of the Department of Defense pertaining to such activities and necessary to facilitate the audit.

SEC. 808. DEFINITIONS.

For the purpose of this title:

(1) The term "Board" means the National Security Education Board established pursuant to section 803.

(2) The term "Fund" means the National Security Education Trust Fund established pursuant to section 804.

(3) The term "institution of higher education" has the meaning given that term by section 1201(a) of the Higher Education Act of 1965 (20 U.S.C. 1141(a)).

SEC. 809. FISCAL YEAR 1992 FUNDING.

(a) AUTHORIZATION OF APPROPRIATIONS TO THE FUND.—There is hereby authorized to be appropriated to the Fund for fiscal year 1992 the sum of $150,000,000.

(b) AUTHORIZATION OF OBLIGATIONS FROM THE FUND.—During fiscal year 1992, there may be obligated from the Fund such amounts as may be provided in appropriations Acts, not to exceed $35,000,000. Amounts made available for obligation from the Fund for fiscal year 1992 shall remain available until expended.

AUTHORIZATION OF APPROPRIATIONS.—There is authorized to be appropriated for fiscal year 1993 to the National Security Education Trust Fund established by section 804 of the David L. Boren National Security Education Act of 1991 the sum of $30,000,000. (NOTE: This authorization was not appropriated for fiscal year 1993. The Fund remains at $150,000,000.)

Selected Bibliography

AID-University Cooperation in Technical Assistance. *Building Institutions to Serve Agriculture*. LaFayette, Ind.: Purdue University, 1968.

America in Transition: The International Frontier. Report of the Task Force on International Education. Washington, D.C.: National Governors' Association, 1989.

Ball, Donald A. and Wendell H. McCulloh, Jr. *International Business: Introduction and Essentials*. Homewood, Ill.: Irvin, 1990.

Barber, Elinor G. and Warren Ilchman. *International Studies Review*. New York: Ford Foundation, 1979.

Bergman, Larry. *Planning a Tragedy: The Americanization of the War in Vietnam*. New York: Norton, 1983.

Bok, Derek. *Higher Learning*. Cambridge, Mass.: Harvard University Press, 1986.

____. *Universities and the Future of America*. Durham, N.C.: Duke University Press, 1990.

Bornet, Vaughn Davis. *The Presidency of Lyndon B. Johnson*. Lawrence: University Press of Kansas, 1983.

Boyer, Ernest L. *College: The Undergraduate Experience in America*. New York: Harper & Row, 1987.

Brademas, John with Lynne P. Brown. *The Politics of Education: Conflict and Consensus on Capitol Hill*. Norman: University of Oklahoma Press, 1987.

Burn, Barbara B. *Expanding the International Dimension*. San Francisco, Calif.: Jossey-Bass, 1980.

Califano, Joseph A., Jr. *A Presidential Nation*. New York: Norton, 1975.

Clowse, Barbara B. *Brainpower for the Cold War: The Sputnik Crisis and National Defense Education Act of 1958*. Westport, Conn.: Greenwood Press, 1981.

A Crisis of Dollars: The Funding Threat to International Affairs in U.S. Higher Education. New York: EWA, 1968.

Czinkota, Michael R. and Ilbba A. Ronbainen. *International Marketing*. Chicago, Ill.: Dryden Press, 1990.

Deagle, Edwin A., Jr. *A Survey of United States Institutions Engaged in International Relations Research and Related Activities*. New York: Rockefeller Foundation, 1981.

Divine, Robert A., ed. *The Johnson Years, Volume One, Foreign Policy, the Great Society, and the White House*. Lawrence: University Press of Kansas, 1987.

Donovan, John C. *The 1960's: Politics and Public Policy*. Lanham, Md.: University Press of America, 1980.

Finn, Chester E. *Scholars, Dollars, and Bureaucrats*. Washington, D.C.: Brookings Institution, 1978.

Frankel, Charles. *High on Foggy Bottom*. New York: Harper & Row, 1968.

____. *The Neglected Aspect of Foreign Affairs: American Educational and Cultural Policy Abroad*. Washington, D.C.: Brookings Institution, 1966.

Gardner, John W. *AID and the Universities*. New York: Education and World Affairs, 1964.

Geyelin, Philip. *Lyndon B. Johnson and the World*. New York: Praeger, 1966.

Gladieux, Lawrence E. and Thomas R. Wolanin. *Congress and the Colleges*. Lexington, Mass.: Lexington Books, 1976.

Goodwin, Richard N. *Remembering America, A Voice from the Sixties*. Boston, Mass.: Little, Brown, 1988.

Graham, Hugh Davis. *The Uncertain Triumph: Federal Education Policy in the Kennedy and Johnson Years*. Chapel Hill: University of North Carolina Press, 1984.

Groennings, Sven. *Group Portrait: International Education in the Academic Disciplines*. New York: American Forum for Education in a Global Age, 1989.

Harari, Maurice. *Global Dimensions in U.S. Education: The University*. New York: Center for War/Peace Studies, 1972.

Hayden, Rose L. *Federal Support for International Education: Assessing the Options*. Washington, D.C.: National Council on Foreign Studies, August 1985.

Heginbotham, Stanley J. *The National Security Education Program: A Review and Analysis*. New York: SSRC, 1992.

Holderman, James B. *Critical Needs in International Education: Recommendations for Action*. Report to the Secretary of Education by the National Advisory Board on International Education Programs. Washington, D.C.: Government Printing Office, December 1983.

Humphrey, Richard A., ed. *Universities and Development Assistance Abroad*. Washington, D.C.: ACE, 1967.

International Education Act of 1966. New York: Education and World Affairs, 1966.

Jain, Subhash C. *International Marketing Management*. Boston, Mass.: PWS-Kent, 1990.

Johnson, Walter and Francis J. Colligan. *The Fulbright Program: A History*. Chicago, Ill.: University of Chicago Press, 1965.

Kearns, Doris. *Lyndon Johnson and the American Dream*. New York: Harper & Row, 1976.

Knowles, Asa S., ed. *The International Encyclopedia of Higher Education*. San Francisco, Calif.: Jossey-Bass, 1977.

Lambert, Richard D. with Elinor G. Barbar, Eleanor Jorden, Margaret B. Merrill, and Leon I. Twarog. *Beyond Growth: The Next Stage in Language and Area Studies*. Washington, D.C.: Association of American Universities, 1984.

Lambert, Richard D. *International Studies and the Undergraduate*. Washington, D.C.: ACE, 1989.

____. *Points of Leverage: An Agenda for a National Foundation for International Studies.* New York: Social Sciences Research Council, 1986.

Leestma, Robert. "OE's Institute of International Studies." *American Education.* USOE. Washington, D.C. (May 1969): 5–8.

Lindquist, Clarence B. *NDEA Fellowships for College Teaching, 1958–68; Title IV, NDEA of 1958.* Washington, D.C.: U.S. Department of HEW, OE, 1971.

Lippman, Walter. *Public Opinion.* New York: Macmillan, 1965.

McCaughey, Robert. *International Studies and Academic Enterprise: A Chapter in the Enclosure of American Learning.* New York: Columbia University Press, 1984.

McDonnell, Lorraine M., Sue E. Berryman, and Douglas Scott, with John Pincus and Abby Robyn. *Federal Support for International Studies: The Role of the NDEA Title VI.* Prepared for U.S. Department of Education. Santa Monica, Calif.: Rand Corporation, 1981.

McPherson, Harry. *A Political Education.* Boston, Mass.: Little, Brown, 1972.

Michie, Allan A. *The University Looks Abroad: Approaches to World Affairs at Six American Universities.* New York: Walker and Co., 1965.

Miller, Merle. *Lyndon, an Oral Biography.* New York: G. P. Putnam's Sons, 1980.

Perkins, James A. *Strength through Wisdom: A Critique of U.S. Capability.* Report to the President from the President's Commission on Foreign Languages and International Studies. Washington, D.C.: Government Printing Office, 1979.

A Quarter Century: The American Adventure in Academic Exchange. Washington, D.C.: Board of Foreign Scholarships, 1971.

Redford, Emmette S. and Richard T. McCulley. *White House Operations, the Johnson Presidency.* Austin: University of Texas Press, 1986.

Reischauer, Edwin O. *Toward the 21st Century: Education for a Changing World.* New York: Alfred A. Knopf, 1973.

Seaborg, Glen T. *Stemming the Tide.* Lexington, Mass.: Lexington Books, 1987.

Sidey, Hugh. *A Very Personal Presidency.* New York: Atheneum, 1987.

Smith, G. Kerry, ed. *Agony and Promise.* San Francisco, Calif.: Jossey-Bass, 1969.

Sovern, Michael I. *Annual Report 1982–83 Academic Year.* New York: Columbia University, 1983.

Sufrin, Sidney C. *Technical Assistance — Theory and Guidelines.* Syracuse, N.Y.: Syracuse University Press, 1966.

Thomas, Norman C. *Education in National Politics.* New York: David McKay, 1975.

Tolo, Kenneth W., ed. *Educating a Nation: The Changing American Commitment.* A Symposium on Education. LBJ School of Public Affairs and University of Texas at Austin, 1973.

U.S. Congress. House. Committee on Education and Labor. Task Force on International Education. *International Education: Past, Present, Problems and Prospects. Selected Readings to Supplement H.R. 14643.* Eighty-ninth Congress, Second Session, October 1966.

Valenti, Jack. *A Very Human President.* New York: W. W. Norton, 1975.

Ward, Robert E. *National Needs for International Education.* CSIS Monograph. Washington, D.C.: Center for Strategic and International Studies, Georgetown University, 1977.

Weidner, Edward W. *The World Role of Universities.* New York: McGraw-Hill, 1962.

Wennergren, E. Boyd, Donald L. Plucknett, Nigel J. H. Smith, William L. Furlong, and Joan H. Joshi. *Solving World Hunger: The U.S. Stake*. Washington, D.C.: Consortium for International Cooperation in Higher Education, 1986.

Wicker, Tom. *JFK and LBJ: The Influence of Personality upon Politics*. New York: William Morrow, 1968.

Wood, Richard H. *U.S. Universities: Their Role in AID-Financed Technical Assistance Overseas*. New York: Education and World Affairs, 1968.

Index

ABOUT THE AUTHOR

Theodore M. Vestal is Associate Professor of Political Science at Oklahoma State University. In the Department of Health, Education, and Welfare in Washington, D.C., he worked on implementation of the International Education Act of 1966. He was an executive of the Peace Corps in Ethiopia, Resident Director of New York State's Educational Resources Center in New Delhi, and president of the California Institute of Integral Studies in San Francisco.